WHAT I

MARK HERZLICH

WITH ALEX TRESNIOWSKI

WHAT IT TAKES

Fighting for My Life and
My Love of the Game

 NEW AMERICAN LIBRARY

New American Library
Published by the Penguin Group
Penguin Group (USA) LLC, 375 Hudson Street,
New York, New York 10014

USA | Canada | UK | Ireland | Australia | New Zealand | India | South Africa | China
penguin.com
A Penguin Random House Company

First published by New American Library,
a division of Penguin Group (USA) LLC

First Printing, June 2014

REGISTERED TRADEMARK—MARCA REGISTRADA

LIBRARY OF CONGRESS CATALOGING-IN-PUBLICATION DATA:

Herzlich, Mark.
   What it takes: fighting for my life and my love of the game/Mark Herzlich; foreword by Tom Coughlin.
      p. cm.
   ISBN 978-0-451-46879-6 (hardback)
   1. Herzlich, Mark. 2. Football players—United States—Biography. 3. Ewing's sarcoma—Patients—United States—Biography. I.Title.
   GV939.H467A3 2014
   796.332092—dc23   2014006534
   [B]

Printed in the United States of America
10   9   8   7   6   5   4   3   2   1

Set in Warnock Pro
Designed by Alissa Rose Theodor

To the twelve million new cancer warriors each year who are searching for hope in the face of fear—don't ever stop fighting, because you are stronger than you know and you all have what it takes

FOREWORD

As a head football coach in the NFL I've been around a lot of tough men. You don't make it to the NFL, and you certainly don't last, unless you're exceptionally tough. Mark Herzlich, whom I've had the privilege of coaching on the New York Giants, is one of the toughest men I know.

I was well aware of Mark's many accomplishments long before he joined the Giants. I used to be head coach at Boston College, and though I left before Mark got there, I kept track of the team and I heard a lot about number 94. Mark was a tremendous football player for the Eagles, a first-team All-American and the Atlantic Coast Conference Defensive Player of the Year in 2008. He was highly regarded by everyone in the Boston College community, and his future seemed limitless.

But in 2009 Mark's life took a drastic turn. He learned he had an extremely rare bone disease, and he was told he'd never play football again. For a time his survival was not a sure thing. For someone like Mark—so young, so strong, so full of promise—it was a staggering blow. Doctors recommended a surgery that would end Mark's football career, just as he was discovering how good he really was.

Mark had other ideas. Despite what doctors told him, Mark truly believed he would play football again, so he made some very difficult decisions about his treatment. He didn't take the safe road; he went with the riskier, harder course of action. And even while he was undergoing weeks of grueling treatment, he would often hit the weight room to stay strong for his eventual return to the field. Mark never lost sight of his goal, and he never stopped pushing himself past the limits other people set for him.

It is a testament to Mark's belief in himself and his strength of character that he made the decisions he made and fought as hard as he did.

There would be other setbacks for Mark. Even after he somehow made it back to the football field, he wasn't selected in the NFL draft. That was when the New York Giants entered the picture. At the urging of our team president, John Mara—like Mark, a Boston College alum—I met with our general manager, Jerry Reese, and discussed the possibility of giving Mark a chance to play for the Giants. There are only a few open spots in any training camp and dozens of good players waiting to take them. But the vote on the Giants was unanimous—we were all in favor of giving Mark a shot.

After that he faced another obstacle—the NFL lockout. Because of the lockout, our training camp was condensed, and we never had a chance to work with Mark in the off-season. The first time we saw him was when he showed up at camp. We had questions about Mark's physical condition, and we were eager to see him play. Because of everything he went through, we were even prepared to give him a little leeway.

Yet Mark never gave any indication he needed any leeway. Quite the opposite: Mark was relentless.

He wasn't far removed from his treatments, and he had to deal with other physical setbacks along the way. But it was clear Mark worked extremely hard to get himself into NFL shape. It was clear he didn't just want to play again—he wanted to play at the highest level. In that first training camp Mark's endurance was unbelievable. I am still in awe of that. If it was ninety-five degrees and unbearably humid, Mark was still out there, pushing himself harder and harder every practice, every day.

Mark faced extraordinary adversity and answered it with an extraordinary show of will, faith, and strength. On the field Mark personified toughness.

But that is only half the story. In 1996 I created the Jay Fund Foundation, which provides financial, emotional, and practical support to families of children stricken with cancer. Each spring, the Jay Fund hosts a fundraising dinner and golf classic. Mark is on the Jay Fund advisory board, and he has become one of the stars of our annual event. It is quite a thing to see how the children respond to Mark. The kids cling to him, drawn in by his big heart and his openness. And Mark doesn't just spend time with them—he becomes a friend. Mark stays in touch with some of the kids who most desperately need companionship as they fight their own battles to survive.

That positive, never-say-no attitude is something I see in Mark with each play on the field and each interaction off it. What he's been able to accomplish in football, and how he has used that platform to provide hope and inspiration to kids and families everywhere, is truly remarkable. Mark is a giver. He gives of himself tirelessly, and if you ask him to do something to help other people, he will never refuse.

One of the jobs of a head coach is to evaluate skill and talent. But it's just as important to evaluate a player's character. With Mark, that part was easy. He is clearly a man of great courage and compassion—a man whose bravery and achievements make him a hero to children and grown-ups alike.

I truly believe Mark's story will motivate and inspire anyone who reads it, and that is why I am proud to introduce him to you. I have coached football for almost forty-five years now, and there are few players I admire as much as Mark Herzlich.

Tom Coughlin
Head coach, New York Giants
February 2014

WHAT IT TAKES

INTRODUCTION

Let me tell you what it feels like to hit someone.

First of all, it's silent. Or at least it is for me. I don't hear the sound of bodies colliding, the rumbling thunder of impact. The first sound I hear is the deep thud of my opponent's body hitting the ground, followed by gasps as he struggles for air. Maybe it's the adrenaline that blocks out the sound, or maybe it's my euphoria at delivering the hit. Either way, it's silent.

A good hit is also strangely effortless. If I do it right it feels like the man I'm hitting evaporates into me. There is no resistance, only the purity of my own movement and momentum. Many of the guys I hit stand three or four inches taller and outweigh me by twenty to fifty pounds, but none of that matters. A perfect hit absorbs the extra mass and feels like nothing at all. Like the time I drove my right shoulder into the chest plate of a three-hundred-pound tight end so perfectly flush, his arms flailed forward and his head snapped back, his helmet unbuckled and sailed into the air, his body recoiled like a crash-test dummy, and his feet were the last things to hit the turf.

And I didn't hear or feel a thing until it was all over.

For much of my life I've been a football player. My position: linebacker. Physically devastating another man's body is my job description. It is also something I truly love doing. To be honest, I can't say I've ever felt guilty about inflicting pain on a football field.

I understand football is a violent sport, and I'm aware of all the research into the damage high-speed collisions can cause the brain and body. I firmly believe we should do everything possible to make football a safer sport on every level. But when I step between the white lines, my view of the world is filtered through the steel mesh of my face mask, which blocks out everything except the bodies I need to displace in order to get to my endpoint: the ball carrier. There is no room for regret or caution or apology on a football field. As a player I've entered into a covenant not to resist pain and damage, but to overcome it. My opponents have entered into the same agreement. We all operate under the same code.

Believe me, I've been on the receiving end of plenty of brutal, bone-crunching hits—hits that temporarily flattened my lungs and scrambled my brain and sent tremors of pain radiating through my body. And after each one, I've risen up from the hard ground and walked off the pain. It's a point of pride to get right back up after a big hit. That's because a football player is not conditioned for self-preservation. He is not taught to protect his body. A football player is trained to surrender his body to the game, to hurl it at brick walls of bone and muscle again and again and again. In football, your body becomes your weapon. Your strength becomes your faith. Your toughness becomes your salvation.

Now let me tell you about the hit that took all that away from me.

The hit that left me fighting for my life.

❦

It didn't happen on a football field. It happened in a small room with an examination table, two chairs, a window, and a metal light box mounted on the wall. My mother, Barb, sat in a chair, while my father, Sandy, stood by the window, staring out absently. I sat on the exam table, waiting.

On that day in 2009 I was a star football player at Boston College. I was a first-team All-American. I was the ACC Defensive Player of the Year, and I was a finalist for the Butkus Award for the nation's top linebacker. I was six-foot-four, two hundred forty-eight pounds, and in peak physical condition. On almost every day I played or practiced football, and at night I dreamed about it, and in the mornings I woke up desperate to play it again. My life was football and my future was football, and nothing else. I was projected to be a top-ten pick in the upcoming NFL draft.

Four doctors in white lab coats came into the small exam room. I didn't know what was happening, but I knew four doctors couldn't be good. One of them took two MRI results and jammed them in the top of the light box, then turned it on. Images of the two longest bones in my body—my left femur, or thighbone, and my right femur—were lit up. But the two bones looked completely different. It was as if they came from different bodies, or even different species. I knew that couldn't be good, either.

The doctor got right to it. He explained that I almost certainly had an extremely rare disease that affects fewer than two out of every million people in the world. Only two hundred and fifty or so cases of the disease are reported each year. Depending on further tests, my chances of surviving the disease could be as low as ten percent.

The news blindsided me. I felt an instant rush of heat through my body, and before I knew it my hands and neck and forehead were sweating. I felt a strange weightlessness, like when you're leaning back in a chair and it's about to tip over. I felt dizzy and distant and disconnected from everything.

"Mark is a very good football player," were the next words I understood, coming from my father. "He was hoping to make a career of it. When will he be able to play football again?"

The doctor's startled look snapped me back to consciousness. He explained that if I survived—*if* I survived—the damage from the disease and the treatment would leave me "unable to participate in physical activity."

"What do you mean, 'physical activity'?" I heard my mother ask.

The doctor hesitated for just the slightest second.

Then he said, "Mark will never be able to play football again."

Just like that, it was over.

I was twenty-one years old.

❦

The story I'm about to tell is not really a football story, though there's lots of football in it. And it isn't a medical story, either, though the diagnosis I received is the reason I wrote this book. To me this isn't really even a story, in the way it is to others. To me, this is my life. It's made of flesh and blood.

Mostly, this book is about something we all have to do at some point in our lives—face a terrifying obstacle and find out how tough we are. Face our deepest fears and find our strongest faith. Face a troubling enemy, and find our true identity. Reach deep to find what it takes to fight for your life.

I grew up in a middle-class town in eastern Pennsylvania, not far from Valley Forge, where George Washington made camp during the Revolutionary War. I had what you would call a white-picket-fence childhood, with two loving parents and a younger brother, Brad, and a big backyard, where Brad and I pretended to be big stars like Barry Sanders and Marshall Faulk. But I had only one true sports hero—my father, Sandon Mark Herzlich Sr. My full name is actually Sandon Mark Herzlich Jr., so right from the start we had a special bond. My dad wasn't a professional athlete, but he was strong and fit. He played lacrosse on a local club team, and I loved going to see him play. In fact, my earliest and most vivid memory of him is my mother pointing him out to me on a lacrosse field.

"He's right over there, Marky. Can you see him?" she said, holding me up in the air. "Wave hello to Daddy."

The man I saw waving back at me had huge biceps and defined legs. His face was hidden behind a shiny helmet, and he carried a gleaming metal lacrosse stick, like he was some kind of a warrior, which I guess he was. And when he ran off and started playing, he was fast and strong and powerful—to my young eyes like the Hulk and Superman rolled into one. He was the epitome of a pop culture icon—the rugged manly man. On the field that day, I got my first inkling of what I believed it meant to be a man.

It meant being just like my dad.

My dreams were shaped on that lacrosse field and many other fields like it, and ever since I can remember I wanted to be an athlete just like my father. And through hard work and tireless devotion I put myself on a path to achieving that dream. But then came the diagnosis, and everything I'd believed in—everything I'd thought to be true—came crumbling down.

I thought I was indestructible. I learned none of us is.

I thought life was something I could control if I worked hard enough. I learned it wasn't.

I thought I knew what it meant to be tough. I learned I didn't.

This is a story about everything I learned once I realized I didn't know anything.

The reason I wrote this book is because I believe there is something in my story that speaks to all of us. Adversity is a great equalizer, and illness doesn't care who you are. We all face challenges, some not so important, some life-or-death. We're all eventually on the receiving end of a *hit*—a knocked-down, laid-out, brought-to-our-knees, bruised and bloodied hit.

And when that happens—when we wind up in the darkest, loneliest place we've ever been, facing the fight of our lives—we're forced to ask ourselves, "What am I going to do now? Am I going to fight this thing? Am I going to beat it? Am I tough enough to beat it?

"Do I have what it takes?"

What I discovered, and what we can all discover, is that we're capable of so much more than we ever dreamed. We're stronger than we ever imagined.

We're tougher than we ever could have known.

My own journey took me to unexpected places and rocked my mind and heart and soul. It altered the way I look at life and it altered the arc of my dreams. The people I met along the way—the doctors, nurses, new friends and supporters—changed me to my very core.

What I'm about to describe to you wasn't just a detour in the journey of my life—it was the event that taught me what that journey is all about.

And at the end of it all, there is another unforgettable moment that happened on a sports field—a moment so surprising and logic-defying, I'd hardly believe it if it hadn't happened to me.

My illness changed me in other ways, too. It brought me closer to my extraordinary family—and without my family I don't know where I'd be. It brought me closer to my friends, and it brought me closer to God. It was only after I got sick that I was able to pray and speak to God and walk through the door He opened for me at birth. It was only then that I walked with Him through the valley of the shadow of death.

And it was only after I'd lost all my physical strength and toughness, and was left feeling less like a man than ever before, that an amazing woman came into my life and taught me what it truly means to be a man.

Because, you see, I also thought I knew what it meant to be in love, and to have someone love you. But I didn't.

Finally, and perhaps more than anything else, my story is about the blessings we sometimes take for granted in our lives. Because sometimes it's only in hardship that we discover how truly blessed we are.

❦

When I was in the darkest stretch of my fight I received a lot of letters from other people going through their own hard battles. Many of those letters came from kids. One of them was from an eight-year-old boy named Logan.

Logan sent me two photos of himself—one that showed him with no hair and pale skin, and one that showed him in a football uniform, running on a field with a full head of tousled brown hair, a determined look on his face.

In his jangly script, he wrote:

> *Mark:*
>
> *I have leukemia. I know what you're going through. I just want to tell you, never give up and always be positive. I know it is tough but you're tougher and you will win this fight.*
>
> *P.S. I'm in remission. I lost my hair but now I have lots of it.*

I haven't been able to write back to every Logan out there who sent me a letter, so this book is my way of doing so now. This book is the letter I have wanted to write to hundreds of students, children, patients, teachers, moms, dads, grandmothers and grandfathers, doctors and nurses, fans and friends—all of whom have touched my life in remarkable ways.

I hope what you're about to read gives you even a fraction of the strength and inspiration and hope their letters gave me.

CHAPTER ONE

In my life there is before and there is after, and that divide started with pain.

It was right after the New Year—a time for dreaming and looking ahead—and I was home from Boston College for winter break. At the time my mother was coaching squash in our hometown of Wayne, Pennsylvania, and I challenged her to a game. My mother, like my father, was an athlete. She had played squash, field hockey, and lacrosse at Wesleyan University, and had eventually been inducted into the school's inaugural Athletic Hall of Fame, alongside football coach Bill Belichick and marathoner Bill Rodgers. She was a sophomore when she played lacrosse for the first time ever, and by the end of her senior year, she was playing for the national team. My mother was fast and aggressive, and she had unbelievable eye-hand coordination, and on the squash court, I was technically no match for her.

Even so, I was determined to beat her. And in sports, determination can go a long way. We got on the court and my mom put the tiny black squash ball wherever she wanted—high, low, deep, shallow, everywhere. All I could do was chase down every shot and wait until she made a mistake, which I happily did. I still had a chance to beat her when I lunged for one of her perfectly placed shots.

As I lunged I felt a sharp pain in my left leg.

Pain, I have come to learn, is a deeply personal thing. The only one in the world who can feel it is you. No one knows how much you hurt, and no one can ever know. You can share your thoughts with others, and you can share your joy and happiness. But you cannot share your pain. It is yours and yours alone, and your relationship with your pain may be the most personal relationship you ever have.

As a football player, I was no stranger to pain. By then I'd probably played in a couple hundred football games in youth leagues and high school and college, and I'd been banged up in all sorts of ways. Twisted ankles, broken bones, mangled fingers, you name it. And over the years I'd learned that in football, pain is something you play through. Pain is something you endure. You don't allow pain to take you off the football field. You don't complain about your pain or use it as an excuse. In football you swallow your pain and you play as if you're not in pain at all.

In my freshman year at Boston College, one of my teammates, Brian— who happened to be the Big East Rookie of the Year and a top NFL prospect—made the mistake of telling a reporter about his pain. He explained that he'd been playing at less than a hundred percent strength, and that the team's trainers made him go out and play anyway, and that was why he needed shoulder surgery in the off-season. The day his quotes appeared in the newspaper, our head coach, Tom O'Brien, huddled us together for a team meeting on our practice field.

"You all know how I feel about the media," Coach O'Brien said to start things off. "Don't tell the press anything. Not your opinions, not your injuries, not your feelings or philosophical observations. Nothing."

Then Coach picked up a copy of the newspaper and said, "Brian, stand up."

Brian did as he was told.

"You told a reporter you weren't feeling a hundred percent," Coach said, his face turning red. He pointed to the team's defensive line coach,

Keith Willis, who had played in the NFL for several years. "Keith, were you ever feeling a hundred percent when you played in the NFL?" Coach hollered.

"No, sir," Keith said.

"Bill!" Coach continued, pointing to our linebacker coach. "Have you ever played at a hundred percent?"

"No, sir," Bill said.

Coach O'Brien went around the room and asked the same question of every coach there. Big, tough, strong, hard men. And every one of them said the same thing: "No, sir."

Then Coach turned to Brian.

"How the hell could you ever be a hundred percent before the last game of the season?" he screamed, his eyes bulging and his veins popping. "Don't *ever* blame trainers for your bumps and bruises!"

I sat there, stunned. I was just a freshman, and I was shocked to see a player as good as Brian publicly shamed that way. After that, I never complained about any of my injuries. I learned to play through them. The culture of football demands that you deal with pain like you deal with any other minor annoyance—you block it out of your mind so you can go out and play the game.

So when I felt the sharp, unusual pain on the squash court, I really didn't think much of it. It bounced right off the imaginary wall I'd built around the pain center of my brain. It felt like something pinching on the inside of my left knee, almost like I'd banged it against a helmet during a tackle. It just didn't feel like anything major. But when I told my mother about it, she immediately shut me down.

"Let's take a break," she said. "You just finished a whole season of football."

Reluctantly, I left the court without finishing the game. The next day I felt better and I asked my mother for a rematch.

"We'd better not," she said. My mother was determined to protect me from myself. She knew I was so headstrong, I'd play through the pain, and she didn't want me hurting myself any further.

"C'mom, Mom, just one more game," I pleaded. "I've got to end on a good note."

"No way, mister. Not gonna happen."

My mom took me to my favorite lunch spot, Nudy's, instead. I ordered my usual, the bacon-ranch fajita wrap, and decided to take my mom's advice: I rested my knee for the remainder of my winter break, and when I didn't feel the sharp pain again, I wrote it off as a onetime thing. When I returned to Boston College for winter conditioning drills, I told the team's medical staff about the pain I'd felt, but assured them it had gone away. Telling a trainer about your pain is different from complaining— you want them to know how you feel so they can have a record of your injuries and adjust your workload. The goal is always to be ready for game day, and telling your trainer about any pain is the responsible thing to do. A couple of medical staffers looked over my knee and listened to my assurance that it was no big deal.

They agreed and gave me the thumbs-up to practice and play.

My first winter workout began with six eighty-yard sprints. The players formed a straight row along the goal line of our domed practice field, the really big guys on the left, the not-quite-as-big guys in the middle, and the smaller skill guys on the right. I was in the middle with the linebackers, fullbacks, and tight ends. My group had to run each sprint in under ten seconds, with a forty-five-second rest in between. I dug my right toe into the turf as I loaded up on my left leg, and when the whistle blew I ran the first sprint pretty easily. I knocked off the second and third sprints with no problem, either.

For the fourth sprint, I cocked my left hand back over my head as my right hand touched the turf to stabilize my torso. I wound my body into a coil of potential energy. At the whistle my muscles tensed and fired. My left arm swung out in front of my body, propelling me forward. My right knee shot up toward my face. Finally, my left leg straightened, launching me.

And that was when I screamed.

I felt a fiery pain in the same spot I'd felt it on the squash court. Even so, I kept running and finished the sprint. I went ahead with the fifth and sixth sprints, too, but instead of pushing off hard at the start I began slowly and built up speed after forty yards or so. I wasn't about to bow out of the first practice of the year, pain or no pain. I told myself I was just clearing away the cobwebs of the winter break.

But after the sprint drill, the pain was still there, and I had no choice but to tell the trainer about it. If they'd asked me to run six more sprints, I'm pretty sure I couldn't have done it. The trainer told me to go to the weight room and finish my workout there.

"Go do some lifting and see how it feels," he said.

In the weight room, I went over to the big leg-press machine. I wanted to test my leg. I sat down at the bottom of the machine and put my feet up against a platform that held the weight. I'd loaded only three hundred and fifteen pounds, which for me was a good warm-up. Ordinarily I could press as much as six hundred pounds. I released the lock and let the platform lower so that my knees were bent and ready to push the weight back up. But the instant I tried to push the weight, I realized I was stuck.

The pain in my left knee was so sharp, I couldn't even push the platform a single inch.

I took my left foot off the platform and used just my right leg to push it back up and lock it. I got off the machine and limped over to our strength coach, Jason Loscalzo, or "Loco," as we called him.

"I don't know what's going on, but I can't work out my legs," I told him.

Loco sent me to the trainer, who gave me an ice pack and told me to ice my knee and keep track of the pain.

The ice didn't help, and neither did rest. The pain in my knee not only continued—it got worse. I went back to practice and I kept doing workouts, and for a few days the pain was manageable. But after a while, it wasn't. The pain began to colonize my entire leg. It moved up from my knee to my thigh, and it wouldn't go away. I'd sit in a classroom at Boston College and feel my leg start to throb. Or I'd be in my dorm room playing video games with my roommate, Codi, and I'd feel the pain attacking my leg.

Even in the dead of night, when I was fast asleep, the pain would appear and stab me in the leg, like Freddy Krueger torturing my thigh with his sharply bladed gloves, and I'd wake up with an awful howl.

"Shut up, man; I'm trying to sleep," Codi would say, and I'd grab my knee and rock back and forth in bed and try to keep my moans as quiet as possible. But nothing I did could make the pain go away. I had no idea what was wrong with me, and neither did anyone else. All I knew was that I was in excruciating pain that was only getting worse.

My screams got so bad, Codi finally had to go sleep in his girlfriend's room.

For the next several weeks, I wrestled with the pain and lived with the pain and hated the pain and played video games late into the night to take my mind off the pain. I tried to understand the pain, to somehow make sense of it, because not knowing what was wrong or how to fix it was the worst thing of all. I'd had back problems before—could this be some lingering symptom of that? A slipped disk? A pinched nerve? There had to be a logical explanation. Pain doesn't just happen.

And some nights the pain—my constant companion, my torturer—would let me sleep for a while, an hour or maybe two. But always it came back, hard and angry and all at once, and I'd wake up in the dark, screaming and clutching my knee, at three a.m., at four a.m., then at five and six.

The weeks turned into months. I went to see my trainers, and I went to see an orthopedic surgeon. I had an MRI on my back and I was given an epidural. I worked with a chiropractor and I saw a spine specialist. Finally I had an EMG—an electromyogram—to try to diagnose the source of the pain. A few days later, the EMG test results came back.

They were all negative.

As far as the medical community could tell, there was absolutely nothing wrong with me. There was no reason I should have been in pain, much less unbearable pain. No medical professional could verify that I was even *in* pain. There was no conclusive proof that I was, other than my own testimony. And if the doctors say there is nothing wrong with you, then there is nothing wrong with you—or at least, that's how it goes in football. I began to suspect some people didn't believe I was injured. I wondered whether I was making too big a deal of my pain.

Four months after first feeling the pain, the time came to play in Boston College's spring game. It was the year's culminating event and a glimpse at what the next season's team would look like. In those four months my pain had steadily worsened. Some mornings I couldn't even get out of bed, and most days I could barely walk. But if I wrapped my knee up tightly and swallowed four ibuprofen, I could get out on the field and hobble around like a peg-legged pirate and somehow make it through football practice. At the next-to-last practice before the spring game, I lagged behind all the other linebackers, but I managed to stay on the field to the end.

Afterward, I went up to the trainers and said I felt fine.

"I want to play," I told them.

That afternoon the medical staff cleared me to play in the spring game.

That night, like every night, I woke up screaming in pain.

❦

The first time I baffled doctors was way back on September 1, 1987. The doctors told my parents they could expect to meet me sometime in the middle of September, but I decided to enter the world a full two weeks before then. My mother paged my father, then working as a sales rep for Ralston Purina, and told him she was in labor. He got the page in an airport, raced home, and found her cleaning up the house.

"What the heck are you doing?" he said. "Drop the vacuum! We have to go to the hospital *now*!"

"In a minute," my mother said. "Just let me finish this."

My father dutifully waited until my mother finished her vacuuming.

"Okay, now we can go," she said.

I was born in St. Luke's Hospital in Chesterfield, Missouri, about a half hour from our home in the suburb of Kirkwood. "It's a boy!" the doctor exclaimed at nine twenty p.m. (my folks had readied the name Kaylee just in case it went the other way). Right from the start, I was a big boy—nine pounds, seven ounces, and twenty-one inches long. When my father's brother, Adam, held me for the first time, he marveled at my size.

"Boy, oh, boy, look at this kid's legs!" he said. "This kid is cut!" By "cut" he meant my muscles were defined.

My mother heard him say it and panicked.

"Oh, my God, he's cut? Where is he cut?" she said, reaching for me.

"No, Barb, not like that," my uncle said, pinching one of my calves between his thumb and index finger. "Looks like you guys put a golf ball in here!"

From very early on, my life was about sports. For some reason my parents put a tennis ball in my crib with me instead of a rattle, so I learned how to hold a ball before I learned how to walk. By the time I was one year old I could dribble a full-size basketball on our stone driveway and hit a tennis ball right in the center of the racket. My father remembers a game I invented for myself as a two-year-old—I'd take one of those big, bouncy latex balls and lob it in the air, then throw a tennis ball and try to hit it before it landed. Apparently I got pretty good at it and could hit the bouncy ball most of the time. My father tried it once and missed the ball by two feet.

He never played my little game again.

The truth is, I owe any physical prowess I have to my parents. In fact, sports played a part in bringing them together.

My mother and father were both freshmen at Wesleyan University in Middletown, Connecticut, in 1977. One fall Saturday, my dad, a nose tackle for the Wesleyan Cardinals football team, played in a game against the coast guard. My dad was six feet tall and two hundred and twenty pounds, but still somewhat undersize for his position. He also lacked some of the natural finesse that exceptional athletes seem to possess.

But whatever he lacked in ability, he more than made up for in hustle. My father has the most stubborn work ethic I've ever come across. He was what coaches call a "high-motor guy." That meant he made up for his deficiencies with endless hard work and a death-before-surrender attitude. He was a fighter, a gamer, a blood-and-dirt player. When I was younger I believed his toughness came from his upbringing in a rough part of Connecticut, where he was born. I imagined him constantly being forced to defend himself. But when I finally asked my mother about his childhood, she scoffed.

"He likes to *think* he grew up in a rough neighborhood," she said.

I asked my father about it, and he confirmed my mother was right.

"I just grew up with a bunch of other knuckleheads like me who were always starting fights," he said.

Wherever he got it from, my father was one tough man. In that game against the coast guard he played with his usual reckless abandon and at one point collided head-on with a coast guard player. I don't know what happened to the other guy, but my father got banged up pretty good. The

Wesleyan Cardinals won the game 24–7, but afterward my father couldn't remember a minute of it.

That night my dad somehow managed to drag himself to a party hosted by his fraternity house, Delta Kappa Epsilon. A pretty girl named Barb Martin, who played in a Wesleyan field hockey game that day, showed up at the frat party, too. She was looking for someone to take her to the dining hall for a bite to eat. My father, still woozy from his concussion, volunteered.

I don't know whether his likely concussion had anything to do with it, but from what I hear, my father was incredibly charming that night. Over burgers he told corny jokes and made my mother laugh nonstop. The next day they ran into each other again on campus, and my mother was friendly and all smiles.

My father couldn't figure out who she was.

Eventually my father's brain got unscrambled, and he dated my mother for the next seven years. One day he took her to the beach, got down on bended knee, and asked for her hand in marriage. As their families got to know one another they discovered an extraordinary coincidence that tied them together long before my mother and father were even born. Both of their grandparents fled the war in Europe, sailing out of the same city—London—in the same year—1940. After some more digging they learned they'd left from the very same port, on the very same boat—the RMS *Scythia*—on the very same day, April 17.

That our two families were intertwined by a historical coincidence made a great impression on me. There was something deep and important that connected my two families, and indeed my mother and father. Of course they argued, as all couples do, and I'm sure they had dark days or even dark months. But from my point of view, they only seemed to fall deeper and deeper in love as the years went by. Their marriage wasn't successful because Cupid's arrow randomly struck them back in 1977.

Their marriage was successful because they each made a solemn commitment to make it work. Even before they were married my dad sat down with his soon-to-be in-laws and promised, "I will never divorce your daughter. I love her and I will always fight for us." And that's just what he did.

My parents taught me a great love for sports early on, and they also showed me a loving, strong marriage. I may have always dreamed of being an athlete, but that wasn't my only dream. If I think about it, the first and most important goal I ever articulated to myself was the goal to grow up and have a family of my own that was as loving and committed as the one I grew up in. The values important to athletes like my mom and dad, I would learn, are the same values that go into making a great family. Dedication. Discipline. Loyalty. Hard work. Humility. Respect. Passion. To me, sports and family weren't two different things—they were part of the same value set, the same lifestyle.

My childhood was all about sports and family, and for as long as I can remember, I always wanted to succeed in both.

❦

When I was six, my father's company transferred him to eastern Pennsylvania, and today that's what I call my hometown. We settled in the Philadelphia suburb of Wayne, a pretty, quiet town filled with hundred-year-old spruce trees and two-story homes with picket fences and front lawns. It's a solidly middle-class community with its share of doctors, lawyers, and financiers commuting to work in Philadelphia. The King of Prussia Mall isn't too far away, and the kids in town hung out there, meeting up with friends and making an evening out of the two or three dollars you had in your pocket for pizza. Few businesses stayed open past nine p.m., so nightlife usually meant being with your family in kitchens, living rooms, and backyards.

That may sound boring to some people, but it never was for me. That was because I loved playing games.

My neighborhood was filled with backyard trampolines and pools and basketball hoops and Ping-Pong tables, so even before I was old enough for organized leagues I could busy myself from sunup to sundown playing games. Almost every kid under the age of ten played T-ball or soccer or swam for the local team. Then came the peewee games and high school teams. Playing sports was just what kids in Wayne did. It was as natural to us as breathing.

Looking back, I'm pretty lucky to have grown up where I did. But even if I'd grown up in Siberia I'm sure I would have followed my dad into sports.

I completely idolized the larger-than-life image I had of my father growing up. He was handsome in a clean-cut, all-American way, with a strong jaw and a classic mustache he shaved off only once, as far as I know (my mother made him grow it back). He projected confidence and authority. He talked fast but he didn't talk often, so when he said something it carried weight. There was nothing frivolous about him. If you put a cowboy hat on him he wouldn't look out of a place in a Western.

Yet he was also warm and friendly and always laughing about something, and at heart he was something of a jokester. He smiled a lot, as if he knew not to take life too seriously. He was nobody's pushover but he liked kidding around and having fun.

"Mark, guess how many people are dead in there," he said to me once as we drove past a cemetery.

"I don't know, Dad. How many?"

"All of 'em," he said.

The day I went to see my father play lacrosse for the local club team, my mom dressed me up in a white-striped polo shirt tucked into tiny blue shorts. She let me carry my miniature lacrosse stick with a red head and white shaft. I started holding that stick in the morning and didn't let go of it until I feel asleep that night. I can vividly remember watching my father play in the game, and feeling so proud that he was my dad.

After the game he came over and scooped me up off my feet with one arm. Just a few moments earlier, he'd been all brawn and power on the field, but now he was gentle and tender.

"Wanna play catch?" he asked.

He put me down and I ran onto the field. He passed me the ball and I passed it back to him. I played catch with my hero until it was time to go home.

Despite how lasting and powerful that early memory of him has been for me, the truth is that for the first several years of my life, my father worked so hard, I didn't get to see him all that much. His job as a salesman for Ralston Purina kept him on the road for long stretches at a time. One Saturday morning I woke up and went to play in my father's office, since he wasn't home. Or so I thought. My father walked in and surprised me at his desk.

"Daddy, what are you doing here?" I asked.

It was an innocent question, but it hit my father hard. He was away from his family so often, his young son was shocked to see him home on a Saturday morning. My dad reevaluated his priorities, quit Ralston Purina, and became a financial adviser, which allowed him to work more reasonable hours.

After that, my dad was always around when I needed him. Most afternoons we threw footballs or lacrosse balls in the backyard, and some weekends he'd take me hiking in the woods. We'd sleep in cabins and build fires and explore old Indian trails. Eventually, as I got bigger, we became more competitive. My father and I competed at everything—lacrosse, basketball, running, even board games like Boggle and Scrabble. Not once did my father ever let me win at anything. I don't think he was capable of not competing as hard as he could, even against his little boy. In fact, I later realized my father sometimes made up phony words so he could score big points and win at Scrabble.

"Z-Y-P-H-R-A," he'd say. "Zyphra. Fifty-six points."

"That's not a word!"

"Sure it is."

"What does it mean?"

"It's a subphylum of a coniferous tree in the Pacific Northwest."

I knew he was making it up, but with a satisfied smirk my dad wrote down the points. He didn't like to lose, and neither did I. I got my first taste of true competition in the hours I spent with my dad.

My mother was every bit as sports-minded and hands-on as my dad, but she was also a little softer and more tender. Her demeanor was thoughtful and reassuring. She was also our protector, always two steps ahead of the rest of the family, figuring out what we needed. When I was young my mother was the assistant athletic director at Eastern University, a coed college in St. Davids, and she took me to the practices and let me watch the girls play lacrosse and field hockey. And after practices she let me go on the field and pick up a stick and pretend to be one of the players. She was incredibly athletic herself, light and quick and strong, and though she never pushed me into sports, she encouraged my interest in competing. She put me in a position where I *absorbed* sports into my bloodstream.

At the same time neither of my parents was ever boastful or arrogant. In fact, my father was always modest and self-deprecating. "Your mom is the athlete in the family," he'd say. "My skill is running into people with my face." Because of their humility I never, ever felt like I had to live up to any expectation they had of me. I knew they were *already* proud of me, no matter whether I reached their level of success or not. You read stories about athletes who were driven to succeed by some deep desire to make a parent proud, but I can honestly say that is not my story. My folks gave me the support and freedom to set, and reach, my own goals.

❦

They also drew lines I was forbidden to cross. The day I first cursed in front of my dad he stopped everything, took me by the shoulder, and laid down the law.

"That is not okay," he said. "There is a way you talk to your friends and a way you talk to your parents. And the way you talk to your parents is with respect."

Then he added, "Mark, I'm your father, not your friend."

I had a very healthy respect for my dad, mostly because of how big and strong he was. When I was little I liked hiding behind chairs or in closets and jumping out and surprising my parents. One time I jumped out on my father in the living room and scared him pretty good. I thought he'd just laugh, but instead he turned around and got in a crouch and cocked back his right hand. He was ready to strike. My father had never raised a fist to me or laid a finger on me or even spanked me, and he never would. But seeing him react like that kind of spooked me.

Instantly, my father was mortified.

"Jeez, Marky," he said, unclenching his fist. "You scared the heck out of me."

My dad was thirteen when his own parents divorced, and as the eldest boy, he was forced to become the man of the family after his father left. I think that has something to do with the flashes of anger we'd occasionally see. One day when I was eight or nine I made the mistake of being rude to my mom. Nothing made my dad angrier than anyone being rude to my mom. When he came home from work he found me sitting in our little porch off the kitchen.

"I need to talk to you," he said, his eyes narrowing.

He lectured me about treating my mother with respect, and never talking back to her, and always listening to her, and for some reason I felt I had to offer my side of the story.

"Yeah, but she was being a jerk—"

Before I could finish my sentence my father snapped into the same crouch I'd seen when I jumped out at him. His face got red and he cocked back his fist, and at the last second he turned and put his fist right through the kitchen wall.

I was shocked. I'd never, ever seen him that angry.

"Don't ever talk about your mother like that," he growled, pulling his hand out of the crumbling Sheetrock. "You need to treat your mother, and all women, with respect!"

My father got his point across that night.

I don't remember any other time my father got mad enough to put a hole in a wall, but that incident was enough to make me realize there was something else I had inherited from him—something besides toughness and athleticism.

That quick, feral explosiveness my father exhibited on rare occasions— I had that, too. Only in my case it drove me to paint my face with black grease and pound my chest like a crazed person and summon from somewhere deep inside a torrent of pure, seething anger—something I can only call *rage*.

My parents raised me to be a good person, and I think of myself as a good person. But there were times when that goodness went away.

CHAPTER TWO

When I was four, I noticed my mother was putting on weight. Not long after that, my parents sat me down and told me I'd soon have a new brother or sister. One afternoon just a week before the due date, I sat next to my mother on the sofa and put my head to her belly.

"Hey, baby," I said, speaking to my future partner in crime, "see you tomorrow."

"No, Mark, the baby isn't due for another week," my mom corrected me.

But doctors aren't right all the time. The very next day, my mother went into labor and my brother, Bradley Martin Herzlich, was born.

What I remember most about my little brother was how different his personality was from mine. When I was a toddler, all I did was run around the backyard, kicking and throwing balls, but Brad was nothing like that. My mother would plop him beneath a tree, and he'd sit there for hours, happy as could be. He had this fine, downy white hair, like a dandelion, and I always worried one good wind would blow it right off his head. Yet nothing seemed to bother him. He was thoughtful, pensive, content. There's a well-known children's book called *Ferdinand the Bull* about a bull who'd rather sit around idly and smell flowers than engage a matador. My little brother's first nickname became Ferdinand.

Mine, by the way, was Mr. Big.

It was inevitable, I guess, that as Brad grew up he began competing with me. Whatever I did, he had to do it too. If he saw me trying to toss stuffed animals into our Philadelphia Phillies trash can for fun, he had to do it and he had to try to beat me. But I was older and bigger and I almost always won. Brad was a sweet, funny, smart kid and we always got along great, but over the years he found himself trying to measure up to me. He kept track of my accomplishments in sports and he tried to best them. Through no real fault of his own, and in a way he probably couldn't have prevented, measuring up to me became one of the themes of Brad's life.

❦

My father tells a story of watching some seven-year-olds in Wayne playing in a peewee football game. He remembers that after the game, one of the kids on the losing team wasn't in any hurry to follow his father to the car. Instead the boy shuffled slowly behind his dad, head down, shoulders slumped. Finally, the boy's dad chewed his son out—and made him walk home. The car drove slowly beside the boy as he trudged home in his jersey and shoulder pads.

"The kid was scared to death," my father says. "I thought, 'No seven-year-old needs to be yelled at like that. I can do better than this.'"

And so my dad became a coach.

He coached my football and lacrosse teams for as long as I can remember. He and my mom even started the area's first youth lacrosse league. My dad had only three rules: 1) Play hard; 2) Have fun; and 3) Make Coach happy. My dad had no thwarted ambitions or broken dreams that might have made him a more tyrannical coach. For him a good season meant having every kid sign up again to play the next year, because they had had so much fun.

To that end he gave every single kid on one of his teams a nickname. If a kid was fast, he became "Crazy Legs." If he was really fast, he was

"Smoke." There was Jake the Snake, Nick the Tank, and Billy "Madman" Malloy. Brad was "Thunder," while his friend Jon was "Lightning." We all loved our nicknames, because they made us feel like we belonged—like we were something special. Some of the kids who were less sports-minded probably appreciated those nicknames even more than I did, because having one meant you were included. My father was big on inclusion. He felt every child could learn valuable lessons by playing sports, and he didn't think the experience should be limited to just those with above-average ability. He liked handing out awards after games—usually candy bars—and he made a point of spreading the awards around. That didn't always sit well with me. After he gave some other kid a Best Player award, I pouted on the car ride home.

"Dad, *I* was the best player out there today," I finally said.

"I know, I know," my dad said, "but sometimes I have to reward the other kids, too. They're all working hard out there."

I guess there are coaches who might find fault with my dad's approach. Maybe it would strike them as too soft. All I can say is that playing for my father was always a lot of fun, and he never once screamed in my face or made me walk home after a game. Did that approach hold me back as an athlete, or underprepare me for an ultracompetitive world?

No.

You see, by then I was already on a path from which there was no turning back. I was growing bigger and stronger and faster, and I was learning how to tap into my aggressiveness. I was discovering my power.

I forgot to tell you what sports nickname my dad came up with for me. He called me Bear.

❦

At every age I was the biggest kid among my peers. If you lined us all up single file I'd be the head sticking up above the rest. By the age of fourteen

I was already six feet tall. My sophomore year at Conestoga High School in Berwyn, I grew another three full inches. By my senior year I was six-four and two hundred sixty pounds. I never counted them, but most days I'm sure I ate upward of three or four thousand calories. The cafeteria cook at Conestoga—a sweet, funny guy named Chef Jim—sold day-old breakfast sandwiches for a buck apiece. Almost every morning I'd buy five of them—egg, sausage, cheese, and bacon on a bagel, mostly.

"The usual?" Chef Jim would ask.

"Yes, please."

I'd eat three of them straightaway and put two in my pockets for later. Then I'd eat a full lunch, and sometimes a couple of junior bacon cheeseburgers on the way home. I'd top that off with whatever goodies I found in our fridge—leftovers, ice cream, you name it—followed by dinner. This wasn't the healthiest diet, I know, but it did the trick—it made me big. And in football, big was good.

Beyond my size I was also stronger than most kids my age, by a lot. When I was fourteen I joined a team of Wayne-area lacrosse players traveling around the Northeast for different tournaments. One of our assistant coaches was a thirty-year-old guy with a weird clown tattoo on his right calf. For whatever reason this coach singled me out as the biggest kid on the team and challenged me to wrestle him. I politely declined. He kept pestering me to wrestle him, and I kept declining. Finally he got tired of asking. After practice one day he dropped his shoulder and ran right at me. Before I knew it he had his arms around my waist and was trying to wrestle me to the ground.

My instincts kicked in.

I stayed on my feet and put him in a bear hug. In one explosive burst I picked him up, twisted him to the right, and threw him to the ground. I heard the heavy thud of his body hitting the floor, followed by the unmistakable crack of a breaking bone. The coach let out a howl. He went to the hospital and was treated for a broken left fibula, which was the bone right behind his clown tattoo.

That night I told my father what had happened, knowing he'd learn about it sooner or later. I expected he'd be furious. But as I told the story I noticed he wasn't as angry as I figured he'd be. Some part of him was impressed that his fourteen-year-old son had put a man twice his age in the hospital.

Even my own teammates were sometimes on the receiving end of my explosiveness. In my junior year at Conestoga our football team was playing one of our biggest rivals, Strath Haven High. A freshman on our team, a kid named Chris, was playing defensive end alongside me. Play after play, he kept lining up in the wrong spot. I felt my anger bubble up.

"Chris, move over!" I barked, to no avail. Chris stayed in the wrong spot and the opposing running back broke clear for a five-yard gain. On the next play, Chris was out of position again.

"Chris, you're in the wrong spot! Move over!"

Too late: The Strath Haven running back headed straight for where Chris should have been and gained another four yards.

I'd seen enough. As we lined up for the next play I walked up behind Chris, picked him up by his belt loop with one hand, moved him to the right spot, and dropped him there.

But I wasn't finished. After the play I was still fuming.

"Get off the field!" I yelled at Chris. "Get a sub! Now!"

Chris, red in the face with humiliation, ran off the field.

It took me a long time to realize what I had done was wrong. No one deserves to be humiliated that way, no matter how many mistakes they make. But back when I did it I had no control over this explosive side of myself. I hadn't yet learned to harness it and channel it and deploy it only when I needed to. Back then, I was all raw anger and power and emotion.

❦

There's a photo of me from when I was seven and in elementary school. I have chubby cheeks and a goofy smile. But what's important is what I wrote next to that photo in a book my mother kept. In crayon and with backward Ss, I wrote:

I want to be a proferrional football player.

My dad and I both loved lacrosse, but the sport that truly bonded us was football. My dad is a New York Giants fan, and when my mother was pregnant with me, he'd put his head to her belly and say, "Go, Giants!" Way back in 1991, when I was just three years old, I fell asleep on my dad's lap as he watched the Super Bowl between the Giants and the Buffalo Bills. In the final seconds, the Bills kicker tried a forty-seven-yard field goal that would have won the game. The football soared toward the uprights, looking like it might sneak through. At the very last instant, it sailed right.

"No good!" ABC sportscaster Al Michaels yelled. "Wide right!"

At that moment my father jumped up and screamed loud enough to wake the neighborhood. I was startled awake and started wailing. That was my first experience with true fandom—my first taste of the passion of football.

Given my size, there was no way I wasn't going to play football in high school. But in my freshman year, the team was pretty dismal. Our season was seven games, and we lost the first six in a row. I wasn't all that upset, though, because back then my heart wasn't fully in the game. I'd had the chance to play on the varsity team as a freshman, but that would have meant sacrificing much of my summer to practice with the squad, and all I wanted to do was go to sleepaway camp in Maine. So I played freshman football instead. And now that we were losing every game, I was even less interested in the sport. I kind of sleepwalked through the season.

When I came home after our sixth straight loss, my mom told me my father wanted to talk to me in his office, on the top floor of our split-level Colonial. I couldn't recall ever being summoned to his office before. I found him sitting behind his big mahogany desk, doing some paperwork. He didn't look happy.

"Sit down, Mark," he said. "So tell me, what did you think of the game?"

My dad had left work early to attend the game, so he knew as well as I did that we'd played terribly. There weren't enough officials on hand, so the refs asked my dad to handle the first-down chains on the sidelines, and, still in his work suit and tie, he got an up-close view of the action. I knew he didn't like what he saw, and I told him I didn't think our team played well.

"I gotta say, I didn't see much effort on your part," my father said. "I didn't see any intensity or any pursuit of the ball."

I was taken aback. "I did exactly what the coaches told me!" I said in my defense. "It's not my fault we stink! Besides, what difference does it make? We're going to lose our last game anyway. It's just freshman football."

"Stop!" my father said, suddenly dead serious. "Don't you dare talk like that."

My dad didn't raise his voice or get all worked up; he just leaned in and forced me to focus on what he was saying.

"I don't care whether you make tackles or score touchdowns or even win the game," he said. "I do care that you play with passion and a love for the game, whatever game it is. You played today like you were completely uninterested. You didn't show any *wanna*."

Wanna was a term my father liked to use with his Little League players, and I'd been hearing it since I was seven. It was his way of teaching us that winning, in and of itself, was not what our goal should be. The goal was to test your own limits and see what happened if you gave a hundred percent. It was all about desire, and my dad's name for that desire was *wanna*. He believed *wanna* was the most important aspect of football—the thing that made someone good, or even great. It was less about skill than it was about devotion and effort. Before you could win, you had to *wanna* win.

"I watched you today, and I could tell you just didn't care," my father went on. "If you want to play like that, it's up to you. But if you do, I'm not going to come watch you play anymore."

My father could hardly have said anything more crushing than that. The idea of his not wanting to watch me play was unthinkable. He'd always been the loudest, most supportive dad of them all. But sitting there listening to him, I knew deep down he was right. I didn't play the way my father had taught me to play. I had disappointed my biggest fan. His words sent me into something like a panic.

"No, Dad, wait. I want you to come to the next game," I said. "You *have* to come. Give me another chance."

In our last game, I was a changed player. My father's talk flipped a switch. I played with passion and determination and more focus than ever. I knocked down two passes, had an interception, and led the team in tackles. Conestoga won the game, saving us from a winless season. My father was there and watched me play and congratulated me afterward. It was the best victory of my young life.

After that, football was never the same for me again. It went from being just another sport to being my passion. It was like I had discovered a formula that no one else knew—if I played with every ounce of effort in my body, I could dominate on a football field. It was all there, all inside me, just waiting to be tapped. All I had to do was summon it, and everything else would fall into place.

And in this way, football became the outlet for all the raw power and drive and energy I'd had so much trouble harnessing. The nice, sweet, obedient kid I was at home went away, replaced by a mean and relentless creature. I found I was able to put myself into a rage state before games, and I discovered I could stay in that rage state for as long as the game lasted. On the field in warm-ups I'd pace back and forth, revving up my motor. I'd look for the running back on the other team and think, *I'm going to take this guy and drive him into the ground.* I'd imagine the other players were bad people who were trying to hurt me. I worked myself into such an agitated state that I actually saw red. I wanted to access and project every ounce of fury I could muster, and sustain it for as long as I could.

It all came together in my junior year at Conestoga. We were the best team in our league, with nine wins and no losses, and we were playing the worst team, Haverford High. The game should have been a cakewalk for us, but halfway through it, Haverford was winning. I felt the fury rise up in me, and I thought, *How dare these inferior players get the best of us?* I sought out the opposing running back, as I usually do, and I marshaled all my focus on him.

In this case it was a poor kid named Scott Lipschutz.

Sometime in the third quarter, the Haverford quarterback got the snap and handed the ball off to Scott. He saw a gap in the middle of our defense, and he went for it, but I was two steps ahead of him. Before he could see me or change direction, I was on him. I threw all my might at him with a form hit—I put my shoulder into his chest and the top of my face mask under his chin. His feet picked up off the ground, and we both sailed into the air for a moment before crashing to the turf, me on top of him. I jumped up and raised my arms and screamed a primal scream. Poor Scott lay on the ground, clueless as to what just happened. His teammates helped him up, but he staggered into our team huddle instead of his own. I put my arm around his shoulder and walked him back to his huddle.

"This way, buddy," I said.

His coach took him out of the game, sat him on the bench, and tried to get him to remember his own name. Conestoga went on to win the game. When I saw Scott a year later, he told me it took him a full week to get over that hit. For seven days he couldn't remember the game at all. When I heard that, I felt a twinge of guilt.

But to be honest, it was only a twinge.

Mostly what I felt was pride. My hit on Scott was one of those pure hits I neither felt nor heard—in fact, it was the first such hit I'd ever experienced. It was me executing a tackle to perfection, funneling all my strength and drive and knowledge into one moment of flawless football. Looking back, that was the moment I truly fell in love with the game.

Look, I realize what I just described is a moment of brutality. I took a young kid who wasn't nearly as big and strong as me and pummeled him with all my might, most likely giving him a concussion. To some, that might seem like an odd thing to be proud of. To some, it might even seem like a bad thing.

But the truth is, I really didn't feel bad about doing it. I never felt I'd done something wrong. When the game was over, I immediately slipped out of my rage state and went over and shook hands with all the Haverford players, including Scott. I never once carried the emotion of a game into my life off the field. I went right back to being Mark Herzlich, Barb and Sandy's big, sweet kid. I never gave my parents any problems, and I never got in any serious trouble—not once. I wasn't rebellious, and I didn't go drinking in the park like some of my classmates. If anything I was kind of a nerd. Off the football field, I was a good kid.

But on the field, I was a monster.

❦

At Conestoga High our team won back-to-back championships in my last two years. I was named the team's defensive MVP three years straight. As early as my sophomore year I began getting recruiting letters from some of the nation's top college programs. I had a chance to get a full scholarship to a Division I school and get my education for free. My future was falling neatly into place.

But futures, I would discover, don't always fall so neatly. I did accept a scholarship to a top college, but within just a few days of my first football practice there I called my father at two a.m., desperate and confused.

"What's up, buddy? Everything all right?" my dad asked.

"Dad, I don't know if I can do this," I said. "I don't know if I'm cut out for football. Maybe football isn't the way to go."

I was looking for my father to give me permission to do something I'd never imagined I'd do.

Quit football.

CHAPTER THREE

I'd like to say that as a star of my high school football team I had girls lining up to be my date for our homecoming dance. That's the way it is on TV shows and in movies, where the letter-wearing jocks always get the prettiest girls. But my life wasn't like the movies. Finding a date was a nightmare.

The problem was me—I just wasn't very good around girls. On the football field I overflowed with confidence, but that confidence didn't bleed over into my regular life. I was self-conscious, and when I tried to talk to girls, I tended to mumble. I also tried a series of terrible, misguided hairstyles. One year I bleached my dirty blond hair white! Trust me when I say that wasn't a good look.

As bumbling as I was around girls, I had no choice but to try to find a date for homecoming. Showing up alone would have been embarrassing, since all my friends already had dates. The first girl I targeted was Rachel, a pretty blond freshman. After ten minutes of getting up my courage, I sat down next to her in the cafeteria.

"Um, Rachel, hi. How's it going?" I said, trying not to mumble.

"I'm good," she said. "Um, how are you?"

"I'm good, too. Listen, do you want to go to homecoming with me?"

I looked into Rachel's eyes and what I saw there was confusion.

"Uh, well, can I . . . I don't know. Maybe?" she finally said.

"Okay. Well, can I give you my number?"

"Sure, okay."

I scribbled my home phone on a piece of loose-leaf and handed it over. Rachel took it and ran off with a group of giggling girls. I spent the next three days waiting for her to call me. She never did.

I asked two other girls to the dance, and they both said no. I spent a lot of time wondering why I had so much trouble finding a date. I can joke about it now, but back then I really felt like something was wrong with me. How could I be so confident on the football field and so awkward and inept around girls? And on top of that, I was a hopeless romantic; I often envisioned meeting the girl of my dreams on a beach and sweeping her off her feet. I had an image of love and romance that was pretty much the exact opposite of my actual dealings with women. Part of me wondered whether I'd ever be able to change that.

Luckily, there was a girl at Conestoga who was also having trouble finding a date for homecoming, and we agreed to go together. Both of us wanted to go with that special someone, but that wasn't in the cards for either of us. I picked her up and met her parents, and we went through all the rituals of homecoming, though in all I probably spent twenty minutes with her the whole night. Mostly I hung out by the buffet with my best friend, Zack.

Yet I wasn't fated to be alone forever after all.

One summer my family went on vacation in the Dominican Republic, and we stayed at a resort in Punta Cana. White sand, bright sun, turquoise water.

"Maybe you'll find yourself a girlfriend down here," my mom said. "How about that girl there?"

My mother pointed to the water. I saw a girl with long dark hair skipping along the sand, walking in a zigzag pattern as the surf rushed up the beach. She was gorgeous. I sat there and tried to work up the courage to approach her. *Just go up and introduce yourself,* I said to myself. *It's as easy as that.* But no matter how much I psyched myself up, my legs just wouldn't cooperate. I sat there and watched her disappear down the shoreline.

Later that evening, I saw her again, standing by the courtyard bar with a guy. I assumed he was her boyfriend, but I just couldn't let another opportunity pass. Somehow I found the nerve to shuffle over and prop myself next to her.

"Hello," I said. "Can I buy you a drink?"

"Yeah, sure," she said.

I looked at the guy next to her and stuck out my hand.

"Hi, I'm Mark."

"I'm Matt," he said. "And this is my sister, Caitlyn."

Well, how about that?

Caitlyn and I had an amazing time that night. The more we talked, the more confident I got. After a while her brother said he was tired and went to bed, so Caitlyn and I walked down the beach. We talked about anything and everything, and I didn't even mumble. I'd never had this kind of connection with any girl before. We walked slowly back to the resort, and under the moonlight, we kissed each other good night. I fell in love on the spot.

Caitlyn and I exchanged numbers, and we promised to keep in touch. After a few days of not hearing from her, I called and left a message. Then I left another one. And another. Caitlyn never called. I was eighteen, and I got swept up in the romance of how we met, and not hearing back from her kind of wrecked me. I tried to convince myself I was silly to expect anything more than that one kiss, but that didn't work. It still really hurt.

Four months later, out of the blue, Caitlyn finally called. I didn't ask why she'd been out of touch, and she didn't volunteer it. We just picked up where we'd left off and agreed to get together as soon as we could.

✤

My vision of what a college would look like was beautiful Gothic brick buildings, big leafy trees, kids in North Face jackets milling around the lawn, and, of course, a state-of-the-art sports facility. I found all of those things at Boston College.

Founded more than a hundred fifty years ago, with a campus nestled in a historic district in the village of Chestnut Hill, Massachusetts, Boston College was the first school I visited as a senior. The head football coach, Tom O'Brien, let me watch one of his practices and arranged for me to stay with a player. The team took me along to a college party and treated me like one of the guys. After I participated in the New Jersey Nike All-Star Combine, an event where college-bound athletes showcase their skills, Boston College called and offered me a full scholarship to play football.

I accepted it.

The only thing left between Boston College and me was graduation from Conestoga High and the traditional postgraduation trip to Mexico. Outgoing seniors had a tradition of going to Cancún right after graduating for one last great party before shipping off to college. I'd looked forward to the trip all year and saved up enough money to pay for it myself. I knew my parents weren't crazy about the idea, but they let me make my own decisions. I started searching for flights and hotels online.

But just before I booked my stay, I realized what it would mean if I went on the trip. I was due at Boston College early to start football practice, and going to Mexico meant I'd have less time to spend with my family before leaving. It was going to be hard enough saying good-bye to my mom and dad, but the thought of seeing less of Brad bothered me more than anything. I thought of Brad as more than just a brother. He was my friend and my partner in crime, and I was his protector. One of the reasons I never drank or did drugs is because I never wanted Brad to think he had to just because I did. In neighborhood pickup games I always made sure to pick Brad on my team. As my profile at Conestoga grew, and more and more people wanted to talk to me about football, I became sensitive to how Brad might feel left out. At family dinners I'd make a point of steering conversations away from me and toward Brad and his successes. I worried that once I left for BC the pressure of measuring up to me would still be there for Brad without me around to try to lessen it. Suddenly the thought of jetting down to Mexico didn't seem so appealing. That afternoon I found Brad in his room and popped in to see him.

"Hey, how would you like to go camping, just me and you?" I asked.

"Yeah," Brad said, "I'd like that."

So instead of going to Cancún, I went camping with Brad in the Poconos. We went hiking in a state park, rented a canoe and fished downriver, roasted hot dogs over a campfire and made s'mores. At night we reminisced about all the fun we'd had as kids and retold funny family stories. It was a great time, much more fun and meaningful than a few silly days in Mexico would have been. I took the trip because I wanted Brad to know the bond we shared would never be broken, not by time or distance or anything. I wanted him to know just how much he meant to me.

Early that summer it was finally time for me to go to college. Brad and my dad helped me pack the silver conversion van with all my stuff—duffel bags of clothes, a small TV, a minifridge, all kinds of sneakers. There wasn't enough room for everyone, so my mom was going to drive me while my father and Brad stayed behind. As soon as I squeezed the last duffel bag into the van, I felt a sudden unexpected wave of emotion.

I've never been much of a crier. I've always internalized my emotions. I don't know why; it's just the way I am. I always felt like whatever bad thing happens to me, I can handle it. I don't have to ask for help or make a big deal of it. I'm tough. I don't need to cry.

But standing in our garage, I was overcome with emotion. All at once I realized I wasn't going to be living with my parents anymore, and I probably never would again. The thought of that was almost unbearably sad. I took a deep breath and tried not to burst out crying.

Then I hugged my dad good-bye. I started to whisper that I loved him, and the tears just came. I started sobbing, and I could feel him sobbing too. A couple of tough guys, crying in each other's arms. I'd seen my father cry from time to time but never like this.

"I love you, Dad," I said.

"I love you too, Bear. I am so proud of you."

After a long time, we stepped away from each other and wiped our eyes. I gave Brad a good long hug; then I got in the passenger seat. My mom pulled the car out of the driveway and drove away. I looked over my shoulder until I could no longer see my home.

❧

I will never forget the day a five-year-old kid called me fat.

The truth is, growing up, I *was* fat. Like all my buddies, I hit a big growth spurt and my body filled out, but unlike most of them my stomach hit a growth spurt, too. My upper body was pudgy and poorly defined. I tried to stand up tall, thinking that might make my stomach look less prominent. But that didn't help much. I also wore mostly XXL shirts to hide my rolls of fat. That didn't work, either. One afternoon I was standing in front of our house in Wayne when a group of young kids from the neighborhood passed by.

"Hey, you," one of them yelled from the street.

"Who, me?" I said.

"Yeah, you. You're fat!"

I don't think he was trying to be mean, but the little guy hit a nerve. I wanted to say something back, but getting into a screaming match with a five-year-old didn't seem like a good idea. And if I was being honest with myself, I knew the kid was right. I was fat.

"Don't worry about it," my mother would tell me, sensing how self-conscious I was about my body. "You're going to keep growing. It's just a phase."

I tried to believe her, but there wasn't much evidence she was right. My stomach just kept expanding with every day-old egg-cheese-sausage bagel I ate.

The spring before my freshman year at Boston College I went to meet with the school's linebacker coach, Bill McGovern. I walked into Bill's office standing six-foot-four and weighing two hundred and sixty pounds.

"How much you weigh?" he asked, eyeballing me.

I told him.

"And you can still run?" he said.

I squeezed out an unconvincing "Yes."

"If you can run, we'll play you at linebacker," Coach said, referring to the only position I ever wanted to play. "If you can't, we'll put you on the defensive line."

It stung that Coach McGovern saw me as one of those big, slow bodies on the scrimmage line, because that wasn't how I saw myself. I was a linebacker, the quarterback of the defense, the guy with speed and power who prowled the line and made lightning-quick tackles. I knew just what the coach was telling me to do.

Lose weight.

That spring, for the first time, I vowed to get in shape. My best friend, Zack Migeot, suggested we play pickup basketball, and that was what we did every day for three hours. I also stopped eating junk food. Before long my doughy stomach was gone, replaced by the hint of a six-pack. For the first time ever, I was excited to take off my T-shirt in public. When I showed up at Boston College, I weighed two hundred and thirty pounds. and my body fat was only eight percent. Coach McGovern put me in the linebacking corps right away.

I believed I was ready for college football.

I was wrong.

My first ever workout at Boston College that summer was an agility workout. I was the only freshman who'd elected to come to training early, so I was the youngest and least experienced player on the field. I was sweating pretty good before the workout even started. A field thermometer read ninety-three degrees.

My first agility drill was the four-corners drill. Four cones were set up to form a box, and I had to sprint from the first one to the second, shuffle to the third, backpedal to the fourth, then high-step it back to the starting cone. I handled this drill fine and moved on to the ladders. I ran through stepladders laid on the grass, careful not to trip on a rung. I handled that drill, too, and moved on to the next station.

That was where I encountered a drill I'd never seen before—the L-drill.

Three cones were set up on the grass: one at the start, another five yards in front of it, and the third five yards directly to the right of the second cone, forming an L. The drill was pretty simple—I had to run to the first cone, sprint around the second cone, sprint around the cone to the right, come back around the second cone, and finally sprint back to the starting cone. I began the drill and realized the quick changes of direction were harder than they looked. After one loop I was winded; after the second and third, I was gasping. After my eighth loop, I felt like my legs were going to fall off. When I finished that loop, I fell to my right knee and just passed out.

I woke up a few seconds later with a trainer standing over me. He told me to go to the locker room and get checked out. As I staggered off the field, I could hear some of the other players laughing. Back in the training room, they had to dump ice water over me and stick an IV in my arm just to keep me hydrated. After a half hour the other players came in from the workout I'd failed to finish. I looked up and saw an enormous man walking over to me.

His name was Gosder Cherilus, and he was six-foot-seven and three hundred fifteen pounds. He was a senior offensive lineman, and he might have been the biggest human I'd ever seen. Gosder came over to where I was sitting and leaned over me, blocking out the overhead light with his massive body.

"Don't ever do that again," he said.

"Do what?" I asked.

"Don't ever stop halfway through a drill. Don't ever quit on your team."

Then Gosder turned and walked away.

I guess I hadn't been expecting sympathy, but I didn't expect to get scolded either. But the reality was, I had made a terrible impression on the veterans on my first day of practice. I thought I was in great shape; I thought I'd already put in the hard work the spring before I got there. But now I realized the hard work was just beginning. I sat in that locker room, ashamed and dejected. In high school everything had seemed to come so easily to me. But suddenly I wasn't even sure whether I belonged at this level. For the first time in my life I began to doubt myself.

I went to the next day's practice as nervous as I'd ever been on a field. I wasn't used to being this anxious, and the anxiety made it hard for me to concentrate. During one run play, I was supposed to push back against Josh Beekman, a big offensive lineman and at the time an NFL prospect. When the coach blew the whistle, I rushed right at Josh and hurled my body at him. He didn't budge an inch, and I crumpled at his feet. I'd never been stopped so violently before. All the things I had done so well in high school were suddenly hard, if not impossible, to pull off in college. It was like I was completely starting over.

I toughed it out and got through my first week of practice. Coach McGovern and head coach Tom O'Brien never said anything to me that wasn't a screamed instruction to get in the right position. After one practice the coaches set up a big screen and we watched tape of the workout. I saw myself projected on the screen.

"Herzlich, what the heck are you doing here?" Coach McGovern asked.

I didn't know what he was talking about, so I said, "I don't know, Coach."

"It's obvious you don't know," Coach said. "Get up here, Herzlich."

I shuffled to the front of the room.

"Get in the linebacker stance, Herzlich."

I got in the hulking, crouching stance that I'd used all through high school. Coach McGovern folded his arms across his body.

"You've got to be kidding me," he said.

I could hear the other players laugh. Coach McGovern showed me the proper linebacker stance, which was knees bent, feet shoulder width apart, weight on your toes so you can move in any direction, and palms hovering above your thighs. By comparison my stance looked like a guy waiting for a bus.

"Sit back down, Herzlich," Coach McGovern said, totally exasperated.

I went back to my chair and hung my head and waited for the tape session to end.

That night, back in my dorm room, I didn't sleep much. That whole first week I got only a few hours' sleep each night. I woke up going over plays in my mind, dwelling on each mistake, cursing myself for each missed chance. In my mind all I saw were players who were bigger and stronger and quicker than me, and the doubt I felt about my own abilities was crushing. I'd wake up sweating and agitated, unable to find any solution to what seemed like an insurmountable challenge. As I tossed and turned in the darkness, one thought came to me over and over.

You are out of your league.

On my fifth night of camp at Boston College I woke up at two a.m. I lay in bed and stared at the ceiling and searched for answers. I felt alone and scared, and I needed help. I needed to do something.

I picked up the phone and called my father.

"What's up, buddy?" he said in a groggy voice. Just hearing that voice made me feel better. "Everything all right?"

"Dad, I don't know if I can do this," I said. "I don't know if I'm cut out for football. Maybe football isn't the way to go."

"Wait. What are you saying?"

"Maybe I should have played lacrosse. Maybe I shouldn't have quit."

"Mark, slow down," he said. "Let's talk this over."

My dad listened patiently as I talked about my troubles at practice. When I was finished, he took a deep breath.

"Mark, remember when you used to play hide-and-seek with your little buddy Andrew in St. Louis?" he asked.

I thought back to my early years in Missouri, when my first friend and I learned to play hide-and-seek. I remembered being frustrated when I couldn't find Andrew, and I remembered what my father told me back then.

"Don't stop looking," he said. "Keep going. Don't give up."

He taught me the same lesson when I started playing backyard basketball with Zack in Wayne, and he taught it to me again when I started playing football in high school. At every step of the way my father taught me the same lesson: Don't give up. Don't ever give up. Keep going.

"You've never given up when things got hard before," my dad said.

"You're not going to give up now. I know you, Mark, and I know what you're capable of. I know you can do this. Just stay up. *Stay up.*"

My father's words drained the anxiety right out of me. For the second time in my life, something my father said flipped a switch in me. It's not that his message was so profound—it's that it came *from him*. If he believed I could do something, I had to be able to do it. My father's belief in me was like fuel.

From that moment on, I devoted myself not just to making the team but to being a star again. Once the doubt was cleared away I was able to focus better and push myself harder. I played with a lot of passion in high school, but now I conjured up an even more intense rage state in which to function. I became more driven, more possessed, more monstrous. A better, badder Bear.

It didn't happen overnight. My struggles at practice didn't just go away. But as the summer days passed, I struggled less and less. Bit by bit I got stronger and sharper and more confident. At night I devoured our playbook and learned how to play all of the linebacker positions—outside, inside, strong side, weak side. I wanted to be ready when my chance finally came. Coach O'Brien told me I'd play a lot on special teams as a freshman, but all along I had my eye on a starting linebacker spot. I kept my head down, worked hard, and waited my turn.

Late in my first season at BC, our senior defensive captain, Jo-Lonn Dunbar, hurt his hamstring in practice before a game against the University of Maine. I got the nod to start in his place. The college game is so much faster than the high school game, and if you're not ready, you can get totally lost on the field. The play can pass you right by. But the thing is, I was ready. I felt free and loose on the field. I made a bunch of tackles and I had my first collegiate interception. BC won the game 22–0.

I missed a couple of tackles, too, and I thought a lot about my mistakes during the next week. I ran those plays in my mind again and again.

But I didn't let those missed plays eat away at my confidence. I didn't let my mistakes consume me. Instead I consumed them. I used them as motivation to improve.

I started one more game that season, and at the end of the year, I received an honorable mention for the national freshman All-American team.

My father had been right. I did belong.

CHAPTER FOUR

During my first summer at Boston College, I invited my brother, Brad, to come for a visit. Brad was a freshman at Conestoga High School, and he'd just started playing linebacker—my position—for the football team. I wanted him to get a taste of the big-time college football experience, same as I was getting.

I knew full well that people at Conestoga were going to compare Brad to me. It was inevitable. Even in seventh grade, Brad's football coach moved him from defensive end, where he felt comfortable, to inside linebacker, the position I played. If I had success there, the coach must have reasoned, Brad would have success there, too. That wasn't a fair burden to put on Brad. He wasn't as physically big as I was, and he should have had the chance to discover and refine his own set of skills. But at every turn someone would make the comparison between us.

"Was your brother this size when he was your age?" they'd ask him, implying their hopefulness that Brad would one day be as big as me.

The truth is, Brad never had anything to apologize about as an athlete. He never did get as big or burly as me—he topped out at six-foot-two and around a hundred ninety pounds—but he was every bit as tough as I ever was. I remember practicing lacrosse with my dad in the backyard, me trying to score a goal, him defending me. We made Brad, then twelve, the goalie. There he was, this scrawny little kid in an oversize helmet and pads, trying to stop a ball coming at him at ninety-plus miles per hour. I got a lot of shots past him, but I also hit him a few times, and I'm sure it had to hurt. But Brad never complained or said he wanted to quit. He didn't throw down his stick and march off. He hung in there. He toughed it out. That's who my brother was.

Still, people based their expectations of him on my accomplishments, and there were times that wore Brad down. My mother assured him God gave all of us different gifts, and he'd figure his out soon enough. Eventually he did. While a lot of what I did on the field was instinctive, Brad was more analytical. He had an incredible ability to run through scenarios in his mind and anticipate plays and situations. At first all that thinking tended to paralyze him, particularly when he played baseball, a sport that gave him too much time to think. But he got better and quicker at making decisions, and even more adept at analyzing scenarios, and before long Conestoga's head football coach, John Vogan, trusted him to pretty much run the whole defense.

When Brad came up to see me at BC, I gave him the grand tour. I walked him through Alumni Stadium and right past a Heisman Trophy. I brought him into the locker room, where some of the biggest human beings either of us had ever seen marched past us on the way to the football field. I'm sure Brad must have felt like a boy among men, because sometimes that was how I felt, too.

Finally, I took Brad out on the field. Our quarterback at the time was a junior named Matt Ryan, who went on to become an All-American and eventually a franchise quarterback for the Atlanta Falcons in the NFL. Matt basically ran our players-only practices, and I asked him whether it would be okay if Brad sat around and watched. Matt is one of those truly decent guys, and he had a little brother of his own, and of course he said yes. By then Matt was a fairly famous college player, and when Brad saw him, I could tell he was a bit starstruck.

All of a sudden I saw Matt walk over to where Brad was sitting on the bench.

"Hey, why don't you come out and run patterns with the guys?" Matt said.

Brad jumped off the bench and ran out on the field.

I felt my heart seize in my chest. I could see the excitement in Brad's face, but all I could think about was his hands. Brad didn't have the best pair of hands, which in football speak means you can't catch very well. We used to laugh about it at home, because Brad always seemed to let balls slip right out of his grip. Now here he was, about to have a world-class athlete throw him a pass. If he dropped it, I knew he'd feel miserable. Matt whisked Brad to the front of the line of receivers. My heart seized again.

Then I heard Brad whistling.

I knew that when Brad got nervous about something, he'd whistle quietly to himself. It was a nervous tic, and I'm not even sure he knew he did it. I ran over and gave him my pair of extra-grip gloves, then stepped back and held my breath and hoped for the best.

Matt yelled, "Hut!" and Brad took off downfield on a forty-yard pattern.

I watched Matt throw a hard, perfect spiral in Brad's direction. When the ball was in the air, Brad still had his back to the play. For a moment I worried it might hit him in the head. But at the last instant, as we're taught to do, Brad looked over his shoulder for the ball. He had about one second to react.

Brad stretched out his arms and snagged the ball right out of the air, as if he'd done it a million times. On the sidelines, I felt like crying.

"Yeah, Little Herz!" I heard one of my teammates yell.

"Better than his brother!" someone else chipped in.

Brad nonchalantly jogged back to Matt and flipped him the ball. Then he jogged over to me. He had a big smile on his face, and he wasn't whistling anymore.

"You sure picked a good time to figure out how to catch a ball," I told him. "Great job, dude. Proud of you, as always."

Then Little Herz and I high-fived.

Years later Brad wrote an essay about that moment. "At the time Mark was the youngest player in a new system, and he was trying to get the respect of his teammates," Brad wrote. "Nonetheless he brought me along because he knew how much it would mean to me, regardless of the impression the other players might get. Mark was willing to put his own standing at risk out of love for me, demonstrating that family comes first and that one must put the feelings of others over one's own."

Matt Ryan and I, Brad concluded, "allowed me to become an all-star, if only for one summer night."

❦

After my freshman year at BC, I began to get a little recognition on campus. Not much, but a bit. I was a starting linebacker as a sophomore, and once in a while a student would see me and say, "Hey, Mark, good game," or, "Mark, sweet hit!" I was finding it easier to meet new people and make friends.

Still, I didn't have all that much of a social life. I was too busy with football and classes, and I didn't like going out and drinking all night. The football team had a hot tub in the locker room, and before practices the guys would sit around and indulge in "hot-tub talk"—basically everyone bragging about what wild party they went to or what beautiful girl they hooked up with. I rarely had anything to contribute, so mostly I just sat and listened.

The one thing that eased the sting of feeling like a social outsider was my girlfriend, Caitlyn.

Caitlyn was enrolled at a college near BC, and that made it easy for us to see a lot of each other. She was my first real girlfriend, and I was crazy in love with her. If we weren't on a date, we were on the phone, talking about classes and football. It felt really good to have someone to share my life with. That was a new feeling for me.

Then, out of the blue, Caitlyn called and said we had to talk.

"I need space" is what she told me.

I never saw it coming. She told me she still loved me and assured me there wasn't anyone else she was interested in. She said she just wanted to put our relationship on hold. Not being able to see her or talk to her every day gutted me. I couldn't stop thinking about her, and I couldn't think about anything else. When I couldn't stand it anymore, I'd call her, but she wouldn't pick up. After a few days of complete misery, I got on my 650cc Suzuki Burgman scooter and drove to her dorm. I stopped by a CVS and picked up the biggest bouquet of flowers I could find.

I knocked on her door and her roommate answered.

"Where's Caitlyn?" I asked.

Her roommate just stood there and said nothing. I could tell she was searching her brain for a lie. Then I heard laughter. I went inside and found Caitlyn in her bedroom with another guy. They were lying on the bed looking at something funny on a laptop. It was a Facebook page called "Sweet Moped Dude." There was a photo of a Suzuki moped—my Suzuki moped. This guy was not only stealing my girl—he was mocking me about it.

"Mark, wait," I heard Caitlyn yell, but I was already out of the room.

I would learn Caitlyn was dating that guy, and over the next few months, she dated other guys, too. I was heartbroken. Now and then Caitlyn would take pity on me and call me or invite me over, but that only made things worse. It only made me want to be with her more. We went on like that—on and off, back and forth—for a long time, so I never got the chance to get over her. One day I saw the guy I caught her in her dorm with playing guitar on a campus lawn. As I walked by him, I heard him sing:

I hooked up with your girlfriend;
That's right. I hooked up with your girlfriend.

I outweighed him by fifty pounds, and yet he was laughing in my face. Part of me wanted to smash the guitar over his head. I take that back—every fiber in my body wanted to do it. Instead, I just kept walking. It was a good thing for Guitar Guy that we weren't on a football field. I was glad I had enough self-control to let the matter go. But in that moment my sense of self changed. I didn't feel like a big, tough football player. I felt weak and vulnerable and small. Whatever self-confidence I'd built up seeped away. Heartbreak took over.

At football practice not too long after that, the linebacker coach, Bill McGovern, whom we called Govs, told me to wait around afterward. I was sure he could tell I was having trouble focusing on the field, and I wondered whether he was going to kick me off the team. After practice, while the other players went in and showered, he pulled me aside.

"Mark, you haven't been yourself lately," he said. "Is something going on you want to talk about?"

I'd had it drilled into me that a football player doesn't complain. If he's in pain, he eats the pain and plays. And if that pain is emotional, that's even more reason not to bring it up. My instincts told me to tell Govs I was fine.

But there was something about the way he approached me that reminded me of my father. Most of the time, all Govs did was yell at me and the other players. His cheeks would blaze red, and his blue eyes would ice over. But that gruffness was gone now. He didn't want to intimidate me. All he wanted to do was listen.

"Well," I said, "there's this girl." And after that it all came out.

Govs sat patiently and let me tell my story: about how much I loved Caitlyn, how she was popping in and out of my life, how this guy with the guitar was mocking me. When I was through, he took a breath and finally spoke.

"Here's the thing, Mark," he said. "Caitlyn does not make you who you are. I understand how you feel, and I know it seems like your whole world is hanging in the balance. I'm sure Caitlyn is a great girl and all, and if somewhere down the line she wants to be with you, that's great. But if she doesn't want to be with you, that's great, too. Because you are your own man, Mark. Your life is yours, not hers. Don't ever forget that."

As he spoke I felt relief wash over me. I felt like I could breathe freely for the first time in weeks. Here was a guy whose job was to teach me how to smash into other human beings with maximum force. But after practice that day, Govs didn't treat me like his player. He treated me like his son. Beneath the gruffness and toughness, there was a ton of heart.

I felt a lot better after that talk, but I didn't get over Caitlyn right away. That took a while. Bit by bit I was able to get my mind back on football. I got a new roommate, a guy from California named Codi, and we became best friends. Codi had been a freshman quarterback at the University of Idaho when he learned his father had stage-four testicular cancer. He quit the university and went home to be with his dad. Not many people with stage-four cancer recover, so Codi prepared for the worst.

Somehow, Codi's dad's cancer went into remission. After that, Codi transferred to Boston College and wound up sharing a dorm room with me. He was smart, laid-back, and sort of goofy, like me, and we became fast friends. We set up our schedules so we'd have the exact same routine—classes, practices, parties, meals. We were both too big for our standard-issue dorm beds, so we smuggled in two queen beds and fastened them to the smaller frames. Our room was so small, the two queen beds almost touched.

My sophomore year at BC, I solidified my position as one of the best defensive players on the team. I started all fourteen games for the BC Eagles, and I had the second-most tackles on the team with ninety-seven. Twelve of those were for loss of yardage. I also had four pass breakups, two forced fumbles, and two fumble recoveries. After that season I was one of forty-two college players around the country who were put on the watch list for the prestigious Lott Award, which recognizes defensive players who exhibit "integrity, maturity, and tenacity." I liked that last one most of all—tenacity. My profile at BC, and across the country, was growing. For the first time, I began to think I might have a shot at playing in the NFL.

The only downside to the increased attention was the effect it had on Brad. I don't want you to think he was obsessed with measuring up to me or anything like that. It's just that no one ever let him forget who his brother was. Whether or not he felt it himself, other people wanted him to be like me, and they didn't hesitate to tell him so. There was practically no way for him to escape that pressure.

In my sophomore year, I got a call from Brad. The Conestoga Pioneers had just played a rival team and gotten crushed. Apparently Brad blew a couple of assignments. At the time he was wearing the number 22, which had been my number at Conestoga. He chose that number because it made him feel connected to me.

But after the defeat Brad called me to apologize.

"Mark," he said, "I'm sorry I dishonored your number."

I felt terrible hearing him say that.

"Whoa, hold on," I said. "That is not my number. It is *your* number now. You don't need to honor it for me. I am always proud of you, no matter what happens on the field. Besides, twenty-two looks better on you anyway."

We talked about the loss, and I could tell Brad felt better. Not too long after that, he came up to Boston to visit me again. I took him to a party at my dorm, Edmonds Hall. It was crowded and hectic, and someone I didn't know went up to Brad and asked whether he was my brother.

"Yeah, Mark is my brother," he answered.

Then the guy asked, "What does it feel like to know you will never live up to your brother?"

When I heard that, the fire inside me started to rage. I was going to do to this jerk what I should have done to Guitar Guy. But before I could do or say anything, some of my teammates jumped to Brad's defense and chased the guy out of the dorm. Brad shrugged it off, but I could tell it stung a bit.

Growing up I had a church card hanging in my bedroom. It showed a winged lion, which symbolized Mark the Evangelist. Underneath the line was the name Mark, and beneath that were two words: *The Defender*. And that is how I saw myself when it came to my little brother—Mark the Defender. Growing up it was my job to protect Brad from all harm. But how could I protect him from people comparing him to me?

❦

The average football play lasts just six seconds. As a linebacker, if I do my job correctly, the only portion of those six seconds that I actually touch another human being is the last half second.

That's not to say the other five and a half seconds don't count. They count a lot. So do the fifteen seconds or so before the quarterback yells, "Hut," and so do the other thirty seconds in between plays, and the three or four hours directly before the game, and the hundreds and hundreds of hours before that, and the endless play visualizations that wake you from your sleep in the middle of the night, night after night, week after week, month after month, a relentless expenditure of drive and effort and brainpower and obsessiveness that finally converges, on game day, into a single crucial, explosive, dynamic, thrilling half second.

A linebacker lives for that half second.

The mind of a linebacker is a calamitous place. The position I play is, I think, as challenging as any on the field. On the offensive side the quarterback position is highly cerebral, and the best QBs are quick, lively thinkers. But in the end a quarterback's burden is more mental than physical. Quarterbacks exist *not* to get hit by other players—the rules of the game, and the schemes of an offense, are designed to keep the quarterback from getting hurt. Yes, quarterbacks do get sacked, and sometimes they get hit so hard, the crowd lets out a unified groan. But a quarterback can make it through a game with only one or two trips to the turf, and sometimes without getting touched at all. The QBs I've known have been not only incredibly smart, but also as tough as any player out there. They have been phenomenal athletes. Still, at the end of a game, a QB's uniform is likely among the cleanest on the field.

A linebacker, on the other hand, exists to instigate contact. A linebacker has nearly as much of a mental burden as a QB—reading the offense, envisioning the play, calculating angles—but he also has the physical burden of enduring several savage hits each game. A linebacker *knows* before he ever sets foot on the field that he's in for many, many brutal collisions. Pain is a guarantee. The mind of a linebacker accepts that reality and learns to ignore the pain.

For me, all the action happens in my head before it ever happens on the field. Long before I put on my uniform, I've already watched dozens of hours of film of my opponents, studying their moves, charting their tendencies, getting a sense of where they will be at any given time. I focus on the running backs and pay attention to what they do in certain situations. I catalog the opposing team's plays and run them again and again in my mind, until I know them as well as they do. I prepare so much and so thoroughly that I feel I can anticipate anything and everything that could possibly happen in the game. That anticipation is the whole *key* to my success as a linebacker. I have to know what's going to happen before it happens. I have to know what the running back decides to do before he even decides it.

For me, being in a football game is like watching a big action movie. You *know* what is going to happen at the end, even if you don't know exactly how it's going to happen. But the outcome is never in doubt. The good guys will win. The outcome has already been decided in your mind.

So as I stand on the field, waiting for a play to begin, I've already watched so much film and obsessed over so many plays, I feel like I can deduce what's about to happen just from tiny visual clues provided by my opponents. As the quarterback approaches the center for the snap, I look at his eyes and watch him read the defense; I see him look left and right and over the middle, and I watch for him to linger for just a millisecond in any direction. I look at the running back to see whether he is leaning, ever so slightly, almost imperceptibly, any one way. I survey the offensive linemen to see if they, too, are tipping their hand by subconsciously moving a fraction of an inch left or right. I look at eyes and faces and hands and feet and shoulders. I look for shudders and leanings and twitches and tells.

Then my focus goes from narrow to wide. I survey the play in its entirety. I look at all the players and how they're positioned, and scan for gaps and clues and revealing angles. And right around this time, all of the information I've been gathering on the field, together with all the information I've stored in my endless hours of preparation, begins to coalesce not into a number or a statistic but instead into a feeling. I begin to *feel* the play that's about to happen. As strange as this may sound, I almost become *one* with the play. I merge into it, become part of it, fit into its scheme. The universe shrinks to the size of the play, ten square yards, twenty-two men massed together, about to ignite. My mind seamlessly slips out of analytical mode and into instinctual mode, removing any obstacles to quick, decisive action.

Then the play begins.

Linebackers are taught not to move until we see the running back's first step, see what direction he takes. My body wants to jump the instant the play begins, but I'm trained to wait. And once I see that first step, I see the whole play. I have seen it a thousand times in my mind already. And suddenly the play itself begins to move me into position. It's almost like a magnetic pull, shifting me to where I need to be. An offensive player has been tasked with blocking me, and he will come at me and try to take me out of the play. But I already know he's coming. I'm already one step ahead of him. I swat away his clutching hands and move past him, closer to my target.

And maybe another offensive lineman spots me and rushes me, and I maneuver past him, my momentum unstoppable, the magnet pulling harder. And then it's just me and the running back, on a collision course. Five and a half seconds have gone by.

And that is when I harness all of my pent-up anger and emotion and devotion and obsessiveness and explode *through* the running back, destroying his progress, obliterating his plan, ending the play.

Then I get on my feet and do it all over again.

The mind of a linebacker is also a dark place. I can't deny that when I bring someone down I feel a strange sense of joy. A good tackle is immensely satisfying, mentally and physically. The destruction I cause on a field is not random or sloppy. It is precise and surgical. It is the culmination of tremendous preparation and effort. When a play unfolds just like I saw it in my mind, and the magnets pull me into position, and my whole being gets absorbed into the play, blocking all else out, the outcome is undeniably thrilling.

Because I know I'm not just a factor in the play. I am the *determining* factor. The play begins and ends with me.

❧

In my junior year at Boston College, everything came together. Our coaches decided to move me from middle linebacker (which we call Mike) to strong-side linebacker (Sam). At first I worried about changing position, because I felt good about what I'd accomplished at Mike. But my very first practice at Sam was a triumph. It felt completely natural and effortless, and it was the final piece in the puzzle. I'd found my natural spot on the field. Before long I began to feel invincible. I remember giving advice to a freshman player named Luke Kuechly, and what I told him was that, if he kept pushing himself, there would come a time on the field when he felt invincible. Well, that was the zone I was in. I believed that no one—no one—could stop me.

The night before Boston College played Georgia Tech, the team ate at a local hotel, like we usually do on the road. The next morning ten of our guys were sick as dogs, and I was one of them. I couldn't even look at food without wanting to throw up. Still, there was no way I was going to let a little food poisoning keep me from suiting up. The training staff stuck a needle in my arm and intravenously fed me nutrients so I'd have the energy to play. Then I got into my rage state, which muscled the sick feeling out of my stomach. I had fourteen tackles that day, and the Boston College "Screamin' Eagles" won the game. I was right—nothing could stop me. Not even an infectious food-borne bacteria.

One of our next games was against Clemson a day after Halloween. The night before, one of our coaches, Jeff Jagodzinski, screened the great Batman movie *The Dark Knight* for the team. *The Dark Knight* featured Heath Ledger as the Joker, and to me he made an amazing villain. He wore ragged, clownish makeup that gave him sunken eyes and a crazy appearance, and he gave you the sense he was capable of utter mayhem.

He was unpredictable and terrifying. And as I watched the movie, I had a thought—*I want to be terrifying, too.*

The next day, before our game against Clemson, I fooled around with my look. Many football players wear something called eye black, which is a smear of black grease applied under the eyes to reduce the glare from the sun or lights and make the ball easier to see. But instead of just putting some under my eyes, I made big black circles around my eyes. That made me look too much like a raccoon, so I turned the circles into triangles. Suddenly I was transformed. I looked menacing. By then I was already shaving my hair into a Mohawk, because I thought it made me look fierce. But once I added the face paint I was transformed. I was *frightening.* My teammate Clarence Megwa came over and liked my look so much he painted his face, too—only he connected his triangles across his brow to make a sort of mask. We looked like a couple of deranged warriors.

That was just the look I was going for.

The game itself was brutal. In the third quarter, Clarence, a wide receiver, ran over the middle and got hit below the knees by a Clemson safety. As he crumpled to the turf, we knew instantly the injury was bad. Clarence lay on the ground, writhing in pain and covering his face and smearing his black grease everywhere. His left leg had snapped, and both his tibia and fibula had been shattered.

I don't know whether Clarence's injury distracted us, but we lost the game to Clemson, 27–21. After that, the news got worse. Clarence had suffered a compound fracture, and one of the broken bones had penetrated his skin and caused an infection. The infection got so bad, doctors put Clarence in a drug-induced coma for a week. We didn't really talk about it, but all of us realized there was a chance Clarence could die. Football players often refer to the sport as a life-or-death battle. They talk all the time about going to war. But that's just hyperbole. We don't expect to die on the field. Yet here was my friend, in a coma, and all from a single hit. The mood in our locker room was grim. We prayed for Clarence and we told ourselves he was tougher than the infection.

Despite Clarence's injury we still had to play a game that Saturday against Virginia Tech, one of our biggest rivals. It was our most important game of the year, and it would be televised in prime time on national TV. Before the game I decided I had to do something to honor Clarence. So I painted my face with the same black mask he'd worn the game before. Then, with a silver Sharpie pen, I added Clarence's number—11—just beneath my eyes. I told everyone we were going to win this game for Clarence.

That night I was possessed. The mask turned me into an assassin. On one play I jumped right over a running back who tried to cut-block me and sacked Virginia Tech's quarterback. I batted down a couple of passes and made a bunch of other tackles. It was the best game I'd ever played, and later the Atlantic Coast Conference named me its Defensive Player of the Week. Most important, Boston College won the game. The next day I saw my face on TV and in newspapers. Sportswriters wrote about my intensity—and my Mohawk and spooky black mask. I knew I was onto something with the face paint—it was an outward symbol of my inner rage. After that I wore the mask for every game. It became my signature.

And the best news of all—Clarence got better and even played football again.

The Boston College Eagles had a great season my junior year, and even though we lost the ACC Championship Game to Virginia Tech, we were considered one of the top teams in all of college football. The Eagles finished as the fourth-ranked defense in the whole country. I truly valued the team's statistics and accomplishments above my individual stats, but even so, if I'm being honest, I couldn't help but keep track of how the sporting world viewed me as a linebacker. A Web site called Rivals.com ranked fifty college players at every position throughout the season, and at the start of the year I was ranked number forty-eight. Each week I kept checking back, and each week I crept higher and higher, until finally, one week, I was ranked number one. By the end of the season I was consistently among the top three linebackers in the country.

I led the Eagles with a hundred and ten tackles, six interceptions, eight pass breakups, two forced fumbles, and two fumble recoveries. That December the ACC voted me its Defensive Player of the Year, a huge honor. I was also named an All-American, and I was a finalist for the Butkus Award, which honors the best collegiate linebacker. Footage of my best plays was all over ESPN and YouTube. Beyond that, I became a kind of unofficial spokesman for the team, and even for the school. I was elected to BC's Student Athlete Advisory Committee, and I moderated discussions between athletes and faculty. I went on service trips to hospitals and spoke at local banquets. Without even realizing it I'd become the leader of our football team, and possibly the best-known student in the whole school. I discovered I had a huge following of fans not only at Boston College, but across the country.

Just three years after I called my father wanting to quit football, I was considered one of the best college linebackers in the nation.

All of which left me with an excruciating decision—stay at Boston College for my senior year, or leave early and join the NFL.

The allure of the NFL was powerful. Little kids everywhere tossing footballs in their backyards dreamed of one day playing in the NFL. And now, after three good seasons at Boston College, it was my dream, too. I could imagine myself going pro and becoming a great player. I'd be an instant millionaire, and kids would buy my jerseys and want to be me. Nothing but fame and glory awaited. It was an intoxicating dream.

But there were other factors involved. By then there was little question that I could play in the NFL. The only question was, how high would I be drafted? Some analysts were saying I'd be a certain top-ten pick—but only if I stayed for another year of seasoning at Boston College. Others thought I'd be a first-round pick if I entered the draft that year. There were no guarantees either way. And the farther you fell in the draft—into the second or third rounds, or even lower—the less money you were going to be offered to play.

What's more, the average pro football player's career is only three or four years. The guys who last ten or fifteen years and earn a fortune are few and far between. The game is just too violent and demanding, and careers are ended in the blink of an eye. On top of being uncommonly gifted and athletic, you also have to be uncommonly lucky. The odds are against you from the start.

But if I stayed at Boston College and earned my degree, at least I'd have something to fall back on. Getting a good education was a big reason I had picked BC in the first place.

The NFL has a process that allows college players to submit their names to professional scouts for all thirty-two NFL teams. The scouts look at your footage and give you a nonbinding grade that represents where they think you'll end up in the draft. I decided to submit my name, and if I came up as a first-rounder, I would most likely have left Boston College.

When the results came back, I was pegged as a second-rounder.

I was disappointed. Maybe pro scouts didn't think I was big enough, or maybe it was because that year's draft featured a lot of great linebackers. Either way, my big decision became a lot easier.

Fortunately my family was financially sound, so they didn't need me to earn a big paycheck right away. Plus, the thought of spending another year at Boston College was appealing. For one thing, I was still upset that I hadn't won the Butkus Award. I felt like I had unfinished business at Boston College. All I had to do was have another great season, and then for sure I'd be a first-round draft pick after my senior year. The NFL wasn't going anywhere.

That December, I made my decision—I was returning to Boston College.

That decision made a lot of people happy. My parents both supported it, and my roommate, Codi, was thrilled. And to the student body at BC I was now a returning hero. I lay in bed and dreamed ahead to what my senior year would be like. I envisioned us finally winning the ACC Championship Game, and I imagined all the highlight-reel sacks and tackles I'd make. I saw myself getting even stronger and more powerful. And I saw myself growing: as a player, as a student, as a man.

My dream of senior year was a sweet and wonderful one.

That dream was still playing in my mind when I went back home to Wayne for winter break and challenged my mother to a game of squash.

CHAPTER FIVE

When I was little I liked dressing up as Superman. Actually, I liked dressing up as anyone. Some days I'd be a Ninja Turtle, with a green mask and sword. Other days I insisted on wearing suspenders—I don't know why; I just liked them. My mom had to sew buttons on all my shorts so I could wear my suspenders.

But my favorite costume of all was Superman. My mom made me a beautiful flowing red cape, and she made a second one for our border collie mix, Koni. My cape had a big S on it, while Koni's had a K for Krypto, Superman's dog. It was not unusual to see me bouncing around in my red cape, red-and-white-striped shorts, red-and-white sweatband and wristbands—plus my suspenders and my Ninja Turtle sword for good measure. If I wanted to really make my costume special I'd sometimes paint my face.

I was three years old when I discovered I wasn't actually Superman. I was all dressed up in my cape and shorts and sweatbands and standing on our sofa, preparing to fly like a bird or a plane, just like Superman. I jumped off the sofa and smashed my forehead against the corner of our coffee table. Blood everywhere. My mom took me to the hospital, and I got my first set of stitches.

I learned the hard way that a red cape doesn't mean you can fly, and face paint doesn't make you a superhero.

But I was just a kid then, and somewhere along the way I had forgotten that lesson.

✤

It's not surprising that when I felt that sharp, pinching pain behind my knee on the squash court with my mother, in January of 2009, I didn't think anything of it. Before that day, I had no history of significant illness at all. In my sophomore year at Boston College I started getting back pain, and a doctor diagnosed a bulging L4-L5 disk and recommended a spinal epidural, which helped. But other than that—and childhood bumps, breaks, and bruises aside—my medical history was clean. As far as I knew, I couldn't have been healthier.

I listened to my mother and rested my knee for a few days, but when I went back to Boston College in mid-January to start winter conditioning, the pain came with me. At my first workout, I could barely finish a set of eighty-yard sprints because the pain was so bad. And it wasn't only at practice or when I was exercising—my leg would start to throb as I sat in a classroom, or when I was playing video games with Codi, or in the middle of the night. If my screaming didn't wake Codi up, I'd wake him myself and ask him to play video games so I could get my mind off my pain. We'd play until Codi passed out with the controller still in his hand.

After three weeks I had no idea why I was still in pain, and neither did the trainers at BC. They sent me to the team orthopedic surgeon, who I'll call Dr. R. Because I'd had back issues before, Dr. R took an MRI of my back and found nothing wrong. Then she prescribed an epidural, or an injection of anesthetic to block my pain receptors. A nurse stuck me with an enormous needle and asked whether I felt better. The truth was, I didn't. I could still feel the pain in my leg. That was one of the first times I got angry about what was happening.

What the hell is going on inside me? I thought. *Why does nothing help?*

Meanwhile, I couldn't practice with my teammates, and I couldn't run or lift weights. I felt like some kind of leper. All I could do was get in a pool and swim. Instead of a helmet I wore goggles. Working out in a pool felt completely strange—no coaches yelling at me, no loud music to pump me up, no nothing. The tranquillity should have calmed me down, but it had the opposite effect. My thoughts got louder underwater. With every stroke and leg kick, I tried to calibrate whether the pain felt better or worse. After an hour of swimming my body would be okay, but my mind would be exhausted.

Five weeks after I first felt the pain, the trainers sent me to see a chiropractor. I got on my Suzuki and drove along icy roads to his office. He was a pleasant, slightly spacey guy who promised he'd fix my pain with something called the Graston Technique. Then he brought out some smooth chrome tools that could have passed for torture devices.

"Okay, Mark," he said before starting, "this is going to be pretty painful."

And it was. He dug the devices into my body like he was scooping out a cantaloupe, and for the next hour, all I felt was excruciating pain. It was a deep, weird, crunching sensation, like someone was using a cheese grater on me. I tried to be tough and I didn't complain, but after an hour, my shirt was soaked through with sweat and I couldn't be stoic anymore.

"That was absolutely miserable," I told the chiropractor.

"Yeah," he said, chuckling, "it is pretty bad."

I subjected myself to the Graston Technique twice a week for the next six weeks, and each session was more torturous than the last.

And at the end of six weeks, the pain in my leg was still there.

❦

With only five weeks to go before Boston College's spring game, I still held out hope that someone would figure out what was wrong with me and fix me so I could play. Still, I'd barely worked out with the team at all, and when I did, I could put out only a fraction of the effort and energy I usually devoted to practice. I was way behind all the other players.

At practice one afternoon, Mike McLaughlin, our six-foot-one-inch starting middle linebacker, suddenly crumpled to the turf while running a W drill—backpedal five steps, run forward five steps, backpedal five more, and on and on. I saw him clutching his leg, and when I got closer, I could see his calf muscle looked like it had rolled up like a pull curtain and lodged itself behind his knee. Mike had ruptured his Achilles tendon. Just like that, he was out for a year.

Govs approached me not too long after that.

"So how's everything going, Mark?" he asked.

"Good."

"Listen, I know you haven't been doing much this off-season, but are you going to be ready to go for the spring game?"

I wanted to say yes, but I hesitated, because the truth was, I didn't know.

"We don't want you to hurt yourself," Govs went on, "so if you're not ready, I understand. But we'd love to have your leadership out there."

Govs used the magic word: *leadership*. He knew I was the only player on the team with enough experience to step in for Mike. I went straight from our talk to the trainer's room.

"What do I have to do to get myself ready to play in the spring game?" I asked. The trainers recommended another epidural.

I started working out with the team, even though I couldn't really keep up in the workouts. Many days I left practice to swim in the pool. With less than four weeks to go before the game, my teammate Marty Bowman, a fifth-year senior and one of the squad's most respected leaders, found me outside the locker room. He was one of those guys who was always cheerful and smiling, but he wasn't smiling that day.

"Some of the guys think you're taking the easy way out," Marty said. "There's talk you let last year's success go to your head and you're faking this injury to get out of spring ball."

I didn't know what to say. I got up, nodded at Marty, and walked away. Marty didn't know how bad my pain was; no one did, except for maybe my roommate, Codi, who had just moved out because of my midnight screaming. That my teammates would think I was dogging it made me sad. I didn't want my teammates thinking I was letting them down.

Still, I could see why they might think that. I wasn't on the field with them, and I couldn't produce a reason for why I wasn't. Neither could the trainers and doctors. From the outside looking in, it wouldn't be that hard to conclude that I was faking my pain, or at least exaggerating it, to get out of our brutal winter workouts. I hated that anyone would think that of me, but what could I do to disprove it?

Doctors ran a battery of tests on me. They were all negative. No sign of any problem. My pain was still a complete mystery to everyone. And so I began to question myself. I began to wonder whether the problem wasn't really in my head.

Now there was only one week to go before the spring game. I went to see the trainers one last time, and we talked about my situation. My knee was so stiff, it felt like I had a peg leg, but I told the trainers I believed I could play. They told me to practice and see how I felt afterward. I practiced in pain but finished without complaining.

After that, the trainers cleared me to play in the spring game.

Before the game, on April 24, 2009, I swallowed four ibuprofen, suited up, and started jumping up and down to test my left leg. It felt good, better than usual. The adrenaline coursing through my body must have masked the pain. I ran out on the field and got ready to play. The spring game was an intrasquad exhibition, with our offense playing our defense. It was a way to showcase talent and preview the next football season. But

I didn't approach the game as an exhibition. I approached it like it was a playoff game, and I slipped into my familiar rage state. I played with a lot of energy and led the team with eight tackles and a couple of batted-down passes. Afterward I stayed on the field and signed autographs for three hours. That night I took more ibuprofen, plugged in my heating pad, and tried to sleep.

The next morning I woke up in agony. The pain was more severe than ever. For the first time I felt something like panic. Some of my friends on campus had offered me prescription painkillers, and I'd always said no, but that morning I seriously considered taking whatever I could get my hands on to make the pain go away. Instead I toughed it out and tried my best to resume my regular college life. Two days later I went to a cheer-leading formal, but the pain was so awful, I could stay only an hour. I went back to my dorm and got in bed and thrashed around, sweating and moaning. The clock slowly ticked away hour after hour. The pain just got worse and worse.

Finally I couldn't take it anymore. I needed some kind of comfort. I picked up the phone and called a number I knew by heart.

My father's number.

"Dad, I'm in so much pain," I told him. "I'm scared and I don't know what to do."

My father was aware of how frustrated I was, and I'm sure he was frustrated too. The issue of my pain had been dragging on for nearly four months now. My dad heard the anguish in my voice and took a deep breath.

"All right, Mark," he said, "this is what we're going to do."

I listened intently, ready to soak up my father's wisdom.

"You're going to take that credit card I gave you, the one for emergencies, and you're going to go out to a bar, and you're going to start drinking."

For a moment I thought my dad was kidding, but he wasn't.

"Back in the old days they didn't have pain meds," he went on. "They had whiskey. So go out and drink like the cowboys do in the movies. Drink till it stops hurting. I got nothing else for you tonight, son. But I promise you, everything is going to be all right."

My father had once played a game of football with a hand so infected, doctors considered amputating it. He was the toughest man I knew. He'd always warned me not to overindulge in alcohol, but here he was telling me to go out and get hammered. I almost always did what my father told me. That night I took my father's advice, too.

I called my college buddy Fio, a top athlete on the BC ski team, and told him to meet me at a bar and grill on Beacon Street called City Side.

"Drinks are on me tonight," I said. "I just have to drink this pain away."

I don't remember us having an empty glass in front of us for more than a minute or two that night. I started with two Jack and Cokes and two shots of Patrón tequila. After a couple more shots of whiskey, I felt the pain in my leg start to fade. A couple more and I was out on the dance floor. Fio and I closed the bar at two a.m., and afterward I felt so good, I gave up waiting for a cab and started running home. It had been so long since I'd run—really run—and it felt so good to just cut loose. I was in khakis and dress shoes, but I didn't care. The feeling of being pain-free was exhilarating. I ran with the fresh April wind in my face for a full mile until I reached my dorm. Then I got in bed and quickly fell asleep.

I'm sure you can figure what happened next. I woke up the next morning with a terrible hangover and blinding pain in my leg. I was no longer frustrated; I was desperate. I began to think I'd never, ever be pain-free again.

I went back home to Wayne, where my mother had set up an appointment with Dr. Brad Smith, a sports specialist at Bryn Mawr Hospital.

We sat in Dr. Smith's office for a while and talked about my pain. It felt like I'd had this talk a million times before. Suddenly Dr. Smith got quiet.

Finally he said, "Why don't we try getting an MRI of your leg?"

Remarkably, no one to that point had suggested MRIing my leg, which is where my pain actually was. Everyone surmised that the issue was really in my back. Dr. Smith scheduled an MRI for that very day.

But as I sat in the hallway waiting for the test, my leg began to ache. I was angry and frustrated, and I told my mother I didn't want to wait anymore.

"Let's just go," I said.

"Mark, this test is important," my mother said in her calm voice. "You have to wait."

But I didn't want to. This was just another useless test. A waste of time. My mom patiently made it clear we weren't going anywhere.

A technician finally showed up and took me away. The next hour of my life was misery. The technician laid me down on a hard surface and moved me into the giant MRI tube. The first thing I saw on the surface just inches from my face was scuff marks. It looked like someone had tried to claw his way out of the tube.

"Okay, we need you to be perfectly still for thirty minutes," the technician said.

By then my knee was already exploding with pain.

I did my best to lie still, but it was almost impossible. I was lying on a thin layer of foam, and after a few minutes, it felt like I was lying on concrete. And the more I tried not to move, the more aware I became of my pain, not only in my knee but in my back as well: a deep, dull wave of pain, broken up by sharp, piercing stabs of pain in my leg. The technician gave me a ball to squeeze, and squeezing it meant I wanted to stop the test and get out of the machine. I squeezed that ball as hard as I could. I was only ten minutes into the test.

"Please hurry up!" I begged. "I need to get out of here, *please!*"

The technician told me that if he stopped the MRI I'd just have to start all over again. He gave me a thumbed-through copy of *Time* magazine to distract me.

I lay there frantically squeezing the ball and reading something about high-fructose corn syrup. Every few minutes I would scream and beg some more.

Finally the test was done. I scrambled out of the machine and bolted from the room without saying a word to the technician. I ran past my mother in the hallway without a word to her, either. All I wanted was to get out of that hospital.

That night my mother made lasagna and salad, and we sat down for our usual family dinner. I was too upset to eat much, and I noticed my father and mother didn't eat much, either. The mood in our house was grim. I'd been in pain for months, and not knowing why was taking a heavy toll on everyone. I was angry and tired and bitter, and I'm sure my parents felt the same way, but unlike me they never showed it.

My mother, in particular, turned into a lioness. Within a week or two of my complaining about the pain for the first time, my mom became the chief executive in charge of curing that pain. My mother's family has deep roots in America; three of her ancestors signed the Declaration of Independence, and my great-great-grandfather on her side was a pall-bearer for Stonewall Jackson. Just as my father looks like the Marlboro cowboy, my mother looks like the all-American girl next door. She is sweet and friendly and down-to-earth, but she's also strong and precise and deliberate, and whatever needs handling, she handles it. She is good at stepping into a situation and taking charge.

Just as soon as it looked like my pain might not be a passing thing, my mother went to work. She read books and journals, scoured the Internet for information that might be helpful, called medical professionals right and left, and scheduled all my doctors' visits. She went with me to nearly every appointment, and she kept neat and thorough logs of all my diagnoses and treatments. But she wasn't just a researcher and administrator; she was also a cheerleader. She did everything she could to keep my spirits up without once showing how she must have felt inside.

She made fixing my pain the most important thing in her life, because it was.

But not knowing what was wrong with my leg was tearing a giant hole in me, and I knew it had to be wrecking her, too. My mother is a fighter, and if you give her something or someone to fight, she'll fight until she wins. But that was the problem with my pain: We couldn't fight it, because we didn't know what was causing it. We had no one and nothing to fight.

Only much later did I find out that, the night after my MRI, my mother had a meltdown. She was in the kitchen of our home when, for whatever reason, the pressure of the last few months just got to her. She braced herself against a wall, then slid down into a heap, sobbing. All the anger and frustration poured out. At that moment my best childhood friend, Zack, walked into the kitchen. He saw my mother lying in a puddle on the floor and froze. In the best of times Zack doesn't talk much, but in that situation he had no idea what to do or say.

"Hi, Mrs. Herzlich," he finally said while casually walking over my weeping mother and running upstairs to see me.

Not much later my dad found my mother on the floor. He went over and crouched down next to her.

"I can't do this all by myself anymore," she said.

"Tell me how I can help," my dad said.

"Stay home from work tomorrow. Come with us to the doctor."

My father took the day off and came with my mother and me. He was with us in the examination room when the four doctors in white lab coats came in.

CHAPTER SIX

That day, May 12, 2009, we all went to see a neurologist in the morning. Just as we got back home from that trip, my cell phone rang. It was Dr. Smith, the sports specialist who took the MRI of my leg. He said he needed us to come to the University of Pennsylvania oncology department immediately.

"I'll text you the address," he said. "They have your film, and they'll be waiting for you."

I turned to my father. "Oncology? That's cancer stuff, right?"

"I'm sure it's precautionary," my dad said. "Nothing to worry about."

During the half hour ride to the hospital, my father and I talked football, but my mother didn't say a word. We got to the waiting room, which was packed, and I started playing a silly game called Kitten Jump on my phone. After a long while, I heard a nurse call my name. The three of us went into the exam room and the nurse closed the door behind us. We sat there and waited, not talking. My father stared out the window at nothing. My mother had her hands folded in her lap, as if she had to hold them down. I remember running my finger over a small tear in the laminate coating of the exam table. We heard a noise and the door handle turned. The four doctors walked in.

I felt my heart drop.

One of the doctors wedged the MRI results into the light box on the wall. He got straight to it without a hello or any small talk.

"This is where your pain is," he said, pointing to the femur of my left leg. In contrast to my right femur, which was illuminated in the second MRI result, my left femur was glowing white.

"White shows fluid on the MRI," the doctor went on. "A tumor is made of ninety percent water. That is what you see on your left leg."

Tumor. The doctor said tumor. My hands involuntarily squeezed the edges of the exam table. I was in an oncology department, and a doctor said tumor.

"How bad is it?" I heard my mother ask.

"We don't know for sure," the doctor said, "but there is a ninety percent chance the tumor is malignant."

Malignant? I felt heat surge through my body and sweat form on my forehead. I felt an immense, sudden, paralyzing overflow of dread—the kind you feel when you wake up from a dream where you're dying. My eyesight got blurry and the room started to spin. I felt detached from myself and from the space around me, like I wasn't even there. I felt weak and brittle like I might topple over.

"It's either osteosarcoma or Ewing's sarcoma," the doctor said. "We won't know until tomorrow exactly what it is." I'd never heard of either one. I didn't know what a sarcoma was.

"Mark is a very good football player," my father said. "He was hoping to make a career of it. When will he be able to play football again?"

Just then I saw my mother swing her arm toward my father and give him a hard backhanded slap on the chest. It wasn't a tap; it was a slap, and it was probably involuntary.

"Sandy," she said, looking sternly at my dad, "that's not important right now."

I saw guilt wash over my father's face. But the truth is, he had asked the one question I needed an answer to. I had no questions about the tumor. All I wanted to know was, *When can I play football again?*

"Dr. Smith has raised my awareness of the type of player Mark is, and I understand this is hard to hear," the doctor said. "In my opinion Mark's return to playing physical contact sports is very unlikely. The cancer has damaged his leg, and even without surgery, the leg will most likely be too permanently damaged to withstand the pressures of being hit by three-hundred-pound players. Now, Mark will have to have surgery on his leg in order to remove the tumor, and that will substantially reduce his leg strength even more."

The doctor took a pause.

"Mark will never be able to play football again," he said. "There's a chance he may never be able to run again."

❧

I don't think the doctor could have told me anything more devastating than that, even if he'd said I was dying.

My life was driven by athletics. My entire identity was wrapped up in my physicality. I was big and strong and fast and powerful—that's who Mark Herzlich was. There was no other way for Mark Herzlich to be. Those nine words from that doctor—"Mark will never be able to play football again"—turned my world from a place I understood into a place that made no sense. I can hardly describe what it feels like to have your existence so completely upended like that in the span of just a few seconds. It's like the ground beneath you gives way and swallows you up. All the constants in your life—gravity, stability, a sense of belonging, a sense of yourself—disappear. In an instant, your own life is alien to you.

The doctor went on with his diagnosis. I didn't hear much of it, but I later found out what he said.

"It's a miracle that Mark has been able to play football on that leg at all," he told us. "The tumor has severely weakened the bone. Had the bone broken, the cancer inside the femur could have gotten into Mark's bloodstream. If that had happened, Mark would have only a short while left to live."

The subject of treatments came up. My mother was already asking what came next.

"Depending on whether or not the cancer has metastasized, which we will determine after a full-body scan, we will take various procedures into account."

"Like what procedures?" my mother asked.

"Certain surgeries to salvage the leg. But making sure the cancer doesn't spread is the most important thing to consider. So even a procedure like amputation can't be ruled out."

After hearing the word *amputation*, I didn't want to hear anything else. I just wanted to get out of that room.

I don't remember saying good-bye to the doctors, though I'm sure I did. Or maybe I didn't. I do remember walking out ahead of my parents, and nearly sprinting toward the elevator. My mother stayed behind to handle the paperwork while my father tried to catch up with me. Before he got to me, I put my headphones on and played a song on my phone. I didn't want to talk. We waited somberly for my mother, and then we went down in the elevator and got in the car and drove home.

My parents didn't speak during the car ride, and I wouldn't have heard them if they did. I was blasting a song at full volume: "You've Got a Friend." James Taylor. One of my favorite songs as a kid.

When you're down and troubled, and you need a helping hand . . .

I wanted so badly for the music to bury my thoughts, but it couldn't. One after another, questions lit up my brain. *Why me? What did I do to deserve this? What happens if they cut off my left leg? What if the cancer has spread?*

If the sky above you should turn dark and full of clouds...

Some of what the doctors told us in that room finally registered for me. If the cancer hadn't spread, my chance of survival was seventy percent. That did not seem very encouraging. A thirty percent chance to die? That felt like a lot. And if the cancer did spread, then my chances of making it were only ten percent. Ten percent! Sitting in that car I was facing the very real possibility, and maybe the probability, that I wouldn't be alive a year from now. I could die—I could really die.

Winter, spring, summer, or fall, all you have to do is call...

I remembered the lyrics from my childhood. Listening to this song was how I first learned the order of the seasons. I remembered hearing it in the kitchen with my mother, me holding her hands and standing on top of her feet as she danced around. And that was when a terrible, terrible thought overcame me.

I might not ever be able to dance with my children like that.

❦

As soon as we got home I burst out of the car and ran into the house. I headed straight for the stairs to my room. Brad was on the staircase coming down. My parents had asked him whether he wanted to come with us to the hospital, and he'd said no. I knew he was worried about me, and maybe even scared about what the MRI would reveal. But at that moment I didn't want to stop and talk to anyone. I brushed past Brad and just blurted it out.

"I have cancer," I said.

Then I ran into my bedroom and shut the door.

I wish I hadn't told Brad about the cancer in such an abrupt way, but I did. Brad was the one person in our house I could show my worst side to and not worry about the repercussions. As brothers we'd learned to put up with each other's nonsense. We didn't hold grudges, and we didn't take things personally. We just knew that no matter what we'd always be okay with each other. Maybe that's why I chose to be so insensitive to him. Still, I wish I hadn't.

Brad didn't follow me upstairs. Instead, he went downstairs and found my parents on the front porch. They sat and talked about what the doctors had said. My mother, father, and Brad all knew better than to come and talk to me in my room. They knew I needed to be alone, and they didn't bother me.

In my room I lay on my bed, surrounded by my football trophies and awards, and I tried to get a grip on what was happening. But what was happening was unlike anything I'd ever experienced or imagined. Up until that point, my life had been fairly easy and smooth. Sure, I had trouble talking to girls or meeting new people, but that was minor stuff. I'd never been through anything that a phone call with my father or mother couldn't make better.

But now I was facing something vast, something enormous. It was too big for me to comprehend, much less handle. And there was no one I could turn to for help. My father didn't know what it was like to be told you might die. My mother had never learned she might lose the one thing she loved doing more than anything. I was in strange and hostile territory all by myself. I lay in bed and stared at the ceiling for two long hours.

All of a sudden I heard a faint knock on the door, and my brother came in. I didn't say anything, and neither did he. He came over and sat on the foot of my bed. I kept staring at the ceiling. I waited for him to say something, but he didn't. He just sat there quietly. I was glad he didn't say anything. But I was also glad he was there.

Finally, he spoke.

"I love you," was all he said.

"I love you, too," I said.

Brad sat on my bed for a few more minutes, then got up and walked out. I didn't have to tell him I didn't feel like talking; he just knew.

All sorts of thoughts swam around in my brain in the hours after my diagnosis, almost all of them bad. I was angry and scared and confused and overwhelmed. I looked up at all the sports mementos in my room, mocking me now with their shininess. I saw framed acceptance letters and gleaming gold trophies and autographed footballs. I also saw photos of me in action. One photo in particular caught my attention.

It showed me in high school, playing fullback in a game against Haverford High. The photo showed me running along the sidelines with the ball in my right hand, while my left arm was extended, ready to push any defender away. In the photo I looked strong and powerful. I looked like I couldn't be stopped. All the promise of my future was right there, in that photo.

But what really struck me about the photo was my left leg.

My leg was planted on the turf, and I was pushing off it with all my weight. The leg was the source of my power. But now that same leg was riddled with a tumor and, according to the doctors, weakened beyond salvage. I felt a million miles away from the kid in that high school photo. I felt removed from all the mementos on the wall.

I looked away from my football stuff but I couldn't get the photo out of my head. I couldn't get *football* out of my head. Then another thought came to me. A clean and simple thought.

I love football.

That was why I was surrounded by letters and banners and photos and trophies—because I *loved* football. It was my passion, my promise, my purpose. My father gave me an out when he told me he wouldn't come see me play anymore, but instead of quitting the game I doubled down and became a football monster. I did that because I loved it. *I loved football.* And that kind of love doesn't just disappear in an instant. Cancer or not, I still loved football. It was as simple as that.

That thought led to a question, different from all the other sad and dark questions I'd been asking myself in my bedroom.

How can I get back to being the kid in that photo?

And if there was an answer to that question—any answer at all—what was stopping me from finding it?

It took a couple of hours of moping in my room, but finally I got out of bed and went downstairs. I found my father and Brad sitting in the kitchen, staring emptily at the counter and not talking. I could hear my mother crying softly in the next room. It was late and dark, and no one had even bothered to turn the lights on. My father and Brad looked up when they saw me come in. No one said a word. I took a deep breath.

"Dad," I finally said, "I am going to be okay."

My mother came into the kitchen and stood next to Brad. The three people closest to me in the world looked at me with their drawn, tired faces and waited for what I had to say next.

"I am going to beat this cancer," I said, "and I am going to play football again."

My father slowly came around the counter and walked toward me. He looked into my face and what he saw there was conviction. The same conviction he saw when I begged him to give me another chance and come see me play again. He knew I meant it then, and he knew I meant it now.

"Okay," was all he said back to me, "let's do this."

❦

When my father said that, he made it clear this wasn't my battle to fight alone. "Let's do this" meant all of us, the whole family. That was immeasurably comforting to hear at that moment. I wasn't alone after all, and I didn't have to beat this thing by myself. I had my family, and my family was made up of a bunch of fighters. My chances weren't as grim as I thought.

That very night we all sat down in the kitchen and came up with a tentative game plan. I would find that, over the next few weeks, the way we approached this battle was not too dissimilar to how any of us approached playing in a game. It was all about preparation, thoroughness, dedication, and passion. It was about *will*. I found that our training as athletes came in handy, now that we were up against our most fearsome opponent of all.

It felt good, really good, to sit in that kitchen and get to work. The two hours I spent in my bed that night were probably the last time I would be that still for that long. I needed to move, to keep going forward. I needed to make progress. Just like the kid in that photo, I needed to generate momentum. That was the only way this thing would work.

As we sat in the kitchen making notes and plotting appointments, I felt the need to tell my family only one other thing.

"The doctors may know cancer," I said, "but the doctors don't know me."

❦

One of the hardest parts of that day was telling my friends I had cancer. It's not an easy thing to bring up out of the blue. Most of all I dreaded telling Zack. Zack grew up five minutes away from me in Wayne, and we met in kindergarten. One of our other friends' father coached a youth-league basketball team, and we were both on it. Both of Zack's parents worked, so after school and sports he started coming over to our house. There we'd just play more sports—basketball, football, lacrosse. And after that we'd play video games. Most days Zack stayed over for dinner. I'm pretty sure that, besides sleeping, he spent more time in our house than his own.

We were always just easy, happy friends. Zack wasn't as big as me, but he was tenacious when it came to sports. He was as competitive as I was. He held his own in basketball, but I pretty much dominated in everything else—though he might tell you otherwise. When we weren't playing sports or breaking windows with lacrosse balls we were out throwing snowballs at passing cars and doing silly stuff like that. We weren't bad kids or even rebellious kids. We just liked being active, and we liked doing it together. Zack's dream was to play in the NBA. Mine was the NFL.

Zack is the kind of guy who can be in a room for an hour and you don't even know he's there. He just doesn't like to talk much. But when he says something, it's usually smart and funny and right on the nose. He's shy and reserved and, like me, not exactly smooth with the ladies. Maybe that's one reason we liked each other growing up. We stayed best friends through elementary school, middle school, and high school, and even when he went away to the University of Pittsburgh and I went to Boston College we tried our best to stay in touch, though neither of us was a big phone talker. A typical phone call between us might include fifteen words combined.

"Hey."

"Hey."

"What're you doing?"

"Nothing."

"Play ball later?"

"Yeah."

"See ya."

"See ya."

The best thing about Zack was that when we got back together in the summers, it was like nothing changed at all. We went right back to competing, joking around, having fun. Even when my profile at Boston College began to grow, Zack never acted differently around me, not even slightly. He was the same guy, always, every day. That is something you can't put a price on. The constancy of our friendship is one of the great blessings in my life.

But now something *had* changed. I had cancer.

My mother called him the day we met with the four doctors.

"Can you stop by the house, dear?" she asked. "Mark has something he needs to talk to you about."

I'm sure Zack found that pretty ominous, and maybe he even ran through different scenarios in his head as he came over. But I'd bet he never thought for a minute I had cancer.

I heard a knock on my bedroom door and Zack was standing there. He came over and sat on the corner of my bed.

"What's up?" he said.

"Yeah, you know my leg has been bothering me," I told him. "So we saw the doctor and he said I have cancer."

Zack was silent. He sat in silence for a good twenty seconds before speaking.

"That sucks," he finally said. "I'm sorry to hear that. So what do we do now?"

I told him the first thing that would probably happen was that I would start chemotherapy.

"Want company?" Zack asked.

I knew Zack had a summer job at the Princeton bar on the Jersey shore.

"What about the bar?" I asked.

"Don't worry about that," Zack said.

"Well, yeah, then that would be great," I said.

"Okay."

And just like that, my friend Zack turned my problem into his problem. He made my life his life. Over the next several months, he was right by my side every step of the way. We didn't talk much about cancer in that time. But we didn't have to.

❦

Next I had to tell my friends and teammates back at Boston College. I really didn't want to have to call a bunch of people individually, so I sent out a group text. Again, maybe not the ideal way to break the news to anyone, but that was what I went with.

"Hey, guys," the text read, "I went to the doctor and found out I have a rare form of bone cancer. Everything's going to be all right; just wanted you guys to know."

My roommate, Codi, was the first one to call. He'd spent the day inner-tubing down the American River back home in Sacramento, and he was just walking back into his home when he got the text. When he read it, he stood in his driveway and cried. Then he called and told me he was there for whatever I needed.

After my parents and I finished plotting out our initial game plan that night, Brad told me he was taking me to the movies. He got some of his friends together, and we all went to see one of the Wolverine films. The truth is, to this day, I cannot remember going to see that movie, though everyone assures me I did. My brother knew I'd just endured one of the worst days of my life, and he wanted to take my mind off everything that had happened. Brad took the first step toward establishing some kind of normalcy that night, or at least what would pass for normalcy for the Herzlich family going forward.

Later that night, when Zack went home and told his parents about my cancer, his mother asked him how my mom was doing. Zack thought about it for a moment.

"Better," he said.

"Better?" his mom asked.

"Yeah, better than she was before. Because now she has something to fight."

❦

A day after I got my diagnosis from the four doctors, May 13, the results of my biopsy came back. They confirmed I had Ewing's sarcoma. Ewing's is a small, round-cell tumor found in bones or soft tissue, mainly in the pelvis, the humerus, or the femur. It occurs mostly in teenagers and young adults, and more often in men than women. It's most likely caused by some abnormal genetic exchange between chromosomes. The disease presents with fevers and inflammation and, in most cases, great pain.

Up to that point I didn't know too many people who had cancer or were sick or had died. My first experience with death happened when I was four, when my family went to see my grandfather Pop-Pop at his home. We were in his kitchen about to have breakfast, and Pop-Pop was drinking milk out of a blue plastic mug. All of a sudden he collapsed on the checkered linoleum floor. I remember seeing the milk from his cup spill everywhere. My grandmother Gandy rushed over to him, and so did my father, who began giving him mouth-to-mouth. My aunt Linda ran to the foyer, grabbed a big jade cross off the wall and brought it back to the kitchen, clutching it in prayer. My mom jumped on the phone and called for help. I just stood there, horrified, before someone hustled me out to the living room. I turned around for one last look and saw the empty blue cup lying on the floor.

Pop-Pop never regained consciousness. He died of cardiac arrest. Just like that, he was gone. Drinking milk one minute, dead the next. It didn't make sense to me, and it was frightening that someone's life could be wiped out like that. At the age of four, I just couldn't comprehend how *final* it all was. I was still too young to realize that death can be a shockingly ordinary thing. It can be quick and ruthless, and it can happen anytime and anywhere.

Over the years my own mortality wasn't a subject I spent a lot of time on. As far as my thought process went, I didn't have an expiration date.

The stronger I got as a football player, the more invincible I felt. Death wasn't something I ever had to think about. It just didn't concern me.

And so I began the process of fighting my cancer with no real sense of my own mortality, no awareness of my ultimate enemy, no respect for the fragility of my life. These were concepts it would take me some time to wrap my mind around. Like I said, I thought I knew a lot about a lot back then. I had no idea how much I still had to learn.

The confirmation that I had Ewing's sarcoma was the bad news. The good news was in the results of a CT scan—my cancer hadn't spread. "There is no evidence of metastatic disease," the doctor's report proclaimed. That meant my odds of survival shot up from ten percent to seventy percent. Still not great, I thought. But it could have been worse.

My family and I had to make a lot of decisions in the next few months, but our basic plan to make me better was broken into two parts: First, defeat the cancer. Then figure out how to heal the leg. Step one did not require a lot of debate.

The way to get rid of the tumor was chemotherapy.

I stayed enrolled at Boston College and took one summer-school class. I had to show up on campus twice to take my midterm and final exams. Otherwise I moved back in with my parents. My BC teammates got together and wrote me letters of support, and those letters helped a lot. They made me feel a little less removed from my life.

We scheduled my first chemo session for May 19, just eight days after the diagnosis. But first I had to have a double port put in. The ports were little tubes that connected to one of my arteries so doctors could pump the cancer-fighting medicine right into my system. The day before my first chemo session I went to the Hospital of the University of Pennsylvania for the procedure.

It was the first surgery I had ever had.

The nurse gave me a low dose of anesthetic, and before I knew it the double port was already in my body. From the outside all I could see was a raised, bruised bulge on my chest. Knowing there were tubes implanted in my body made me feel like some kind of space alien. On the car ride home the seat belt dug painfully into the wound.

The next morning, May 19, I woke up to the buzz of my alarm clock. The glowing red numbers said six thirty a.m. I rubbed the sleep out of my eyes and threw on sweatpants and an old Boston College T-shirt. My leg hurt badly, so I reached over to the nightstand and popped two Percocet my doctor had prescribed for my pain. I put the chalky pills on my tongue and washed them down with water. I stumbled downstairs and saw my friend Zack sitting at the kitchen counter, eating Quaker instant oatmeal. Zack looked up, nodded, and went back to eating. He looked sleepier than I did. Then my mother bounded into the kitchen, fully awake and alert.

"Morning, Mark!" she said, way too loudly. "Morning, Zacker!"

I ate my own bowl of brown-sugar oatmeal and brushed my teeth. My mother went out and fired up the SUV. Zack got in the back, closed his eyes, and rested his head on the window. I got in the passenger seat, and my mother pulled out of the driveway. Day broke over the neighborhood, burning away the dark of night.

My journey had begun.

CHAPTER SEVEN

I don't know how else to put this except the straightest possible way—my mother saved my life.

She probably saved my father's life, too.

I told you my dad once played football with a badly infected hand. Now let me tell you how it got infected. When he was nineteen, he was out drinking with a buddy in a low-rent tavern in Hartford, Connecticut. Back then my dad worked as a bar bouncer on the side while attending college, and he was popular with everyone who frequented the taverns in that area. After a few shots, my dad's friend got into an argument with some other guy. All of a sudden this guy's friend jumped in and held my dad's buddy so they could gang up on him, two on one.

My dad ran over and punched the man, dropping him to the floor.

The bartender knew my dad and hustled him out the back before the police showed up. Other than a small cut on his punching hand, my dad was unscathed. But two days later, the cut hadn't healed. My father went to a doctor, who told him it was too late for stitches and put a butterfly bandage on the wound. My dad went right back to playing football at Wesleyan University. After a couple of weeks of smashing his hand on the hard turf and banging it on players during tackles, he noticed it was badly swollen. He played football for another week or so before he finally took himself and his damaged hand to an infirmary.

"This is badly infected," a doctor told him. "The bacteria are spreading. We have to get you to an emergency room right away."

If doctors hadn't operated on my father that very day, he probably would have lost two or three fingers and maybe the whole hand. If the bacteria had continued to spread, there was a chance my father could have died.

The thing is, my father would never have gone to the infirmary if it hadn't been for the pestering of the woman who was his girlfriend at the time—my mother. She *made* him go see a doctor.

That was only the first time she saved a life.

A few days before my cancer diagnosis, I called my parents from my dorm room in the middle of a particularly painful night. My mother answered the phone. By then my pain had already been an issue for months, and my mother was deep into the process of finding out what was wrong with me. When we finally hung up, she sat up in bed and turned to my father.

"What if Mark has cancer?" she said.

It was the first time she said that word aloud in relation to my pain.

"He doesn't have cancer," my father said. "No way. He's playing football. How can he have cancer?"

But my mother didn't let it go. She wouldn't have dreamed of telling me about her suspicion, but she didn't let it go.

After I played in the spring game at Boston College, my mother drove up in a big van to help me move all my stuff out of my dorm and into a storage room, since I had to clean out my room during break. As we loaded up the van, I noticed she wasn't talking much.

"What's wrong, Mom?" I asked.

"Nothing."

"You're acting weird."

"Really, Mark, it's nothing. I'm fine."

When we got the van loaded up, I expected we'd go straight to the storage place, but my mother had other plans.

"You know what?" she said. "Let's just leave everything in the van and drive it back home, and then we can drive it back after break. I'm too tired to move it now."

Ordinarily, my mother would have made sure we put all my things in storage before we drove home. She was too neat and organized and deliberate to just let my stuff sit in the van for days. But for whatever reason, she didn't want me to store my stuff. So we drove home to Wayne and left it all in the van.

Not long after that my mother made the appointment for me to see Dr. Brad Smith. After that visit—the visit where he suggested I get an MRI of my leg—she stayed behind to talk to him while I waited in the hall.

"If Mark has cancer," she asked, "will it show up in the MRI?"

"It is highly unlikely he has cancer," Dr. Smith said, "but, yes, it would."

When she came out I asked her what she and the doctor had talked about.

"Oh, nothing," my mother said.

The next day, I got my diagnosis. Once everyone at Boston College found out, someone from the front office called my mother and told her that since I wouldn't be coming back to BC for a while, I had to empty out my dorm room.

"It's already empty," my mother told them. "All his things are here."

Somehow, my mother knew I wouldn't be going back to Boston College. Somehow she knew I had cancer before anyone else did.

And because of that intuition, my mother relentlessly pushed me to see new and different doctors, never letting me rest or get complacent, always driving me to every appointment, staying behind and asking questions, covering every base.

The only reason I went to see Dr. Smith for that crucial visit was because my mother made the appointment for me.

Had she not been so pushy and determined—had she not somehow *known*—another month or two could have passed before I was diagnosed, and the cancer in my femur most likely would have spread.

❦

Heading into my first day of chemo, we had a good team in place. We had a new doctor in charge of my case—Arthur Staddon, a highly respected oncologist at the Pennsylvania Hospital. Dr. Staddon recommended I be treated with a regimen of Cytoxan, Adriamycin, and Vincristine, alternating with VP-16 and Ifex—all very strong drugs used in chemotherapy. The plan was to put me through two rounds of chemo, then rescan my femur and chest to see whether the cancer was receding. After that, I'd have to decide on a treatment to strengthen my leg—most likely some kind of surgery—followed by another four rounds of chemo to make sure the cancer was gone. All told, my treatment was going to take several months—providing everything went well.

The only thing I insisted on was scheduling the chemo to start right away. I didn't want to waste a single minute. Dr. Staddon mentioned I might want to undergo a procedure called "banking" before starting my chemo. Banking is when you store your sperm, in case the chemo wipes out your chance to have kids.

"Every patient I've treated here with the doses I'm giving you has been able to father children afterward," he said, "but if you want to be a hundred percent sure, then you should do the sperm banking."

"How long does that take?" I asked.

Dr. Staddon explained that I'd have to push my chemo back a full week.

"Forget it," I said, without even thinking about it much. "Let's just get started on the chemo."

I would worry about fatherhood some other day. I had a long, long road ahead of me, and I didn't want to start it with a week's delay. I wanted to get going. I wanted to move fast. I'd never felt as much urgency as I did right then. The cancer had been killing me for several months. Now it was my turn. My mother couldn't drive me to my first chemo session fast enough.

We wound our way out of Wayne and headed to Radnor, Pennsylvania, about a ten-minute drive from our home. The building housed all kinds of doctors from the Pennsylvania Hospital, but it also housed a private practice called Pennsylvania Oncology Hematology Associates, or POHA. There are only about twenty-five physicians in the entire country who specialize in sarcomas, which is the type of cancer found in bone, cartilage, fat, muscles, and veins (the much more common type of cancer—breast, colon, lung—is called a carcinoma). Out of those twenty-five physicians, two of them worked at POHA. That's how I ended up there. I was lucky to have a place so adept at handling sarcomas just a short drive from home.

POHA was in a bland four-story brown-brick suite of offices. The place had once been the headquarters of *TV Guide*, but now it looked like any other office building. My mother, Zack, and I walked through the open atrium and veered left toward the reception desk. There were beige walls, brown handrails, and a brown-checkered carpet. Works from local artists decorated the walls. We walked all the way to the back of the building, to the infusions area. Infusion refers to the process of pumping medicine into your body.

A staffer greeted us at the reception desk. I was extremely anxious and maybe even a little buzzed from the two Percocet, so I felt kind of goofy and weird. I noticed she had a tattoo on her wrist.

"Hey, how's it going?" I greeted her. "What's your tattoo?"

She explained it was an old symbol that meant *faith*.

How appropriate, I thought. I never learned her name; from that day forward I just called her Faith.

"Okay, Faith, let's get started," I said.

We checked in and after a while a nurse came by. She was a very sweet lady named Kathleen. She put me on a scale to weigh me—I clocked in at two forty-four, right around my playing weight. Then she gave us a tour of the place: a little cafeteria, a recovery room, and finally, toward the back, the chairs.

The chemo chairs.

I guess the technical name for them is infusion chairs. I saw something like a dozen of them, big, roomy recliner-type chairs, each a bright shade of mint green. They were lined up in rows of three or four and scattered around the room. When we came in there were patients in a handful of the chairs. I tried not to stare at them, but I couldn't help looking at their faces. They were tired, pale, drawn, and bald. They looked miserable. *These are sick people,* I thought. *This is a place for sick people.*

I started to get anxious. The tour was taking too long. All I wanted was to get started.

"Okay, let's go," I said more than once. "Let's get going."

Kathleen noticed my anxiety, but she didn't speed things up. She spoke in a soft, gentle tone that might have struck me as condescending, but instead I found it comforting. Her tone told me she was in charge. As impatient as I was, I got the feeling I needed to listen to Kathleen.

"You're a cancer patient now, Mark," she told me. "And for the rest of your life you will be a cancer patient. Being a cancer patient is forever. We don't have a cure. What we go for is complete remission. But you're going to have to be ready to fight it now, and fight it again. There is no magic drug."

It wasn't exactly a pep talk, but I liked her honesty. She told it to me straight. I could handle that. From that point on I trusted Kathleen. And so far I hadn't trusted very many people in hospitals. Kathleen was raised in Milwaukee and grew up a Green Bay Packers fan. She worked at several different jobs but never felt any were her calling, until her mother-in-law got breast cancer. Kathleen became her caregiver, and found she was good at it. She went to nursing school in Wisconsin, got two degrees, and started out in a hospital psychiatric ward. One day a head nurse shifted her to the oncology department.

Kathleen was hesitant. She knew how emotionally draining it had been to care for her mother-in-law, only to have to watch her die anyway. She wasn't sure she could handle the heavy burden of being around terminal patients. She thought she might be too emotional, too invested. So she went to the head nurse and told her how she felt.

"Let me ask you," the nurse said, "who would you rather take care of you if you were dying—a nurse who acts like it's all business, or a nurse who cries and cares?"

Kathleen has been in oncology ever since.

She took me through the process of chemo, and talked about all the specific drugs I'd get pumped into my body. "They are toxic," she explained. "They are designed to kill bad cells, but they also kill good cells. Like blood cells. Or hair follicles. Your nail beds. Your gastrointestinal tract. You will have diarrhea, constipation, and reflux. There are times when you'll feel bad. But you need to understand what drugs you're getting. This is your body, and this is your fight."

Finally, after a couple of blood tests to check my white cell count, it was time to begin the chemo. We headed toward the chairs. I noticed a small room off to the side, and asked Kathleen about it.

"That's a private treatment room," she said. "Do you want to be in there?"

"Yes," I said immediately. The truth is, I wanted the privacy. If I was going to suffer, I didn't want to suffer out in the open.

We all walked into treatment room S-6. It was a small room with a window, two infusion chairs, an extra chair for a guest, and a small desk with a small TV on it. I picked one of the green chairs and sat down. This was going to be my chair now. This chair and I were going to go through a lot together.

Chemotherapy is administered in cycles. I had an A cycle, which was one session a week followed by a week off. The A-cycle drugs were strong, which was why there was only one session. I also had a B cycle, which was five straight days of chemo followed by a week off. My first round would last one month—an A cycle, a week off, a B cycle, a week off—and then I'd have a second identical round for another month. After that I'd have a checkup to see whether the chemo was working.

On my first day Kathleen got all my chemotherapy drugs ready and carefully double-checked them. Then she gave me some antinausea medication and a steroid. The steroid instantly made me feel better. Kathleen noticed.

"Sometimes the steroid makes it so you don't feel too bad for the first few days," she told me. "But, Mark, you will have your down days. You will get to know your down days. And this is what you have to remember: If you don't feel like talking to anyone on your down days, don't."

That was some of the best advice I ever got.

❧

I took my shirt off and Kathleen put a tube into the port in my chest. Chemo drugs can be administered a lot of different ways—orally, dripped through an IV, pushed through an IV, or even through a port in your head. Some of mine would be dripped into my body, and some would be pushed.

I was also hooked up to something called a saline flush, which all chemo patients get. It's basically a shot of saline that can be flushed through your body before or after treatment, in case something goes wrong, or just to clear away dried blood. The saline flushes weren't exactly painful, but they were horribly uncomfortable. A sharp metallic smell and taste would overwhelm my mouth and nose, like someone was drowning me with cheap vodka. I'd feel the strange, cold shock of saline quickly coursing through my veins. It all felt like an unnatural assault on my body. The flushes lasted only three or so minutes, but I came to dread them nearly as much as anything else.

Kathleen hung a small bag of clear liquid on an IV pole next to my chair, and we got started. My first cycle—cycle 1A—was Cytoxan, Adriamycin, and vincristine. Zack sat in the other green chemo chair, and my mother took the guest chair. We settled in for a long afternoon.

Before long, Zack pulled something out of his bag, and I knew just what it was. It was his Xbox 360 console. Zack plugged it into the small TV on the desk, and put in a video game called Madden NFL 2009. I'd gotten permission from the staff to play video games during my chemo, and I didn't waste any time. Zack and I got right to it, trying to beat each other at Madden and win whatever prize we designated, just like we had a million times before.

"Five bucks?" I asked him.

"Five bucks," he said.

Zack and I played Madden each and every day of my chemo. That video game was a key piece of the puzzle for me. Sometimes our games got so intense, Zack and I would forget where we were and we'd scream after a touchdown or a great tackle. Kathleen would come in and kindly tell us to try to keep it down. And we did—until the next time one of us made a great play.

Not too long into that first session, I got hungry. Going in I already knew something very important about chemotherapy—whatever you ate during the chemo, you would come to associate with pain and misery and ultimately never want to eat again. So I made the choice never to eat any of my favorite foods during the process of chemo. Peanut-butter-and-jelly sandwiches may have been my very favorite food in the world, ever since my mother made them for me when I was young. In high school they were always my pregame ritual: I'd eat one before I left home for the game, and another one right before the game started. So I made sure not to even look at a PB&J during my chemo. I vowed to eat only foods that I wouldn't miss. That first day my mom got on the phone and ordered cheesesteaks from a local diner.

After one bite, I was sure my cheesesteak was rancid. It tasted like tinfoil. I asked my mom and Zack whether their sandwiches were okay, and they said yes. The chemo was already ruining food for me. I poked around the brown paper bag for salt or pepper or anything I could use to make my cheesesteak taste better. I found a few containers of Frank's RedHot sauce. I poured the extremely spicy and zesty sauce over my cheesesteak and took a bite. To my great relief, I could taste the sauce. It was so strong, it overpowered the awful metallic taste. I'd found a secret weapon in my fight against cancer.

Frank's RedHot.

My mother went out and bought a case of it, and from that day forward, I poured it over everything I ate: pizza, saltines, mashed potatoes, didn't matter. It all got dunked in Frank's.

A couple of hours into the chemo session, I started feeling dizzy and dehydrated. My brain started to spin. I felt incoherent, like I couldn't make sense of the reality around me. I couldn't understand what people were saying, and even when I spoke, they didn't sound like my words. Sort of like how you feel when you're really drunk and nothing is stable: a spinning, dizzy, foggy, displaced kind of feeling. I felt so bad, I told Zack I didn't even want to play Madden anymore.

Then I had to go to the bathroom. I was encouraged to drink lots of liquids during my session, and I did just that, raiding the snack room for

Gatorade and cranberry juice. My body easily absorbed all those liquids, plus the chemo liquids, for the first two hours. But after that I felt like I had to go to the bathroom every ten minutes. I pushed myself out of my chair, took hold of my IV pole, and staggered slowly and deliberately out of the room. Zack followed me to make sure I didn't fall. It was only a few feet to the bathroom, but it might as well have been a mile. I had to focus intently to get there. I narrowed my vision, homed in on the bathroom door, and aimed myself before finally lurching forward. Aim, step, aim again, one unsteady step at a time.

Finally I made it to the bathroom, and then I made it back to my chair. I repeated that process every ten minutes. I must have been a sight—this burly six-foot-four-inch football player staggering shirtless past the chemo chairs. But I didn't care what I looked like, and if anyone in the room was looking at me, I didn't notice. My world shrank to a very small patch of space directly in front of me. That's what cancer does to you. It shrinks your world.

After three bags of medicine, my first session was over. All told, we spent seven hours at POHA that day. Most of my chemo days would last six hours. Kathleen warned me that even with the steroid, I might feel particularly miserable after my first day, because it was all such a shock to my system. And she was right—I did feel miserable. I felt nauseated and dizzy and tired and weak and just plain bad.

But on the drive back home, I noticed that I didn't feel like I wanted to die.

That was how I imagined I'd feel. I imagined I'd be throwing up, and un-able to walk, and maybe in a wheelchair, and so sick and spent and beat-up I'd literally want to die. But I didn't feel that way. I felt bad, but not as bad as I'd expected. Even when I got home and went up to my room and lay down, and my head started spinning and my stomach started lurching, I remember thinking, *This isn't too terrible. This is not as bad as I thought. If this is the worst of it, I can handle this. I can get through it.*

My first day of chemo, a Monday, was over. I was a cancer patient now.

❦

As I headed into that first day of chemo, my prognosis was completely up in the air.

Since the cancer hadn't spread I had a better chance of surviving, but there were still plenty of scenarios in which I could die. With regard to my playing football again, most of the professionals around me were pessimistic. In fact, they were downright certain that I wouldn't.

"If things work out okay—no, if they work out *great*—Mark will come out of this walking with a limp," some of the doctors basically told us.

Not playing football. Not running. But walking. With a limp.

I listened to everything they said, and then I ignored it. Because my goals and the doctors' goals were different.

You see, my mind-set had very little to do with cancer. I know that sounds strange, but it's true. In my mind, I had no choice but to beat the cancer, so I skipped right over that part and made my ultimate goal to play football again. I never thought beating cancer would be easy, but I was much more focused on the endgame. The goal for me was not survival. It was playing football again.

I didn't tell a lot of people that was my mind-set, because I didn't think they'd understand.

"Just get better first," they'd probably say. "Worry about football later."

But I didn't want to worry about football later. I needed to worry about it *now*. Because football was everything to me, and a life without football was a life I didn't want to contemplate. Whether that was realistic or not, that was how I approached my disease. I needed to have that goal in front of me so I could get through all the hard stuff along the way.

The first people I told about my football mind-set were my parents. In fact, it was the second thing I said to them the day of my diagnosis, after, "I'm going to be okay." Both my father and my mother told me they believed I'd play again. I may never know if, deep, deep down, they actually felt that way, but I think they did. They knew me well enough to know I'd do whatever it took to play football again, even if no one else in my situation had ever done it. They knew enough not to bet against their son.

"Mark is going to play football again," my father would sometimes tell people who asked about me.

"We just hope he lives and gets better," they'd say, as if my father were out of his mind.

I also told Brad about my goal, and his reaction made it clear I didn't even have to.

"Of course you're going to play again," he said.

My friend Zack believed that, too.

Early on I told only one other person about my absolute certainty that I would play again, and that was my Boston College linebacker coach, Bill McGovern. Like I said, on the field Govs was a terror. He was a former All-American defensive back at Holy Cross, and he thought nothing of chewing out eighteen-year-olds with a string of obscenities. Some of the stuff he yelled at me from the sidelines is completely unprintable, except for the words *you* and *lazy*. On the field Govs was completely intimidating. He was a football guy through and through—hard, gruff, no-nonsense.

But off the field he was one of the warmest guys I ever met. He helped me handle my breakup with Caitlyn, and if I ever had a problem he was always there to talk me through it. He became my father figure away from home, and a really good friend to my family.

After my diagnosis my father called Govs to tell him I had cancer.

Coach was driving at the time, and he was so upset, he had to pull over to the side of the road.

Not much later, Govs called me. We talked about what lay ahead for me, and that was when I told him I fully intended to play football at Boston College again. I really didn't know how he'd react. I didn't know whether he would say, "Mark, just get better. That's all that really matters."

But that wasn't what he said.

"Mark, I have no doubt in my mind you will figure out a way to fight this thing and get back here and play football," he said. "I'm completely on board with what you're saying. We'll see you here next season." After, he sent me Boston College game films throughout the summer to keep me motivated.

Govs may never know how much that meant to me.

My father, my mother, my brother, Zack, Govs, and me—the six people in the world who knew about my football-over-cancer mind-set and who believed I would play football again.

Over the next few weeks of my life, their belief in me would be put to the test.

CHAPTER EIGHT

Two weeks later I was back at POHA in Radnor for my second cycle of chemo. I said hello to Faith at the reception desk, and I gave Kathleen a hug. I saw a patient I recognized from my first day, and I nodded at him. My mother and Zack were with me, and we all settled into room S-6. Zack plugged in his Xbox and powered up Madden 2009.

"Five bucks?" I said.

"Five bucks."

I was on my B cycle now, which meant five days of chemo in a row. It also meant more saline flushes, more dizziness, more drunken stumbles to the bathroom every ten minutes. I noticed Zack had to go to the bathroom a lot, too. He'd taken a liking to the free cranberry juice in the snack area, and he drank a ton of the stuff. I'm sure he drank more of it than any patient there. At one point I looked at him and his lips were purple. Later he came out of the bathroom and told me his pee was purple, too. When he told me he seemed kind of nervous, as if something might be wrong with him. That gave me a pretty good laugh, which was rare in room S-6.

Soon enough I got hungry and we ordered hamburgers, and I doused mine with Frank's RedHot and chewed my way through it. I whipped Zack's butt in Madden and he beat me in NBA 2K9. After two hours the really heavy discomfort rolled in: the nausea and disorientation. Halfway through the session all I wanted to do was go home and crawl into my bed. That was how my whole B cycle went.

I realized I needed to do something to fill my days after my chemo sessions to get my mind off being sick. I couldn't just go have chemo, collapse into bed, wake up, and do it all over again. I needed some kind of outlet. All of a sudden it hit me—golf. I knew my father played a little, and while I didn't know the first thing about it, that hardly seemed like an obstacle now. I had nothing but time to learn how to play. I asked one of our doctors whether it was okay for me to hit the golf course.

"Definitely not," the doctor said. "All the torque and the twisting will hurt the leg too much. You could break it."

I was crushed, and I asked for a second opinion. We called Dr. Staddon.

"I don't see a big issue with it," he said. "Just try not to swing too hard or twist the leg too much. Take a cart. Don't walk. But, yeah, go ahead and play. Just be careful."

I dragged my father to a golf range at a little par-three golf course nearby called Glenhardie. The range was only two hundred and fifty yards long, with a big net at the far end to keep balls from going on a highway. Right away it became my mission to hit a ball over the net. I know—I was twenty-one and way too old for that kind of mischief. But whenever I find myself in a game situation—with a ball and a stick and a challenge—I go back to being eight years old. The thrill of the game overtakes me.

My technique was terrible, but I could still hit the golf ball a mile. Maybe not straight, but a mile. Before too long I was clearing the net. Every time one of my golf balls sailed over it my dad and I held our breath and waited to hear the squeal of tires on the highway. I guess my father should have put a stop to it, but he could see how happy being out there made me, and he let it go. Besides, we never killed anyone—that we know of.

On an actual golf course we were both pretty terrible. Our first time out I think my father shot a 108 and I shot a 120. But I couldn't have cared less about the score. Being outdoors and competing in *something* was the best feeling in the world. I couldn't play football; I couldn't lift weights; I couldn't run. But at least I could try to beat my dad at golf. The sport became the escape I desperately needed. I became gluttonous for golf.

During the course of my treatments I sometimes played thirty-six or even fifty-four holes a day. I know I once played ninety holes in a three-day span. Everyone was happy to see me get so wrapped up in golf, and my grandmother Gandy even bought me my own set of clubs (she bought Brad a set, too, so we could play together). My mother would play with me during the day, and my father would join me after work. Sometimes he had to work late and had time for only three or four holes, but he came out anyway. Sometimes my mother and I played twenty-seven or thirty-six holes in intense, searing heat, and I knew she must have been exhausted. But she never stopped playing, because she knew I didn't want to stop. I even made her play from the white tees instead of the red tees, where women usually hit from.

"It's only fair we hit off the same tee," I explained.

But as the chemo process wore on, I noticed I couldn't play as much golf as I had at the start. I just felt too sick or too dizzy or too weak. I'd play a few holes, then have to quit. Except for my first workout at Boston College, I'd never, ever been too tired to keep playing or practicing any sport. My drive and stamina were the most dependable things about me. The idea of telling a coach or my father, "I'm too tired to play," was unfathomable. It just never happened.

But then one day, on the golf course with my dad, I felt so bad, I just couldn't swing a club anymore. Even then, something in me didn't want to tell him. The words didn't want to come out. I knew he wanted to see me play with as much vigor as possible, because that meant I wasn't feeling so bad. Telling him I felt miserable would have been a blow to him, and I didn't want to do that to him. I stood on a tee box deciding what to do. Finally, my body made the decision for me.

"Dad," I said, "I don't feel good. Can we go inside instead of playing?"

"Yeah, of course," my father said instantly. "Let's go in."

We drove the cart to the clubhouse and sat inside having iced teas. Opening up to each other about how we felt or our vulnerabilities had never been a big part of the fabric of our relationship. But that was changing now. I could no longer internalize everything. I had to share what I was going through with my father, at least a little bit. It was brand-new territory for us both.

What I found was that, as I became more vulnerable around my father, he became more vulnerable around me. And when that happened, my father became more *real* to me. My childhood image of him as a larger-than-life warrior started to chip away. In its place, I saw a real human being. That did not make my father any less of a man to me. But I found that it is easier to love a human being than it is to love an image.

❧

Our family was changing in many ways. First my pain, then my diagnosis, then many sleepless nights consumed us whole. It turned all of our worlds upside down. I could see the pressure it put on my parents, and early on I knew it was killing them not to know what was wrong with me. It was so frustrating for my mother that she often cried about it, though she never let me see that. When I'd come home from Boston College and tell her a trainer told me to take Advil, I could see the anger rise up in her face. Later she would call the trainer and demand answers.

"Advil?" she'd say. "Is that the only thing you can think of?"

Another time, one of my doctors told her I'd be perfectly fine if I just stopped playing football. This doctor had no idea what was wrong with me, yet still stated authoritatively that quitting football would make my pain go away. That kind of thing drove my mother crazy. Instead of answers she was getting half-baked theories. And then she'd hear me moaning in pain in one of my late-night calls. The frustration must have been agonizing, yet she never let me see her get too angry or emotional.

"We need to keep the energy positive," she told me. "Being negative isn't going to help anything."

When things got too heavy she'd lace up her running shoes and go for a long jog. Or maybe she'd find a private place and cry.

My father wasn't as good at hiding his emotions. Before the diagnosis he was angry no one could figure out what was wrong, and after the diagnosis he was furious that four crucial months had slipped away. He was particularly angry with Dr. R, because he felt she'd completely botched the situation.

"A kid comes in and complains of leg pain and you never MRI his leg?" he said. "How is that competent?"

The idea that I might never play football again because medical professionals had completely missed the cancer was practically unbearable to my dad. That is why his first question to doctors was whether or not I could play again. He knew how interwoven my life and football were. To see all that taken away from me must have given him a terribly helpless feeling.

Like I said, my father did his best to follow my mother's instructions—keep the energy positive—but it wasn't easy for him. I could tell when he was angry, and I could tell when he was frustrated. The stress of it all made him overeat, and he started to put on weight. I'd never seen my father be anything other than fit and trim. Now he was literally changing in front of my eyes. We all were, in different ways. Cancer is a completely transformative event. It was like someone put our family in a bubble and started sucking the air out of it bit by bit. The pressure was overwhelming, and it was changing us.

And yet my father never let me see him break down or cry, and for a long time I didn't know whether he ever did. Only much later did I find out that, on some evenings, when things seemed bleak, my father would get up from wherever he was and excuse himself to my mother.

"Where are you going?" she'd ask.

"To the shed," he'd say.

Behind our house we have a small brown wooden shed where we keep the lawn mower and all our lacrosse sticks and bags of fertilizer and gardening tools. My father would go there with a flashlight and close the door behind him. And then, in the privacy of the shed, he would let it all out.

My father would break down and cry.

The shed became my father's spot, and going there became a ritual for him. Eventually my mother went out there, too. My parents did not ever want to cry in front of Brad or me. But on some days they needed a trip to the shed.

❦

From the very start my cancer was a public matter. The day after the diagnosis my father called Barry Gallup, the associate athletic director for football operations at Boston College, and together they crafted a press release. ESPN picked up on it and ran a segment on me. That segment was how many of my friends and my parents' friends learned I had cancer. Ordinarily the news might have slowly leaked out across the neighborhood, and my parents would have had time to figure out a way to let everyone know. But they didn't get that chance. Everyone found out at once.

My mother called all our closest friends and relatives, but after that she asked her friend Christine to send out an e-mail on our behalf. "Dear Friends of the Herzlich Family," it began. "I am very sad to inform you that Mark has been diagnosed with Ewing's sarcoma." It went on to say, "Due to their focus on getting Mark well, the family would appreciate it if in the near future there would be limited contact. We all love and respect the Herzlich family and want to extend our best wishes, but what Barb asks of us right now is to keep Mark in our prayers." Like me, my mother wasn't the type to ask for help. She didn't want our neighbors feeling like they had to drop by with chicken casseroles and fruit baskets.

But once my chemo started, things got pretty hectic around our house. My mother had a million things to do. She had to organize all my medication, and she made a big chart and relabeled every pill bottle with a Sharpie to make it easy for me to know what I was taking. She made all my doctor appointments and kept doing research on Ewing's sarcoma. She couldn't plan any meals for me, because she never knew when I would feel too sick to eat, and besides, she barely had time to shop. The normal pace and schedule of our lives was obliterated.

So after a few days my mother sent out another e-mail to all our friends. "Okay, the men in the house have convinced me that they want to eat!" she wrote. "If people do wish to provide meals, we could do that during the week. But please don't feel that this needs to be done!"

The Wayne community jumped into action. Because we were hardly ever home we set up two big Gatorade coolers behind the house, and our friends and neighbors would come by and put food for us in the coolers. Christine organized a sign-up sheet, and different friends cooked for us on different nights. My only request was nothing with mushrooms. Our friends and neighbors complied.

The outpouring of support was incredible. And the meals they made for us were incredible, too: a delicious seafood pasta and an amazing Mexican taco casserole and countless other dishes. After a while we started referring to our "magic coolers." We'd leave in the morning and when we came home at night they would magically be stuffed with great food.

I'm so touched when I think of how Wayne rallied around my family. If I didn't know what it meant to be a community before my diagnosis, I truly did afterward.

I guess it was kind of inevitable that my fight against cancer would not be a private matter. By then I was known not only to Boston College students but to sports fans around the country. I also understood that a strong young football player getting cancer made for a good story. And so early on I accepted the fact that my story would be public.

Just two days after my diagnosis, when I was in a car with my parents, my cell phone rang. It was a number I didn't recognize. When I answered it, a reporter from the sports network ESPN introduced himself to me. He'd heard I had cancer and he wanted to talk about it. I could have hung up on him, but I didn't. I just sat in the car and calmly told him the truth: Yes, I do have cancer. Yes, it is serious. Yes, they told me I'll never play football again. In the front, my parents were amazed I so willingly spilled my whole story.

After that, ESPN became a part of my journey. When they asked whether a camera crew could follow me around and document my fight against cancer, I agreed. I don't think my parents were crazy about the idea, but they understood why I wanted to do it. For the next few months the camera crew followed us everywhere: to my chemo sessions, to doctor appointments, on the golf course, in our kitchen. They weren't around every day, or even every week, but they were around a lot. It was a weird way to go through an ordeal that is usually extremely private, but eventually we all got used to it. Sometimes it felt like we were trapped in a very sad and peculiar reality show, but most of the time we went on with our lives as if they weren't there.

There is another reason I agreed to make my story public. For a while

I didn't even realize it was a reason, but now I do. When I got my diagnosis I had an identity as a football player. Newspapers wrote stories about me, and TV stations ran my highlights. I was Mark Herzlich, fearsome college football player. That's who I was.

But now that I couldn't play football, what identity did I have? To me, it felt like a giant dark shroud got lowered over my existence. Like I was suddenly dead to the world. I thrived on the roar of the crowd; I fed off the attention of fans. But now all that was going away. People would no longer cheer for me, and before long they'd forget me altogether. I like to think I handled all the attention that came my way with humility, and people tell me that I did, but the truth is, I really enjoyed it. I *loved* being the man.

What was I going to do if I became just a guy with cancer?

On a selfish level I wanted to know people still cared about me. If I felt they did, I'd be able to fight my cancer with more purpose and resolve. The camera crew put more pressure on me, but I welcomed that extra pressure. It made me feel like I had to be positive all the time, and so I was. In this way I was able to hold on to my identity as Mark Herzlich, football player, at least a little bit. And that helped.

Sometime early in my chemo sessions I went with my parents to see Brad play in a lacrosse game. I sat in the stands and felt a twinge of something. I wasn't sure what it was. Maybe it was sadness, or maybe the feeling of being left out. Whatever it was, it was unfamiliar to me. I suddenly felt different, smaller.

After the game my mother and I drove home. I turned to her in the car.

"I don't want to be a nobody," I said.

"Mark, don't be silly. Regardless of what happens in your life, you will never, ever be a nobody."

"I know, Mom," I said. "I just don't want everyone to forget about me."

❦

My second A cycle rolled around. Zack came with me again, and so did my mother. Having Zack there was great for my mom, because she could duck out and go shopping or handle some other business for an hour or two. Zack, meanwhile, never went anywhere. He just stayed and played Madden with me. Or occasionally we'd take a break from Madden and watch episodes of *Dexter*. Zack didn't complain, act bored, or roll his eyes when I got grumpy. He was just *there*. We didn't talk much, but then we never really did. Our friendship was a simple and beautiful thing.

Every now and then Kathleen would come around to see how I was doing. Mostly she'd find Zack and me deeply engrossed in our video game. She'd smile and ask us to keep it down. On the days she saw I was struggling she would ask me to tell her what I was feeling. She called it symptom management.

"Do you feel worse than usual?" she'd ask. "Is it just nausea, or is it something else? Are you worried because you feel worse?"

Usually, I just told her I was okay. I tried not to complain to Kathleen, just like I tried not to complain to my parents or Brad, or anyone, for that matter. I just gritted my teeth and got on with it. What was the point in complaining?

Kathleen saw right through me. On days when I was particularly glum, or when I wasn't very friendly, she'd come by and say, "What's the matter, kid, got a chip on your shoulder today?" Kathleen was kind and thoughtful, but she did not treat me with kid gloves. I realized it was her job to find out how I felt and how I was doing. My stoicism may have seemed noble to me, but to her it was just a nuisance. She had to find a way to break through my wall.

One day, when Zack was in the bathroom or the snack lounge, Kathleen sat next to me in room S-6.

"I know I told you that on your bad days you shouldn't feel the need to talk if you don't want to," she said. "But sometimes, Mark, you have to ask for help. If you feel really bad, you have to ask for help.

"Sometimes," Kathleen said, "the best treatment is just talking to someone."

And with those wise words, another piece of my wall fell away.

Kathleen told me that most chemo patients start to lose their hair in the third week. But after three full weeks, my curly hair was still in place. I wondered whether maybe I wouldn't lose my hair at all. Maybe I'd be the exception to the rule. I'd done some research about chemo-related hair loss, and it wasn't very encouraging. One site even featured fake eyebrows. They looked like tiny furry boomerangs. Losing my eyebrows freaked me out more than anything. I was so afraid of how I'd look. Still, I couldn't ever see myself wearing fake ones. So when my hair and eyebrows were all still in place after three weeks, I felt a surge of hope.

A couple days later I got in the shower and lathered up with shampoo. When I finished I saw huge clumps of hair in my hands. I was shocked. It was happening. Losing my hair would change everything. Losing my hair would bring pity into the mix. Before, no one could really tell I was sick, but now everyone would know. They'd look at my bald head and feel pity for me. On the street I'd go from being normal to being an outcast. I'd feel shame and embarrassment. Seeing my hair in my hands was terrifying. I quickly washed out the shampoo, skipped the conditioner, and jumped out of the shower. I went to bed and tried not to think about what just happened.

The next morning my pillow was covered with hair.

Once again I panicked, but only for a moment. In the light of day, I knew what I had to do next. I went into the bathroom and dug around in the medicine cabinet for the electric clippers. Then I ran the clippers through my hair. I dropped the thin strands to the floor, one after another. Before long all that was left was a layer of stubble.

Then I took a can of shaving cream and lathered up my head. I passed a razor under hot water and mowed it through the shaving cream. When I was finished, I rinsed and toweled off, and looked at myself in the mirror. I was completely bald. It felt like I was looking at someone else. I ran my hands over my shiny head and marveled at how smooth it was. There wasn't much consolation for me at that moment. About the only good news was that I still had my eyebrows.

A few days after that, I woke up one morning and my eyebrows were gone.

CHAPTER NINE

Sometime during my first round of chemo, I started talking to my left leg.

Like everything else in my life, my left leg was changing. It was losing muscle mass, and it was getting smaller. When I looked at myself in a mirror the difference was startling. I had one healthy leg and one diseased leg. I took to referring to it as "the bad leg." Some days I'd look down at it and I'd talk to it out loud.

"What did I do to deserve this?" I'd ask. "What did I ever do to make you go out and grow a tumor?"

While my leg got smaller my upper body got bigger, and not in a good way. Very quickly my stomach got soft and doughy. I tried doing fifty sit-ups every morning and night, but some days I was just too weak. One Friday morning, before the fifth day of my B cycle, I was particularly disgusted by my appearance, and I dropped to the carpet to do my exercises. I got through all fifty, but when I stood up my head was spinning and my stomach was lurching. I bolted across the hall to the bathroom. It was the first time I threw up since my chemo started.

Downstairs my mother heard my heaving and ran up to see what was wrong.

"Maybe you shouldn't go to chemo today," she said.

"No, I'm okay. I was trying to work out. I can't even do that anymore."

I made it through chemo that day, which meant I'd made it through my first two rounds. It was time for my first set of scans to check my progress.

My mother and I drove to Dr. Staddon's office in Radnor, neither of us saying much on the ride over. We both knew what was at stake—either the chemotherapy was getting rid of my cancer, or it wasn't. We sat in the waiting room for a while before Dr. Staddon came out and greeted us with a handshake. I settled nervously into a chair in his office. Dr. Staddon opened a file and leafed through some papers. For what seemed like the longest time he didn't say a word, and neither did we. He just read through these slips of paper on which my life was laid out.

"Well, Mark," he finally said, "I've got to say you are responding very well to the chemo treatments."

That was an incredible relief. I looked at my mom and I saw the color come back to her face, too. Her whole body, tense as a two-by-four a moment ago, seemed to relax—just a bit—for the first time since this whole thing had started. Dr. Staddon explained that all my vital signs were good, and if things kept progressing at this rate we'd be able to more seriously discuss phase two of my recovery. My positive checkup allowed us to begin contemplating the next crucial decision I would face—a decision that was the key to whether or not I'd play football again.

There were two distinct options in front of me. The safest and most common surgery for Ewing's sarcoma patients was something called resectioning. It involved surgically removing the cancerous part of my femur—an inch above and an inch below where the tumor was—to make sure all the cancer cells were gone. The missing bone was then replaced with either bone from a cadaver or a prosthetic. The upside to this surgery was that it had a long track record of getting rid of all traces of cancer. But there was a downside, too.

The downside was that the surgery did not strengthen the leg. It left the leg weakened. I would be bedridden for six months, followed by another six months of painful rehab. At the end of it, if I was lucky, I'd be able to walk with a cane.

Resectioning meant I would never play football again.

The second option was much riskier—a procedure called intramedullary rodding. Instead of removing part of my femur, surgeons would reinforce it with a titanium rod. They would drill a hole through my femur's marrow and secure the rod in place. This option could potentially strengthen my leg and give me the chance to run again, and maybe even play football. But it also left open the possibility that cancer cells could still be present in my femur. And if they were, drilling into the bone would increase the chances of my cancer spreading. And if that happened, I could die.

I asked Dr. Staddon to tell me more about the rod implant.

"This surgery depends on completely ridding your leg of any cancer cells," he explained. "That means you'd have to go through five weeks of radiation to kill all cellular production in that part of your leg."

The first surgery, resectioning, wouldn't require radiation, because they'd remove the part of my femur with any residual cancer cells in it. But the rodding required radiation on top of more chemo. Dr. Staddon explained what that meant.

"You've been doing well with your chemo treatments so far, but the addition of radiation treatments will make your chemo much more intense," he said. "You will have more side effects than before. You will not feel well."

How miserable I'd be wasn't my concern. All I wanted to know was whether the rodding surgery would get me back on a football field.

"Mark, assuming we can get rid of all cancer cells, this other surgery will only increase the *possibility* of your participating in sports again," Dr. Staddon said.

"But it gives me a better shot than the other surgery?" I asked.

"Yes. But there is no guarantee."

There were no statistics for me to look at because of the rare nature of my illness. There were no success stories to inspire me, and no failures, either. It was all uncharted water, and there was nothing to help me with my choice.

And my choice was this—a safer surgery that would rule out football, or a much riskier surgery that would leave that door open but that could also kill me.

Live without football, or possibly die.

It was the most important decision of my life.

❧

It is game day. The day we finally play. My favorite day of all. All I need is for the team doctor to clear me. I wait anxiously in his office. Finally he tells me what I want to hear: My tests look good. My leg is healthy. I am cleared to play.

The team bus is about to leave. I am never late for the team bus, but for some reason on this day I am two minutes late, and when I get there the bus has left without me.

So I dig out my bicycle and start pedaling to the stadium. It's a long way, with lots of hills, and it takes me forever to get there, but I get there. The team is already finished with warm-ups. I race into the locker room and pull on my pads and jersey. I race back out to the sidelines, ready to play. Desperate to play.

Except I have forgotten my helmet. The coach tells me I can't play without a helmet.

So I rush back to the locker room. The trip between the field and the locker room is about a mile. I can't remember their being this far apart, but they just are. I find my helmet and hurry back to the sidelines. The first quarter is already over. I find the coach and tell him I'm ready to play.

"Well, you forgot your mouthpiece," Coach tells me.

So I run back to the locker room, and it's so much farther than even the first time, and I try to run as fast as I can but I realize I'm going extremely slowly, like I'm running in mud, and finally I get there and I grab my mouthpiece and I trudge back to the sidelines. By now the second quarter is over and I find the coach and tell him I'm ready. He asks me where my cleats are.

I make two more trips to the locker room, forgetting something new each time. The last time I stagger back to the sidelines—fully ready to play at last—the football game is over.

I never make it back out on that field.

I had that dream all the time, over and over for weeks and weeks, sometimes with different details but always with the same result. It was my main recurring cancer dream. I had others. There was one where I was being chased by a giant black wolf, and he kept gaining on me, and I could never run fast enough to lose him, so he kept gaining ground and getting closer and the chase never ended. In another one something irreversible happened: Either my dad died and I was devastated, or I killed someone and the cops came after me and I faced spending the rest of my life in jail. Some nights my shirt would be drenched with sweat, and I would have awful, vivid dreams that I was drowning.

I always woke up from those dreams with a horrible sense of dread. I knew that if I went right back to sleep I'd have the same dreams again. They were on an endless, unstoppable loop. Eventually I learned to stay awake once a bad dream woke me up. Anything was better than dreaming. Anything was better than not getting back on the field.

❦

Not long after my talk with Dr. Staddon about the surgeries, my father and I went out and played a round of golf.

On the way home my father pulled into a gas station to fill up. I waited in the passenger seat while he gassed up the car. Out on the golf course we hadn't spoken a word about the surgery options. But both of us knew that was a conversation we would eventually need to have. Time was running out. I had to make a decision in two days, because everything in the next two months of my life depended on that decision. Either I'd get radiation and have the implant surgery, or I wouldn't. Hanging in the balance—my fate as a football player. And possibly my life.

My dad got back in the car, but before he could switch on the ignition I asked him the question we both knew was coming.

"Dad, I don't know what to do," I said. "What would you do?"

My father looked straight ahead, through the dusty windshield. He took a long, deliberate pause. This was not an easy question, and there was no easy answer.

"Well, Mark," he finally said, "I know what I would tell you to do as a father. And I know what I would do if it were me. And they are not the same."

I didn't say anything, and he took another pause.

"As a father, I would tell you to go the safe route," he said. "Get the safer surgery, get healthy and do what is proven to work." He let that statement hang in the air for a moment.

"But if I were you," he went on, and here he paused yet again, considering his words carefully—considering, perhaps, whether he should even continue.

"If I were you . . ."

I stopped him. I told him he didn't need to say anything else. I didn't want anyone feeling responsible for the choice I made, especially if it proved to be the wrong choice. I didn't want my father thinking he could have prevented something bad from happening. Besides, he'd already made his point.

My father turned the key in the ignition and we drove home in silence. I remember feeling a sort of lightness on the ride home. Almost like I'd already made the decision, which in a way I had—long before that day. But talking it over with my father brought me more comfort and peace of mind than any pill or injection ever could. Kathleen, my chemo nurse, had been right—sometimes the best treatment is just to talk.

Especially if the man you're talking to is your hero.

I got home and had a similar discussion with my mother. She knew as well as my father did how important football was to me, and I think some part of her knew what my decision would be even as we sat in Dr. Staddon's office. I told her what I was going to do, and she pulled me close and hugged me and told me she loved me. The deliberating was over. The decision had been made.

Even at the risk of my life, I was going to play football again.

CHAPTER TEN

On July 20 my mother drove me to the University of Pennsylvania hospital for my first day of radiation. We met my radiation oncologist, Dr. Stephen Hahn, who told me I'd be having two radiation sessions a day for twenty-five days—fifty sessions in all.

Step one was making a foam cast of my left leg. The cast was so radiologists could make sure my leg was in the exact same position for every session. I put on a gown and lay down in what looked like an MRI machine. A nurse had me bend my left knee at a forty-five-degree angle, then put something that felt like a beanbag beneath it. She pressed a button and I felt the air getting sucked out of the beanbag, molding it around my knee. That formed the foam cast that would hold my leg in place.

Then the nurse had to mark the spots on my leg where I'd be getting radiation. To do this they had two big machine arms aim laser dots at my leg, and the trick was getting the beams to intersect at certain spots. The nurse kept coming back in and repositioning my leg, and after a while it really began to hurt. The table was hard beneath me, and trying to keep still proved impossible. But the more I squirmed the harder it was to line up the lasers. Twenty minutes turned into an hour. An hour turned into two. My pain just kept getting worse.

Finally, after two and a half hours, the nurse walked out of the room.

I guessed she was frustrated, but then again so was I. After a while she came back.

"Mr. Herzlich, I'm sorry," she said, "but you're going to have to come back tomorrow and we'll try this again."

"What?"

"We couldn't get it done in time. We're sorry. We're going to have to try again tomorrow."

I was distraught. All that needling, grinding pain for nothing. By then I had a very low tolerance for delays. The first few months of feeling my pain were filled with tests and delays and postponements and "try this" and "try that" and everything but direct, meaningful action. So wasting even an hour, much less a day, was almost intolerable to me. I left the hospital in a rage.

Early the next morning, I lay on the flat metal table again and gritted my teeth. I could feel the pain in my left leg but I focused intently on keeping it still. I applied that focus, that intensity, to every single second of the procedure. And when you're counting seconds, they pass *really* slowly. After an hour or so I was mentally and physically exhausted and almost delirious with pain. But then the procedure was over. My leg was properly marked.

Next the nurse handed me what looked like an iron clamshell.

"Time to to put this on," she said.

Dr. Hahn had explained the device was to help protect patients from losing the ability to have children after radiation. In layman's terms it was so they didn't fry my baby makers. I watched as the nurse maneuvered the clamshell over my private parts. The shell was cold and heavy. Once it was in place, the nurse had me lie down on the table, and she moved my left leg into a set position. She put a protective vest over my chest and left for a sealed-off area of the room.

It was time to start the radiation.

I expected some kind of searing pain in my leg, like I'd felt earlier. But for the first ten minutes, I didn't feel a thing. I'd later learn radiation itself is painless. But then I felt a strange pinching sensation around the clamshell. In my mind I imagined radiation was leaking in beneath it and forever ruining my chances to have children. I wondered whether I should have done the banking procedure after all. The pain steadily got sharper, and it took me a while to realize what it was—a sensitive part of my anatomy was being pinched by the metal. I made a mental note to double-check the fit next time.

Twenty minutes later, my first radiation treatment was over. I didn't feel all that bad. Then again, I was only getting started. From the hospital we drove thirty minutes across the city to Pennsylvania Hospital. I was beginning my third round of chemotherapy. I had to skip my A cycle, since those drugs weren't compatible with the radiation. So instead I had three B cycles—five days of chemo in a row—in five weeks. Then, after a six-hour chemo session, my mother drove me back to the hospital at the University of Pennsylvania for another twenty minutes of radiation.

That night I lay in bed and tried to put a label on how I felt. By every measure, I felt horrible: nauseated, achy, weak, brittle, light-headed, overheated, raw. My left leg, in particular, was a wreck. But on the plus side, I wasn't vomiting, and I wasn't in a wheelchair. I was told radiation could make it hard for me to walk, and that I should ask for a wheelchair if I needed one. But I didn't. I walked out of that hospital, and when I got home I didn't throw up. These were small victories, but they were victories.

The combination of chemo and radiation was, as Dr. Staddon had warned, much more intense. The schedule alone was exhausting—constant trips to the hospital, racing from session to session, appointment after appointment. And in the middle of all that, at least for my mother and Zack, hours and hours of interminable waiting. Early on I insisted Zack not come to every one of my radiation treatments. He would have if I let him, but there were just too many, and there wasn't much we could do during those treatments anyway. I knew better than to tell my mother she couldn't come with me. In those five weeks she was my chauffeur, my assistant, my scheduler, my dietitian, my medical liaison, and my morale booster.

Even with Dr. Staddon's warning I was surprised by how much worse I felt. My chemo sessions became much, much harder to tolerate. I went from having a relatively healthy appetite to not being able to see or smell food without feeling ill. Even Frank's RedHot didn't help. I was also far weaker than I'd been at the start. I was always tired, and just walking up a set of stairs totally winded me. During the weeks of my first round of chemo I'd sneak over to the weight bench at the gym and do a quick set, to try to salvage whatever strength I still had left. But once my radiation started I couldn't even lift the weight I'd benched when I was sixteen. All of my power had drained away. I was literally a weakling.

Meanwhile my left leg—the bad leg—was being ravaged. My muscles were atrophying, and the skin on my thigh was sensitive to the touch. One night I noticed the skin was peeling completely off my leg. Doctors had told me radiation gets trapped inside the leg so that it continually heats the skin above it. All I had to do was lightly rub my hand across my leg and layers of skin peeled off, like a wet tissue. My leg felt like someone had left it out in the blazing-hot sun for a month. It was so red and raw and tender, sometimes it looked like it was inside out.

I tried wearing spandex compression shorts to try to give myself some protection, but that made things worse. When I took the shorts off, my leg was a bloody, skinless mess. There was no wound on my leg—the leg *was* the wound. I was lugging around a shrunken, burned, disfigured shadow of a limb.

Three weeks into my radiation treatments I was sitting watching TV in the living room when I felt a wetness in my chair. I got up and saw it was covered with blood. I yelled for my mother, who calmly rushed me to the hospital. All sorts of scenarios filled my head, and I'm sure my mother's, too, on the ride over. What if the chemo was no longer working? Was I bleeding internally? Was I going to lose my leg?

Turned out, it was hemorrhoids. Embarrassing, but normal for cancer patients.

That evening put a real scare in me, and as I did most nights, I took stock of where I was. The mental tally I made was grim.

I was bald and had no eyebrows, and I looked nothing like the Mark I knew or anyone else knew. I couldn't run or lift weights or even walk without pain. I didn't want to eat, so I was constantly devoid of energy. I was drawn and pale, almost ghostly white, except for my leg, which was crimson. I had no strength or power or drive or spark. I was diseased and incomplete.

I was the farthest thing from a football player I could possibly be.

I did what I could to keep my appearance up. I tried using my mother's blush to make my face look less pale. I even went to her beauty salon to try having my eyebrows filled in with a stencil pen. I began wearing baseball caps to hide my bald head. None of that really helped.

On some days, when I caught my reflection in a window or a mirror, all I felt was disgust. I didn't recognize the man I was. And I saw not even the slightest sign of the man I hoped to be.

❦

Somewhere around that time I got a call from a number I didn't recognize. Normally I wouldn't have answered it, but for some reason this time I did.

"Hi, is this Mark?" I heard a man ask.

"Yes, it is."

"My name is Walter Musgrove. I saw your story on ESPN, and I had to call you."

The name didn't mean anything to me, and I figured he was just a well-wisher. My story was out there, and I was used to strangers coming up and telling me they were praying for me. It was reassuring to know I was in people's thoughts.

"You and I share something special," Walter said. "Four years ago I played defensive back for Texas State. Before my junior year, doctors found a tumor in my chest. They told me I would never play football again."

Now Walter Musgrove had my attention.

"A year later," he went on, "after I went through all the treatments and the rehab, I was back on the field for opening kickoff, and I ran down and made the first tackle of the season."

I felt goose bumps. Here was a football player around my age who got cancer, same as me. And here he was, telling me he got back on the football field. He wasn't a doctor. He wasn't giving me odds or probabilities. He was telling me it was doable. He was telling me he had done it.

I was silent for a few seconds, until I figured out what I wanted to ask. "How'd you do it?"

There was a pause on the other end of the phone.

"Mark," Walter said, "do you believe in God?"

I hadn't expected that question, and I wasn't prepared for it. I don't think I even knew how to answer it. But if I said no, I was afraid Walter would stop talking to me. And all I wanted to do was keep talking to him.

"Yes, I do," I answered.

"Mark, the reason I was able to do what I did was because of my faith."

Walter spent the next half hour telling me his story. He was an all-conference defensive back when, during Texas State's final game of the 2005 season, he fractured his collarbone while making a tackle. His team clinched the Southland Conference title and earned a trip to the Division I-AA playoffs for the first time in twenty-two years. It was a bittersweet moment for Walter; he'd helped the team win, but he wouldn't be able to suit up for the playoffs.

"Lord, why?" he asked after his injury. "I made all the sacrifices. Why can't I play?"

Walter had surgery on his collarbone, and during a checkup, a doctor found a tumor on his chest. He had Hodgkin's disease, a cancer that spreads through the lymph nodes. Walter had the answer to his question: If he hadn't broken his collarbone, doctors would never have found the tumor. The injury had saved his life.

Walter went through six months of chemotherapy, followed by three months of physical rehabilitation. But he made it back in time for Texas State's 2006 season opener. That season, he was an All-American team honorable mention.

"Mark, every day that I was sick, I prayed to God," Walter said. "Every single day. But I didn't ask God to just fix everything or make me better or make everything like it used to be. I prayed for specific things. I prayed every day not to lose my hair. And, Mark, I didn't lose a single strand of hair.

"This is what you need to do," he said. "You need to pray. Pray, Mark. Pray."

My conversation with Walter Musgrove woke up something in me that had been dormant for a long while—my faith. Growing up I was raised Protestant, and I would say grace and the Lord's Prayer and go to church and all that, but the truth is, it didn't mean very much to me. As soon as I got old enough to make the decision for myself, I stopped going to church. Maybe I thought about God here and there, but I certainly didn't think about Him very much. Whatever it is that we call faith, it was absent from my life.

After my diagnosis, that began to change—at first for a very practical reason. Once I decided on my "I'm going to play football again" mind-set, I really did view my cancer as something I had to get past before the real battle began. But as much as I tried to stick to that, there were times when the chemo and radiation wore away my resolve. I didn't admit it to anyone, but there were times when I was truly scared.

My life to that point had been all about control. I decided what I put in my body, and I decided what sports I played, and I decided how my future would go. That control was important to me—I needed to be in charge of what was happening around me. I am still that way.

But when I got cancer, I wasn't in control anymore. Even worse, I didn't even know what was happening inside my body. There was no way for me to tell. Was the chemo working? Was my tumor shrinking? Was it growing? Was I slowly dying? I developed a real, palpable fear of the unknown. Even when a doctor showed me an MRI and explained what it meant, I felt the compulsion to have him go over it again, and then again. Did he miss something? Were those really my results? I was irrationally afraid the images on the MRIs might change from one viewing to the next. I no longer trusted them. The fear I felt was too great.

But when I went home, I didn't share that fear with my parents or Brad. They would have wanted me to, and I'm sure they would have helped me overcome it, but I felt that if I did tell them, I was just adding to their burden. People tell me that after a while they forgot I even had cancer, because I never talked or complained about it. That was by design, because I didn't want people to ever tiptoe around me. But there was a price to pay for that approach. Not sharing my fears with anyone meant I had to keep them bottled up inside. I put myself in a corner. I made it so I faced my cancer fears alone.

Out of desperation I finally began talking to someone, and that someone was God. There was no big moment of realization, no elaborate prayer. It wasn't nearly as dramatic as that. The first thing I asked of God was very simple.

"Please, God," I prayed, "don't let me die."

❧

After I spoke with Walter Musgrove, though, my prayers changed. I thought back to the very first time I ever prayed to God, and I realized I'd been very specific even then. I was seven years old, and my elementary school was holding a raffle. The teachers had put all our names in a big fishbowl, and we sat cross-legged on the gym floor while a teacher picked names and awarded prizes. There were small toys and candy bars and things like that, but I focused on the prize I wanted—a big blue stuffed M&M. And for the first time I can remember, I tightly closed my eyes and prayed.

"Please, God," I said, "let me win that M&M."

On the very next draw, a teacher pulled a slip of paper out of the bowl and read a name aloud.

"Mark Herzlich!"

I ran up and the teacher gave me my prize—the blue M&M.

I went back to my spot and clutched my M&M and in my mind I said, *Thanks for listening, God.*

Looking back on that now, I'm amazed I could have believed God would care whether I won that prize or not. How was it possible that God could attend to such a small, insignificant wish? In any case, I didn't really pray much after that. I can't remember ever asking God for anything else. Basically, I didn't talk to God for the next fourteen years of my life.

Then I got cancer. And after fourteen years of not talking to Him, I was now supposed to ask Him to save my life?

I tried not to think too hard about the mechanics of praying. About how God could care about the fate of one man out of seven billion—much like it was illogical to think He cared whether I won that M&M or not. After talking to Walter, I just decided to make prayer a part of my daily ritual. The first night I did it, I lay in my bed and formulated the prayer in my mind. It was almost like I was writing a letter or a diary entry.

Dear God, I formulated. *My name is Mark. I am praying to be healthy again and to play football again. Sincerely, Mark Herzlich. Amen.*

That was my first formal prayer to God after my diagnosis. I repeated that prayer every night and every morning. Not out loud, but silently, to myself.

And it felt good.

Prayer became a real source of solace for me. At first I half expected God to answer my prayers with some kind of sign. Something to tell me He was listening. Something tangible, even cartoonish, like a thunderbolt or all the lights going off in my room. Nothing like that ever happened, so I forgot about looking for a sign. But as soon as I did, I realized the sign was in front of me all along.

In addition to my regular prayers, I began talking to God whenever I felt particularly scared or weak or despairing. All the feelings I refused to share with my parents and Brad, I began to share with God. I didn't feel bad about dumping all that on Him, because He was God and I knew He could handle it. I didn't have to worry how He'd feel. In the middle of my bad nights, when I felt most anxious and afraid, I would talk to God.

And as I talked to Him the fear and anxiety and despair would go away.

And *that* became the sign. God was taking my burden from me. The relief and comfort I felt after talking to God were as real as anything I could have hoped for. I began to believe God was listening to me—that God had my back. Plain and simple, my prayers were working. I became less fearful of not being in control, because I realized I never had been. God was always the one in charge.

Basically, I was just dipping my toe into the subject of faith. I was discovering what and where my faith was. I can't say I passed my entire cancer experience through a filter of religion or spirituality. I can say only that once I brought God into the equation, things began to change. It struck me that, even early on, I never blamed or cursed God for my illness. I had a lot of questions for the universe, but I never thought it was God who gave me cancer. I don't think any of us know what God's plans are, and I don't think those plans are for us to know. We just aren't privy to how God works.

What I do know is that, once I got cancer, I needed God's help.

❧

Are answered prayers miracles? Is that what we're really praying for—a miracle? What is a miracle, anyway?

I had a lot of time to think about questions like that. I had endless hours to wonder how God moves all the little pieces around on this earth. Look at Walter Musgrove. He thought he'd been dealt the worst possible hand, and with pain in his heart he asked, "Lord, why?" But in fact he'd been given the best hand of all—the chance to go on living. What he thought was bad news was actually a blessing.

Or how about this: I mentioned how, after my junior year, I submitted my name to the NFL to see where the league's thirty-two top scouts predicted my being drafted. The answer I got back—the second round, not the first—was extremely disappointing. Maybe even crushing. It made me wonder whether I was even as good as I thought I was. A bit reluctantly, I tabled my NFL dream and stayed in college.

A few months after that, and long after I'd been diagnosed, my father ran into one of my assistant coaches at Boston College. My dad didn't even know who he was, but the coach knew my father. He pulled my dad aside and asked how I was doing. Then he told him he had a friend in the NFL front office.

"I just want you to know, the NFL is notoriously conservative when it comes to rating college juniors," he said. "They will look at all the grades the scouts give and they will always go with the lowest grade. That's just how it works."

My father wondered what he was getting at.

"My friend told me that when he dug around, he saw how many scouts predicted Mark would be a first-round pick," he said. "Do you know how many it was? It was thirty-one. Thirty-one out of thirty-two. Only one guy thought Mark was a second-rounder."

At first this news made my father angry. "How could one idiot scout mess up the whole thing?" he asked. But then he thought about it some more, and he realized something profound.

If it weren't for that one idiot NFL scout, I'd have been rated a first-round pick and almost surely would have left Boston College and signed up for the NFL draft. And the minute I did that, I would no longer be a college student, and—back then—no longer eligible to be covered under my parents' health insurance. Presumably I would soon have been covered by whatever NFL team picked me.

But the chances are, my cancerous tumor would have been discovered at the preseason combine in Indianapolis, which is where teams make sure they're not getting damaged goods. And once it was discovered, no team would ever have signed me. I'd have been stuck between two worlds, without health insurance. I'd have been facing a monstrous cancer battle with no way to pay for it. I can't imagine what that would have done to our family.

What I thought was terrible news was actually a huge blessing.

"People think miracles are these enormous events, like parting the Red Sea," my father said when recounting the story of the thirty-two scouts. "But I'm convinced life is full of these tiny coincidental miracles. Little miracles—that's how God works. A series of little miracles."

CHAPTER ELEVEN

After twenty-four days of two-a-day treatments, it was finally time for my last blast of radiation.

Prior to my very first session, a nurse told me to bring a book, because it got pretty boring just waiting for the radiation to end. At the last minute before heading out to treatment I looked through a bookcase in our home for something, anything, to read. One book called out to me like no other.

It was titled *Never Give Up*.

The author was a New England Patriots football player named Tedy Bruschi. I knew all about him. He was a linebacker, like me, and with the Patriots he won three Super Bowls and earned two Pro Bowl selections. Just a few days after playing in one of those Pro Bowls, in 2005, Tedy got a blinding headache. His body went numb and his vision was blurred. At the hospital doctors told him he'd suffered a stroke. He was partially paralyzed. Doctors also found a hole in his heart, the result of a congenital defect. Tedy Bruschi had no choice but to quit the game of football. His life was on the line.

But Tedy never gave up on the dream of playing football again. And just eight months after suffering a debilitating stroke he was back out on the field. His first week back with the Patriots he was named the AFC Defensive Player of the Week. Tedy played four more seasons before retiring at the age of thirty-six. Not much later he was elected into the New England Patriots Hall of Fame.

I began reading *Never Give Up* during my first radiation treatment, and I finished it during my final session. I don't know whether I subconsciously timed it that way, but that was the way it worked out. Tedy's story was *enormously* inspiring to me. The way he approached his misfortune, the way he handled losing football, the way he fought back to play again—it was a perfect blueprint for me. A friend of mine from college went on to play for the Patriots, and I asked him to pass a note to Tedy telling him how much I appreciated hearing his story.

There was another professional athlete who made an impact on me during my fight against cancer—Lance Armstrong. Lance was a champion cyclist who battled testicular cancer and against all odds resumed his riding career. Right around the time I lost all my hair, I got a letter from him in the mail. "Mark, you are not alone in this," Lance wrote. "Millions of Americans, including me, have faced the same opponent you're up against now."

Lance went on to give me advice on how to approach my fight. "Be as aggressive about your treatment as you are on the field," he wrote. "Ask questions. Be relentless. Get second opinions." He also opened my eyes to the impact I could have on others. "I am dedicated to the war against cancer because of people like you—survivors who want to live forever and fight like crazy. Your strength is going to give millions of other survivors hope and inspiration. I am one of them. Hang in there. Lance."

I received that letter before all the events that brought the legend of Lance Armstrong crashing down. I know that today so many of his fans feel betrayed by his admission that he used performance-enhancing drugs. But the truth is, I will always, always be grateful to Lance for writing that letter to me. It was like a life preserver thrown into dark and roiling waters. The commodity that is most valuable to people with cancer and other diseases is hope, and hope is fueled by inspiration. Other people's stories of adversity and triumph really, truly matter. Lance's story, and his encouragement, truly mattered to me.

And he made me begin to realize my story could truly matter to someone else.

❦

My long string of B-cycle chemo treatments continued. Around that time I developed an obsession with buying a car. It was no longer safe for me to get around on my moped, so I set my sights on a really good used car. The task of picking one out was really just an excuse, though. What I needed more than a car was something to obsess about. Now that football was out of my life—and I was too weak to play much golf—I needed a new outlet. If I didn't have something to spend hours and hours on I would lose my mind. Car shopping became my thing.

Of course I dragged Zack into it, too. When I finally found a model I liked I sent Zack to the dealership to test-drive it. I must have sent that poor kid to a dozen dealerships, each one in a sleazier part of town than the next. Then I'd badger him for details: "How did it drive? Did it look cool? What about the engine?" We'd talk about cars all hours of the night. I'm sure Zack got pretty sick of driving and talking about cars, especially since he surely knew—as did my mother—that all he was really doing was enabling my obsession. But because he knew I needed an obsession, he never complained and he went to every dealership. In a way Zack became my real-world avatar; he did what I was too sick to do.

It was Zack who suggested we spend some time at his grandmother's place on the Jersey shore. "You can invite some people," he said, "and you can get away from chemo for a while."

I agreed and Zack set it up. My Boston College roommate, Codi, along with some other friends—Alex Albright, Chris Fox, Steve Fiorella, Mike

Morrissey—all crammed into a tiny car and drove five hours overnight from Boston to Wayne to come with us. I'm not sure, but I think one of the guys may have slept in the trunk. When they got to my house we immediately played a game of Wiffle ball in the backyard. I was so happy to see them, and even happier to be able to get out on the grass of the yard and compete with them. Being around them made me forget all about my chemo.

But after just a few minutes I suddenly felt exhausted. My arms and legs felt impossibly heavy. I apologized to the guys and went to my room and took a nap. Later that day we all drove to see Brad play in a lacrosse game. It was a great game, but halfway through it I fell asleep.

The next morning we all piled into a van and headed to the Jersey shore. Brad and Zack were with us, and so was LeRoi Leviston. LeRoi had grown up in the poorer part of Wayne, and he'd had a harder life than I'd had. But I'd known him since the first grade, and we were friends and teammates at Conestoga. He was always incredibly upbeat, and he had a contagious smile. But then his grandmother Flo died, and his family lost their house in Wayne. LeRoi, away at college in Delaware at the time, dropped out and came home to help his family. My mother invited him to stay in our house for as long as he needed, and that was what he did. LeRoi became like another brother to me.

The nine of us drove to the shore and spent a fantastic day on the beach and on Zack's uncle's boat. Much of my time, though, was spent sleeping.

I could tell my friends were upset by my lack of energy. They weren't used to seeing me so weak and listless. Maybe that was when my illness really sank in for them. But for me, seeing them was a tremendous lift. It was the first time in weeks I wasn't surrounded by people whose primary focus was my cancer. Away from my friends I'd become Mark Herzlich, Cancer Boy. But around my friends I was just Mark. And that was an immeasurable relief.

We didn't talk about medical issues down at the shore. We just swapped stupid stories and played games on the beach. LeRoi and Codi had a hilarious rap battle while Chris joined some middle school kids in one of the best sand castle–building contests I've ever seen. After a while we pulled out the sandwiches Zack's mom had made for us. As we ate, Alex told us about a crazy bar fight he'd witnessed in Boston and how his buddy had gotten hit in the head with a baseball bat.

"And I went to see him in the hospital, and they had shaved his head, and, dude, the spot where he got hit had this big, enormous bump," Alex said. "I mean, it was like a giant tumor—"

Alex abruptly stopped. I laughed at the image of Alex's friends with a big bump on his head, but then I noticed no one else was laughing. They were all looking at me. Alex, in particular, looked mortified.

"Mark, man, I'm really sorry," he said. "I didn't mean—"

"It's okay," I cut him off, realizing why he'd stopped. The truth is, I wasn't at all upset that he used the dreaded word *tumor*. I hadn't even made the connection. What did bother me, though, was how it stopped our conversation. The awkward pause, the hypersensitivity—*that* bothered me.

Everyone was still figuring out how to act around me, and that had never, ever been the case before. Before, we'd say anything and everything to one another without the slightest worry. Or we'd tackle one another and horse around and act like overgrown kids. But now things were different. Now my friends had to think about what they said, so they wouldn't accidentally say *tumor*. Or they'd recoil every time they accidentally bumped me or sometimes even when they just touched me. I was suddenly the fragile, delicate one in the group, and I hated that. It wasn't my friends' fault; it wasn't anyone's fault. It was just one more unpleasant consequence of cancer.

My roommate, Codi, figured out quicker than most how to behave around me. Maybe because his own father had gone through cancer, Codi didn't feel like he had to tiptoe around me. In fact, he started teasing me about my illness.

"See that dude down there," he once said, pointing to some man. "That guy is so bald, he looks just like you."

Or if I felt too sluggish to do something with him he'd say, "What's the matter, you got cancer or something? Come on, we're going out."

Sometimes people would hear him talk to me that way, and they'd approach him and say, "Codi, that is *not* okay." But Codi knew that it was okay. It was actually *better* than okay. It was exactly the way I needed him to act around me—the same way he had before I got cancer.

Aside from the trip to the shore I didn't get to see much of my friends once my treatments began. After a while, I really started to miss them. I guess I was pining for the relative simplicity of being around them. When my radiation treatments ended I came up with an idea. I knew my parents wouldn't like it all that much, and I knew my mother in particular might hate it. But the more I thought about it, the more I wanted to do it.

I wanted to go back and live at Boston College.

It had been around four months since I got my diagnosis. I'd spent the whole summer slogging through chemo and radiation. I still had several more chemo sessions to go, but it was August and a new year was just about to begin at Boston College. I asked Dr. Staddon whether I could continue my chemo in Boston. He thought about it for a moment and said he saw no problem with my plan.

As I suspected, my mother wasn't thrilled. My moving back to Boston meant she couldn't be there with me for every step of the treatments. She had run my illness like she ran her field hockey teams—tight, organized, efficient. She created a system that brought some sense of order to the chaos. But if I went back to college she'd have to let go of much of that. She would have to take a step back.

What was more, we'd be taking my case away from two doctors we trusted. One was Dr. Staddon, who handled my chemo, and the other was Dr. Richard Lackman, a nationally known expert in orthopedic oncology, or the treatment of tumors. My mom had asked around about surgeons, and Dr. Lackman's name kept coming up. He was affiliated with the University of Pennsylvania Health System at Pennsylvania Hospital, which meant I wouldn't have to travel far to see him. And when I met him I had a gut feeling this would be the guy.

Dr. Lackman is an easygoing, unexcitable man with a kind of monotonous way of speaking—he's always cool and in control. I liked that. Most of all, I liked how confident he was about the rod-implant surgery. I'm not sure the procedure would have been his first choice for me, and I know for a fact he would have preferred me to make a career out of anything except football. No surgeon is ever going to be thrilled watching his patient get pummeled by giant offensive linemen. Even so, Dr. Lackman recognized my heart was set on a rod implant. And once he accepted that, he conveyed real confidence the procedure would work, and I'd have a shot at my dream.

The way I looked at it, Dr. Lackman was the only doctor with enough guts to do the surgery.

Dr. Staddon and Dr. Lackman—along with Dr. Hahn, my excellent radiologist—were like saviors to us. They were our champions in the medical field. Along the way they also became like part of our family. Taking my case away from them and giving it to new doctors in Boston seemed almost like madness, especially since things were going well. But, like my parents, the two doctors understood why I wanted to go back to Boston College. Physically being on campus brought me a big step closer to my ultimate goal. And psychologically, that would be a boost. They both signed off on the move to Boston. Eventually, so did my parents.

In late August, with two months still to go in my chemo, my mother and I drove up to Boston to meet with the new doctors taking over my case. Dr. Staddon and Dr. Lackman had picked them out and gotten them up to speed on what was happening. On the drive up I was excited, really excited, because the move felt like a real shift to me. It felt like a change in gears. On my calendar I had the last day of my chemotherapy marked in bright red—November 2. After that I'd have the surgery to implant a rod in my femur. And after that, the only thing between me and football was rehab. A few of my buddies were there to greet me when we pulled onto the BC campus. I realized I hadn't felt so good in a long while.

My mother and I settled into the office of our new oncologist in Boston. Dr. Y, as I'll call him, was going to oversee my remaining chemo treatments. He opened my files and looked through my records while my mother and I tried to get a read on him. My mother's goal all along had been to assemble the very best team of doctors she could possibly find, and that extended past expertise and on to vision and wisdom, too. My mother sat there sizing up Dr. Y, and so did I.

"It says here you will have six rounds of chemo," he finally said.

"Yes, that's right," I said.

"Well, I've never heard of doing just six rounds. The standard procedure is seven."

All I could say to that was, "What?" Dr. Staddon had assured us our chemo schedule was sound, and after he discussed it with Dr. Y, we assumed he was on board, too.

"We already talked this over with Dr. Staddon—" I heard my mother say.

"I'm sorry," Dr. Y interrupted, "but this isn't the way we do things here. We will have to add an extra round."

More chemo. More misery. Another delay. I had heard enough. I got up and shook Dr. Y's hand, and as soon as I was outside his office, I turned to my mother and said, "I'm never going to see that doctor again."

My mother didn't try to talk me out of it. All she said was, "Okay."

Next we drove to meet with our new orthopedic oncologist, Dr. P. His colleague, a radiologist, was also there. The topic: the surgery to implant a titanium rod in my leg. We took our seats in the waiting room and listened for my name. An hour passed and we were still waiting. Then a second hour passed. I read every wrinkled magazine in the room while my mother paced the halls. I took out a pen and started playing hangman on my left leg. After a while my mother joined in. I doodled some cartoon figures on my leg while my mom paced some more. She went to the front desk a few times to ask about our doctors, but no one could tell us anything. A third hour passed.

Finally, after waiting four hours, I heard the words, "Mark Herzlich?"

In the office Dr. P and his colleague got right to it.

"I talked this over with your surgeon, Dr. Lackman, and I understand you want a titanium reinforcement," Dr. P said. "But I'm going to tell you the same thing I told Dr. Lackman: I don't agree with his assessment."

I could not believe what I'd just heard. I was already exhausted and anxious from waiting four hours, and upset about the extra chemo, and now this new doctor didn't approve of my surgery? I felt stunned and confused. I looked at my mother and saw the shock on her face, too.

"But Dr. Staddon said the surgery would be all right," she said. "We made this decision weeks ago—"

"I won't do it," Dr. P said, cutting her off. "I won't perform this surgery. It is far too dangerous. If we drill into your femur it could cause the cancer to spread."

I jumped in. "But what if there are no more cancer cells in my leg?"

"You have no way of knowing if they are there or not," he said. Then he turned and looked directly at me. "Mark, if you were my son I would never allow you to have this surgery. I'm sorry, but you'll have to find someone else to do it."

I was rocked. I gripped the sides of my chair. That surgery meant everything to me; it was my ticket back to the football field. If it turned out Dr. Lackman was wrong and I wasn't a candidate for a titanium rod, I would have nothing. My football dream would be over. My mother and I sat there in a daze. One of us, I don't remember which, brought up the other surgical option, resectioning.

Dr. P frowned. He seemed annoyed that we had questioned his judgment, and even more annoyed with Dr. Lackman and his plan.

"The issue now is, you've already done a whole radiation treatment, and I don't know if the resectioning procedure is viable any longer," Dr. P said. "The radiation might prevent the bone from growing and repairing itself, which is necessary for a resectioning."

Now the bottom was falling out. No titanium rod, and no resectioning. For good measure Dr. P's colleague weighed in, saying he'd never heard of a patient getting two radiation treatments in one day, as I had done back home.

"I agree with Dr. P," he said. "You should not have a rod inserted."

So where would that leave me? What would my life be like with a weak, busted, radiated leg? Dr. P gave a hint of that life in the medical report he later filed. "It is our preference that an intramedullary rod fixation *not* be done," he wrote. If a recurrence of my cancer were to happen a "rod fixation would likely lead to contamination of either the joint below or above, or even worse . . . distant metastases." In other words, having the rod surgery could cause my cancer to spread all over my body, and possibly kill me.

"The best modality to pursue," Dr. P went on, is "activity modification."

Activity modification. I would need to "abstain from high-impact

G Fiume/Getty Images

Mom and I greeted Dad at the finish line of a charity run in St. Louis for the American Cancer Society.

I wanted to be just like my dad. For me, that meant matching outfits. For him, that meant painting my wagon "Giants blue" and picking out my sneakers.

One day after school, Zack and I helped my mom dig up a tree in the yard, and we took full advantage of the mud bath left behind.

The end of my dad's lacrosse games meant that it was time to rush the field and play catch with my hero.

Brad and I worked on our game faces at Grandma's house in Rowayton, Connecticut.

Bow tie? Blazer? Coiffed hair? I peaked at age three.

My dad coached all of my youth football and lacrosse teams.

Our mom showed us what it is to be devoted.

Brad and I have been close forever. Sickness, distance, and time could never change that.

I don't remember those early wins and losses, but I remember falling in love with the game that would shape my life.

For LeRoi and me, Senior Day marked our last game of a cherished career together as Conestoga Pioneers.

Friends from high school consider my current Mohawk to be one of my tamer hairstyles.

Seeing this photo on my bedroom wall after my diagnosis, I asked myself, "Is that the leg that's going to kill me?"

J. Meric/Getty Images

In the 2008 ACC championship game, I picked up a Virginia Tech fumble to put Boston College in scoring position. We lost that game, fueling my desire to return to BC for another season.

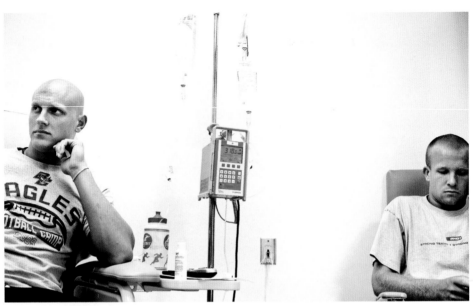

Dexter and NBA 2K9 helped to curb the boredom during the hours and hours of chemotherapy.

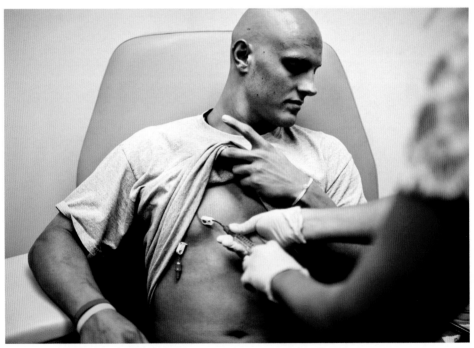

Seven months of chemo treatment never made the daily flush of my port any less jarring.

Codi visited me during treatments and shaved his head bald so that I wouldn't feel alone. He got his tattoo for his dad, who also battled and beat cancer.

We celebrated Brad's senior season on one of my worst days of chemo. He wore my hallmark mask of eye black to honor my battle.

One of my favorite days during treatment! My buddies from BC took me to Zack's house in Avalon, New Jersey: (*left to right*) me, Stephen Fiorella, Codi, Zack, LeRoi, Brad, Alex Albright, Mike Morrissey, and Chris Fox.

Alongside Chris Fowler, Lee Corso, and Kirk Herbstreit on the set of ESPN *College GameDay* at Boston College, I announced to the world that I was cancer-free on October 3, 2009.

Just hours after my announcement, Coach Bill McGovern, a true friend and ally at BC, joined me on the bench as we watched the Eagles prepare for Florida State.

Walking with the team into Alumni Stadium for the first game of the 2009 season was invigorating, even though I wouldn't be playing.

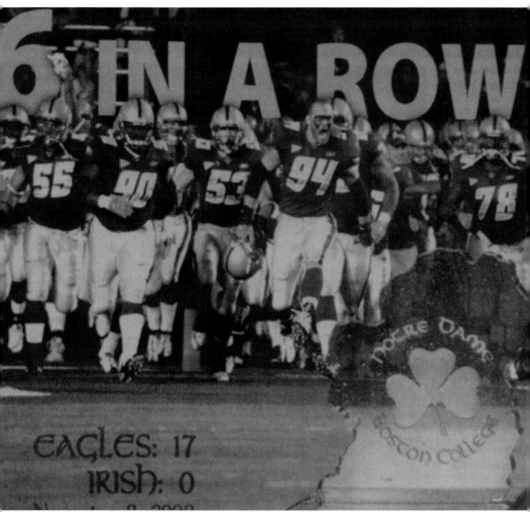

The Heights

This Boston College newspaper hung in my room during chemo treatments. I visualized myself running out of the tunnel again, and it fueled me to keep fighting.

After months of writing, my parents finally met Sister Barbara Anne at my first game back at BC.

My 2009 Halloween costume played to my follicular challenges. Luckily for me, Danielle had a sense of humor; we met later that night.

The summer after chemo ended, Zack, Brad, and I picked up where we left off as if nothing had changed.

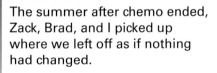

Even after I left Boston to train, I visited often to share in Danielle's senior spring.

My stepgrandfather, Roland, visited BC one final time for my graduation. His recent cancer diagnosis didn't lessen his joy as I entered remission.

Being recognized for my battle wouldn't have been the same without including my family. They always stood by me, whether in chemo or at the Lott Trophy ceremony in California, where I received an honorary award.

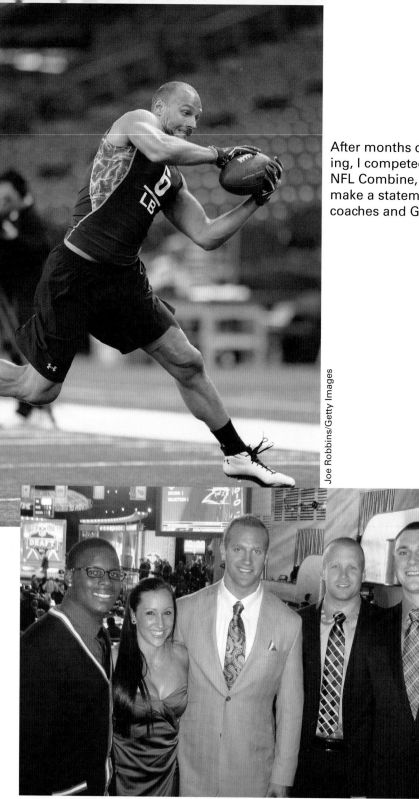

After months of train-
ing, I competed at the
NFL Combine, hoping to
make a statement to NFL
coaches and GMs.

Joe Robbins/Getty Images

LeRoi, Danielle, Zack, and Codi made the trip to Radio City Music Hall to
support me at the NFL Draft.

Starting against the New Orleans Saints in November of my rookie year, I landed a big hit on Drew Brees, one of the best quarterbacks in the league. Later in the game, I broke my ankle and was sidelined for the rest of the 2011 season.

I've had the opportunity to share my story over the last few years in the hopes of inspiring others. I consider it my duty, and my privilege, as a survivor.

Spencer Paysinger and I constantly remind each other that we are in this together. We never fight a day alone.

We came into the league together and won a Super Bowl together: (*left to right*) Spencer Paysinger, Tyler Sash, and Henry Hynoski.

It was amazing to share the Super Bowl victory with Brad.

There's nothing like celebrating with the people I love.

I took a selfie on the float in the middle of the Canyon of Heroes Parade.

I never would have reached the Lombardi Trophy without my family, and I wanted them on the podium with me.

Thanksgiving is a work day for me, but my family trekked to my house in New Jersey to count the blessings of 2013, as they have every year.

We approach life with determination and gratitude, but we never take ourselves too seriously!

If you've seen my Instagram, you're probably glad that I included just one picture of Champ and Scout.

Our journey is far from over, and the future is bright.

sports including football" and settle for "low-impact-type activities such as swimming and biking." My one and only real protection against my femur fracturing and my cancer spreading was "activity modification."

My mother and I left the doctor's office and sat back down in the waiting room. My head was spinning and my throat was bone-dry, so I went to the watercooler. My mother put her head between her legs so she wouldn't hyperventilate. I went to her and put my hand on her shoulder and said, "It's okay. I'll be all right." When we got a bit of our composure back we drove to my dorm. On the way my mother called Dr. Staddon and filled him in on what had happened.

"We have to be able to work this out," she said. "There must be some way to work this out."

In my dorm room I got in bed and tried to sleep. My head swirled with scenarios and diagnoses. The dark dreams were just a few minutes away. I drifted off into some kind of restless, sweaty version of sleep.

When I woke up the next morning, it was my birthday.

I was twenty-two, and I'd just been told the most important decision of my life was a mistake.

CHAPTER TWELVE

M y mother stayed with me in Boston for my first five days of chemo there. But my father didn't come along, so he wasn't there on my twenty-second birthday. That morning, my mother handed me an envelope with "Mark" written on it. Inside was a long typed letter from my dad.

"Sometimes I can't believe you're a grown man of twenty-two," he began. "It seems like yesterday that your mom paged me in the Memphis airport (no cell phones then) to tell me her water had broken."

I sat down and read the rest of the letter, and as I read it I realized these were all the things my father always wanted to tell me, but never did to this degree. It just wasn't our way to have long heart-to-heart talks, and anyway, we knew how we felt about each other. The pride, the admiration, the love—we never hid that. It was there in every hug, every pat on the shoulder, every laugh. But the words—that was a different story. Most of the time we didn't convey our feelings with words. But now my father was doing just that. He was telling me everything he always wanted to say.

"Over the last twenty-two years you have made me very proud," he wrote, "not just with your accomplishments but especially how you've handled both your successes and setbacks. Lots of people know what they want, fewer have the understanding of how to get there, and fewer still will put in the necessary effort to be great. Mark, you are one of a select few."

Then my father wrote about my illness.

"May twelfth will forever be a kick in the nuts for all of us," was how he phrased it. "The past three and a half months are definitely a summer I'd rather have avoided. However, not having that option, I can see some good that has come of it. Your ability to accept your diagnosis (cancer) without accepting the prognosis (your life is going to change forever) is inspirational, and that is why so many people want to talk to you about it."

There was a lot more. My father told me how people came up to him every day, people he didn't even know, to ask about me and express admiration for how I was handling my illness. He predicted that as the days went on more and more people would look to me for encouragement, but like a good parent he warned me that "there are sure to be a few wackos in the woodpile, so just remember your first responsibility is to you." Then he apologized for rambling so long without wishing me a happy birthday. "I'm sorry I can't actually be with you, but I'm also glad that means you're back on campus where you belong. Enjoy the day. Seize the day!

"Love, Dad."

I folded the letter and put it back in the envelope. Then I took it out and read it again. During my journey I would get used to receiving letters from people wishing me well. But the letter from my father was something else. It was the heart-to-heart talk he somehow knew I needed at that moment.

❦

My mom had Dr. Staddon call our new doctors in Boston, and after he did he sent us an e-mail.

"There is no right approach," Dr. Staddon told us. "The most recent data supports the six-cycle approach, compressed, but there are not many older patients in the study, so it is not definitive. I am fine with either six or seven. You have done well on our regimen. Theirs just gives a little more. Both are fine."

In not so many words Dr. Staddon was saying it wouldn't hurt me to have another cycle of chemo. It seemed like he was deferring to my new doctor. But I didn't want to sit for another round of chemo, and I didn't.

By then we'd already scheduled a date for the rod-implant surgery—November 23. That left me enough time to get through my final three rounds of chemo in Boston. I expected my experience at my new oncology facility there would be the same as or better than my experience back in Radnor. But my first week of chemo in Boston was one of the worst weeks I ever had.

My new chemo room was in the basement and had no windows. It was also deathly quiet, with none of the usual rattle of a busy hospital. It felt like a dungeon to me. It felt lifeless. The nurses were nice but I missed Kathleen. I also badly missed Zack. I sat in my chemo chair and fell asleep, and my mother sat beside me and gently patted my head. I woke up with a start, wondering where I was, and when I figured it out I felt a heavy sadness. I was physically and emotionally miserable. My big step forward—returning to college—felt like a big step back.

My mother stayed with me for all five sessions that week and took me to a restaurant afterward. She made small talk when I was too sick to say a word and tried to make me feel comfortable. But I was a wreck, and that was hard for her to see. Her helping me move back into my dorm room made things even worse. The one thing doctors had drilled into us was that chemotherapy would compromise my immune system. I had to be careful wherever I went, because even a small cold could be a big setback. Then my mother walked into my dorm room. There was no Web site or medical book that could have prepared her for that.

The room was a disaster.

There were old pizza boxes and empty beer cans and dirty sweatpants and half-eaten containers of food everywhere. The bathroom was a toxic-waste site. My mother immediately went out and got cleaning supplies and did her best to scour the place. She bought fifteen bottles of Purell and scattered them around the dorm. My roommates saw her cleaning up and promised they'd be as neat as possible, and that made me feel rotten. I didn't want to be the reason they went around picking up every little thing. I didn't want them to feel guilty if they forgot to clean the sink. That stuff had never mattered to any of us before.

It didn't help that around that time, the news reports were filled with stories about a new and deadly contagious epidemic called swine flu. I knew my mother was especially freaked out about that.

"Don't worry, Mom: I won't eat any pork chops or bacon," I told her, trying to lighten the mood. She didn't find that funny.

My first five days back at Boston College were not the triumphant return I'd expected. The chemo treatments just flattened me. One day my mother came to my dorm and found me lying in bed with all the shades pulled down. It was the darkest, dreariest scene you could imagine. She sat on the corner of my bed, and I sat up and put my head in her lap. I was inconsolable, and I knew she felt terrible that she couldn't help me. It was impossible for either of us to be optimistic at that moment. We were in the very worst of it.

"If I could take this from you," my mother said, trying not to cry, "I would."

"I know you would, Mom. I know you would."

My mother says that leaving me in my dorm room after my fifth day of chemo was one of the hardest things she's had to do.

Once she went back to Wayne, my situation got even worse. I still had a ton of chemo left, and I was already sicker than I'd ever been before.

My roommates did everything they could for me, taking me on outings and bringing me food, but a lot of the time I had to excuse myself and collapse into bed. I could hear my buddies laughing and having fun in the common room as I lay in total darkness, shivering and sweating. Sometimes I'd stagger out and stumble to the refrigerator, and dig through all the beer bottles and leftovers for my injections. I'd lift up my shirt, pinch my stomach fat, stick a big needle in, and push medicine to keep up my blood count into my system. Then I'd stumble past the guys and crawl back into bed.

That was when my mind began playing tricks on me. I felt something I never felt before—I felt like I was slipping away. I felt like I was dying. I had the urge to vomit every minute of every day, but I didn't have the energy to make it to the bathroom. I had extreme night sweats and my sheets were always completely soaked, but I was too weak to change them. I was living in filth and darkness, subsisting at a level that was less than human. I was bald and I had no eyebrows and I was pale and fat and fatigued and now the last shreds of my manhood, of my dignity, were being stripped away. I could no longer take care of myself. Recovery didn't seem possible; I forgot what it even meant to feel good. The only conclusion I could fathom, the only next step my mind could envision, was death.

And on those nights when I was sure I was dying I tried to pray, but I was too weak to form the words, so I mumbled some sort of desperate prayer, barely discernible, the slurred sounds of a doomed creature. But they were still prayers. They were still prayers. Somewhere, God was listening. And after I mumbled those prayers I woke up one morning and dragged myself to the phone and made a call and did what I always found so hard to do.

I asked for help.

"Mom, come get me," I said. "I need to come home."

❦

I moved back to Wayne and resumed my chemo treatments at POHA with Kathleen. But I didn't leave Boston College altogether. I was still enrolled as a senior—my classes were Operations Management, Strategy and Policy, a game-designing class called Capstone: Game of Life, and a course on the professional editing system Final Cut Pro—and I split my time between Pennsylvania and Boston. I'd get my chemo treatments in Radnor; then my mother would drive me back to Boston for the rest of the week. The professors allowed me to do all my classwork from home.

I guess the biggest reason I wanted to keep attending Boston College was because it allowed me to go to the BC football games.

I was longing—*longing*—to be a part of the team again, in any way I could. I spoke to team officials and they agreed to let me be on the sidelines for home games, and even to accompany the team to road games. On Fridays I'd endure six hours of chemo, take the five-hour trip to Boston, and get right on the team plane or bus for the trip to whatever city we were playing in.

"How you feeling, Mark?" Barry Gallup, the associate AD for football operations, would always ask as I boarded the plane or bus.

"Good," I'd always answer.

But Barry and everyone else could plainly see I was lying.

The thrill of being back with the players, though, made feeling sick more bearable. Standing on the sidelines at BC games was the most fun I'd had since my diagnosis. I will never forget the first home game I attended after starting my chemo. It was the 2009 season opener against Northeastern. I walked into Alumni Stadium in Chestnut Hill—in street clothes, not in a uniform—and I felt goose bumps on my arms. I was in the locker room for the pregame speech, grinning like a little boy. The guys were all pumped up that I was there. Then I went out on the field with the team.

What I saw amazed me.

There were 33,262 people in the stadium that Saturday. A whole lot of them were wearing Boston College football jerseys with the number 94— *my* number.

A whole lot more were wearing special T-shirts they got from the school bookstore, with the BC changed from Boston College to Beat Cancer. Handheld signs were everywhere: WE'RE FIGHTING WITH YOU, MARK; BEAT CANCER, MARK.

When I looked in the stands I saw my own face reflected back at me— hundreds of students who had painted their faces with my signature black mask.

I was overwhelmed. I hadn't been prepared for such an outpouring of support. I thought, *These kids are pulling for me. The whole school is pulling for me.* There were so many times when it felt like I was fighting my fight alone, completely apart from nearly everyone else on the planet. But that wasn't true. It had never been true. When I got back to Boston College, student after student came up and told me, "We feel like this is our battle as much as it is yours." The entire Boston College family was invested in my progress. They were all rooting for me to win.

All that love fired me up like I hadn't been fired up in a while. On the sidelines for the Northeastern game I became a bit of a madman. I was still bald and chubby and pale and weak and barely recognizable as the Mark Herzlich most people knew, but none of that mattered that Saturday afternoon. All that mattered was that I was back on the field. So I stormed the sidelines, cheering on the players, giving them high fives, yelling advice, screaming encouragement, pointing out coverages, going wild after every score. I was deep—*deep*—into that game.

That season our defensive coordinator, Frank Spaziani, got promoted to head coach. As defensive coordinator, Coach Spaz—a gruff New Yorker with a bushy mustache—had had a yellow towel he always draped over his left shoulder and waved around when he wanted to get a player's attention. When he became head coach, Coach Spaz retired the towel. But instead of tossing it he gave it to me. The omnipresent yellow towel was part of the fabric of our team, and Coach said he wanted me to have it. I was touched. I took that yellow towel, and on the sidelines I waved and twirled it over my head like a crazy person. The crowd would see me running up and down the sidelines waving the yellow towel and screaming at the top of my lungs, and they would let out a huge roar.

People started talking about "the power of the towel."

My mother and father drove up for that first game against Northeastern, and from the stands they watched me act like a lunatic. My mother was grateful to Coach Spaz for giving me the towel, because it gave her an easy way to pick me out on the sidelines. Of course, she worried I was being too physical. She worried I might hurt myself somehow, or maybe even pass out. Quietly she wished I'd slow down a bit. But I never did. It was just too exciting, too emotional, being on the sidelines. I saw that I could actually do something to help the team, even in my addled state— I could be a motivating presence. That became my job at games—to be as intense and ferocious as I'd been as a player, except do it on the sidelines, not the field.

Boston College won that season opener, 54–0.

Our first road game, two weeks later against Clemson in South Carolina, was equally memorable. Before the game Clemson's head coach, Dabo Swinney, brought me out to midfield. He grabbed a microphone and addressed the crowd.

"We hate these guys," he said, referring to our team. "We play against these guys and we compete against them with everything we've got. But this is about more than just football. Good luck, Mark. We're all praying for you."

Then Coach Swinney handed me a check for five thousand dollars, earmarked to Boston College's Uplifting Athletes chapter, a nonprofit group dedicated to raising awareness of rare diseases.

After that other colleges followed suit. The folks at the University of Virginia, whose players are unofficially nicknamed Wahoos, started a "Hoos for Herzlich" movement and presented me with a check for ninety-four hundred dollars, in honor of my number, 94. Much of that came from the players, who gave up their meal money for the cause. Players at other schools, like North Carolina State, Florida State, and Notre Dame, also raised money on my behalf. Charlie Weis, the head coach of Notre Dame, was remarkable. He not only ran a fund-raiser through the school but also personally donated money in my name. That was how it went everywhere. Our fiercest rivals, our football enemies, banding together to support me. I was now part of something that transcended football.

I'm not a guy who cries very much, but there were times after my diagnosis when all the support from people I didn't even know really got to me. It was just a constant, comforting embrace of support everywhere I went. One day my friends and I walked into a liquor store wearing BC T-shirts, and the owner asked, "Hey, do you guys know that kid with cancer? How's he doing?"

"Not bad," I said.

"You're him?" the owner said. "Here, have all the booze you want, on the house!"

I'm not sure alcohol is the best gift to give a cancer patient, but my friends were delighted and I was humbled by the gesture. This guy I'd never met felt compelled to give me something—to *demonstrate* his support for me. I was used to fans cheering me on and telling me I was awesome, but this was very different. This wasn't admiration for me as a player. This was affection for me as a person.

Then there was the holy water. There is a little sandwich shop called Flat Breads near the BC campus, and I used to eat there all the time. I always got the Acapulco Wrap, which was chicken and cheese and avocado and salsa and hot sauce all rolled up. One day the owner, a lovely Italian man named John, pulled me aside. In his hand he had a clear jar three-quarters filled with water.

"I've had this for ten years," John told me. "My daughter went to Jerusalem and got it when my wife had cancer. It's holy water. It helped heal my wife and it brought us all comfort. And now I want you to have it."

John handed me the jar. I thanked him and took it to my dorm room and put it on a shelf right next to my bed, and I wondered if holy water might help heal me, too.

One of the most moving things anyone did on my behalf involved a piano. One day a BC junior I didn't know sent me a message on Facebook. His name was Denny Carr, and he said he wanted to do something to help raise awareness for my disease.

"I know how to play the piano," Denny wrote, "and I'm thinking of doing a piano marathon."

Denny called it "Music for Mark."

The school set up a grand piano in the cafeteria, and Denny played for 9.4 hours straight (in honor of my number, 94)—song after song after song. He set up a jar and people dropped money in it all day. There were sing-alongs and guest performers, and a friend of mine who'd been on *American Idol*, Ayla Brown, showed up to sing. But what affected me most was when I met Denny for the first time.

Denny and I didn't really run in the same circles at Boston College. I was busy with sports, and he was into music and also worked at the cafeteria. Under normal circumstances I'm not sure we would have ever crossed paths. And yet there he was, busting his butt on the piano to raise money and awareness for me. Later on Denny even named a sandwich in my honor—the Mark Herzlich Sandwich, which was tuna salad and cheddar cheese on whole-grain bread with a drizzle of raspberry vinegar.

To have someone like Denny rooting for me to survive was profoundly humbling.

Around that time I got a letter postmarked Indiana and written in immaculate penmanship. It was from someone named Sister Barbara Anne. Sister Barbara Anne was a Franciscan nun living in a convent just a few miles from Notre Dame near South Bend. "I can see Notre Dame's golden dome from our convent," she wrote. "As you well know, Boston College has long been our nemesis. So when we play you on October 24, I will be rooting for Notre Dame—but not nearly as hard as I will be rooting for you."

Sister Barbara Anne told me she herself had been diagnosed with cancer. "It kind of takes the wind out of your sails for a few months," she wrote. But she went on to describe how she'd been fighting it off, and was devoted to fighting it to her dying day. She was seventy-five now, but she still had "a few unrealized dreams I want to see come to fruition. So let's fight this cancer together."

Sister Barbara Anne's letters became a huge source of comfort for me. I don't know whether it was because she was a sister, or because she was so down-home and easygoing. She would tell me all about her life, or about having corn on the cob at a picnic, or about seeing snowflakes outside her convent window.

"I watch the large beautiful snowflakes fall gently to the ground, and I can't help but think of the gentleness of God," she wrote. "As I watch each snowflake descend, I resolve to be more gentle."

Then she wrote something that has stayed with me ever since.

"When I watch the snowflakes I think of you, too, Mark. Because as tough as you are on the football field, I think you have a gentle spirit."

How could Sister Barbara Anne possibly perceive that? Whenever anyone saw me on TV I was usually screaming and painted up and practically frothing at the mouth with fury. My public persona was all about ferocity and toughness. But did I have a gentle spirit, as Sister Barbara Anne suggested? Could I be both tough and gentle? What in the world was it about a snowflake that made her think of me?

The truth is, I wasn't sure. Because everything I'd thought about toughness and manhood, everything I believed to be true about myself, was changing. Some new man was being shaped and formed here, and I didn't yet know who he was.

But of all the amazing gestures of support, the one that hit closest to my heart happened at home.

This was in Brad's senior year at Conestoga High School. For years Brad had been forced to live in my shadow, and even after my diagnosis the comparisons didn't stop.

"Now that your brother's got cancer," one of his buddies joked, "you're going to have to get a better type of cancer."

All the suggestions that he had to live up to my accomplishments made life hard for Brad, harder than it had to be. But to his great credit, he managed, at last, to shrug it all off. He willed himself to step out of that shadow. And one day he simply stopped trying to measure up to me. "I don't need to be Mark," he told himself. "I just need to be Brad."

The person he became was tremendous. At Conestoga, Brad made the Distinguished Honor Roll all four years; was named to the National Art Honor Society; was an AP Scholar with Honors; won awards for personal integrity and work ethic; ran the school's Model United Nations; was president of a campus group called Students Against Destructive Decisions; and was commended by the American Legion for his "honor, leadership, patriotism, scholarship, and service."

And that was just *off* the field. Brad also won a Defensive MVP award, same as I had; he made the All-Central League football team; was a PIAA lacrosse state champion; a three-time lacrosse district champion; and one of the Maxwell Football Club's high school players of the year.

Brad was a brilliant scholar and athlete in a way I'd never been.

I went to one of his football games his senior year at Conestoga. That was when I noticed something different about his appearance. He always wore eyeblack, as most football players do. But now there was more than just a streak of black grease under each eye.

Now Brad had painted his face just like I painted mine.

It was my brother's way of showing support in my darkest hour. "I did it to remind myself that it is a privilege to be out on a football field," he later told me. "I did it because I knew you would give anything to be out there yourself."

Going into his final football game at Conestoga, Brad needed fourteen tackles to break the school's career-tackle mark of one fifty-four. Fourteen tackles is a lot to get in one game, but Brad knew the number, and he went after it.

Brad played the game of his life, and with just a few minutes to go he needed only one more tackle to break the record. The ball was snapped, Brad locked in on the running back and charged. Their bodies smashed together and Brad brought him to the ground. He had his fourteenth tackle. He had broken the school record. He was now Conestoga's leading tackler of all time.

That was a very special moment for Brad, but an even more special moment for me. Because the career-tackle record he broke was mine.

❦

Going to BC football games and being around the BC students was up-lifting, but there were always moments to remind me I was still a cancer patient. I still had more rounds of chemo to go, and I still looked like a very sick person. I remember a moment in my Game of Life class, a course designed to teach us how video games can influence real-life de-cisions. To me, the course was just an excuse to play Xbox games. Even so, one exercise in the class took me by surprise.

The professor split us into several groups of five or six students. Then he gave us a scenario.

"You're stranded on a desert island," he said. "You have limited sup-plies. I'm going to ask you a series of questions to force you to consider how you will survive on this island."

The first few questions didn't faze me. But then the professor asked, "If you had to kill one person in the group, who would it be?"

My group discussed the matter and put it to a vote.

Unanimously, they chose me.

When the professor asked why, a student explained that it was be-cause they were afraid I might not be able to pull my weight, and I might take an unfair amount of resources from the group.

I could tell the students felt bad about choosing me, but I could not argue with their logic. I was the weakest, most vulnerable member of the group. If I were a healthy, vibrant Mark Herzlich, I'd be the last guy they'd ever want to kill. But I wasn't that guy. I was who I was.

About a month into my return to Boston College, I was scheduled for another MRI. The MRI was to see whether the chemo and radiation were working. I couldn't have my rod-implant surgery unless the tumor was gone. This MRI would tell me whether it was. To me, this was the single most important test since my diagnosis.

I came back home to Wayne and met with Dr. Staddon. He told me he was happy I was looking good and keeping my weight up. I struggled through the MRI, trying to keep my left leg still. A few days later I was back at Boston College.

I was still at BC when Dr. Staddon called my mother and told her the results of the MRI were in.

"Can you come down to my office?" he asked her.

My mother drove to Radnor and sat across from Dr. Staddon as he took out my MRI images.

Then he told my mother to brace herself.

CHAPTER THIRTEEN

Do you ever spend any time thinking about how you want to die? I never did, until I got my diagnosis. After that, I thought about it a lot.

My knee-jerk thought was that I'd like to die in my sleep. That has to be the most peaceful way to go. But then I thought that dying in my sleep meant I wouldn't have the chance to say good-bye to all the people I love. Then I thought, *Well, do I really* want *that chance? Wouldn't that be too painful?* In the end I wasn't sure, so I crossed dying in my sleep off the list.

What about getting hit by a bus? I thought about that because one day as I was riding my bicycle while I had cancer, a bus ripped right by me going sixty miles per hour. I felt a blast of air as it passed just a foot or so to my left. And I thought, *What if that bus had hit me and killed me?* There was a certain appeal to dying so quickly and suddenly. I certainly wouldn't want to get hit by a bus and lie around for half an hour, dying and in pain. Or be shipped to an emergency room and get pumped full of painkillers and linger for a while before dying anyway. That would suck. Better to die instantly. Better the bus killed me right away.

But then what would people say about me? What would my legacy be? I would be one of those tragic figures taken before his time. Someone whose legacy was eternally incomplete. I'd be a perfect subject for a sports documentary about athletes struck down in their prime, remembered now for flashes of brilliance—for what they *could* have been. But the thought of that weighed heavily on me. I didn't want to be the subject of a documentary like that. I didn't want to be the tragic figure who never got to grow old and have kids and watch them do all this cool stuff of their own. How horrible to be fixed in memory as someone who had half a life. I'd be a legend, but dying at my peak was too high a price to pay for that.

The only thing I knew for sure was that I didn't want to die of cancer. I knew how terrible the pain in my leg was, and I tried to imagine what that pain would feel like if it spread through my whole body, my arms and chest and back, and there was no drug strong enough to take it away, and all I could do was lie there and writhe in pain until finally I died. There is nothing peaceful or graceful about dying like that.

And then when you die, everyone gathers around and they say, "Well, at least he isn't in pain anymore." And that becomes the defining thing about your passing—that you were in agony, and now you're not, and at least there is that. I didn't want people to have to say that about me. Dying of cancer was off the list, and so were fire and drowning.

Maybe dying in my sleep *was* the way to go, especially if I could do it like they did in *The Notebook*. In that movie the old couple lie in bed looking back on their remarkable lives and their remarkable love, and then they drift off to sleep and just like that their time on earth is done. It is over. They have lived life to the fullest, and now there is no more. Maybe that is the way to go: spent, exhausted, still in love, with images of your happy grandkids dancing in your head.

But when is life ever like the movies?

In the end I finally figured it out.

I thought about the decision I faced—about the two surgeries I could have. Not all that long ago, my doctors told me, someone like me with

Ewing's sarcoma would probably have had his entire leg cut off—and then *still* probably have died. But then the resectioning surgery came along, and that became the common, proven way to fix your leg. There were studies showing it worked; there were statistics and patient files attesting to the wisdom of choosing it. "We know that this has worked before," doctors could say.

But they couldn't say the same thing about the titanium-rod surgery.

That was a much newer, much riskier, far less proven way to go. It was the *unconventional* way to go. Doctors couldn't tell me with any certainty that it gave me a better or worse chance of surviving and getting better, because there was no track record to go on. Choosing that surgery was always going to be a big risk. Some might even say it was reckless.

Yet there I was, the least adventurous guy around, the anti–thrill seeker, the risk lessener, the designated driver—the one who always made the smart, sensible move. So why in the world would I make such a risky, reckless choice? I was twenty-two and facing the single most important decision I would likely ever have to make, and I was making the gutsiest call imaginable. Why? Why do it? Was it just because I loved football so much? Was I really risking *everything* for football?

Yes, I decided, that was part of it, but not the only part. There was something else. And that is how I figured out how I'd want to die.

It has to do with fortitude. It has to do with glory. *This cancer might kill me*, I decided, *but I won't go easily. I will fight as hard as I know how to fight. Either I'll beat the odds and pull off a miracle for all time, or I'll go down in a ball of flames.* Because asking yourself how you want to die isn't the right question.

The right question is, How do you want to *live*?

If I have to go out, I decided, *I'm going to go out swinging.*

❦

It is Monday, September 28, 2009. My mother sits in a neat, medium-size office in Radnor, Pennsylvania. Just a few days earlier I was horizontal in a massive MRI machine, which surrounded my left leg with a powerful magnetic field designed to oscillate and produce energy and stimulate hydrogen atoms in my body, with the ultimate goal of creating image contrast in a photo of my leg. That contrast allows doctors to identify things like fatty tissue and white-matter lesions and, in my case, a tumor. My MRI test produced clear images of my left femur, and those glossy images are now in the hands of Dr. Staddon, who sits across from my mother in his office in Radnor, holding the film so my mother can see.

This is it. The outcome of my battle. My mother braces herself. Dr. Staddon boils down his analysis of the MRI to one simple sentence.

"I am ninety-nine percent sure the cancer is gone."

CHAPTER FOURTEEN

My mother didn't jump out of her chair when she got the news. That's just not her way.

The MRI showed that the tumor was gone, and that was great, but I still had to keep getting chemo, and I still faced the possibility that some cancer cells remained and could grow. My mother knew this was only one rung on a long ladder. She was excited, maybe even thrilled, but she kept her cool. I'm sure she smiled a beautiful smile, and I wish I'd been there to see it, but I'm also sure she snapped right back into business mode.

The first person she called was me, but I was in class and didn't answer my phone. Then she called my father.

"Sandy! Dr. Staddon said he's ninety-nine percent sure the cancer is gone!"

"What? That's what he said? That's great!"

In their excitement they didn't properly coordinate who would be the one to tell me. I think my mother told my dad to call me, but maybe he thought she said she would call. In any case, no one called me. I knew my mother had an appointment with Dr. Staddon that day, so basically I knew my results were back. But I made a point of not sitting around waiting for the phone to ring. Instead, I went to the movies in Cambridge with my roommate, Codi, and his girlfriend, Molly.

We were in line waiting to buy tickets to some movie when Codi's cell phone rang. It was his father calling from Sacramento.

"I just got my fifth annual checkup," his dad told him. "I am cancer-free."

For recovering cancer patients, the five-year mark means everything. Doctors feel that if your cancer hasn't come back after five years, you have a good chance of living for many more years. It is not a guarantee, by any means, just an optimistic signpost. If you're cancer-free for five years, you can safely feel you are on the other side of the disease. You can more freely say, "I beat it."

Codi's father had just passed that signpost.

Molly and I hugged him and told him how happy we were for him and his dad. Of course, that call reminded me about my own MRI results. A bad thought swept over me: *Are my folks not calling me because the news is bad?* I excused myself and found a quiet spot and phoned my dad.

"Hello," he said in a chipper voice.

"Hey, Dad."

"Oh, Mark, I'm glad you called. I have something to tell you."

My heart sank with a thud in my chest. The results *were* in. So why had he waited so long to tell me?

"Mark, I got this rebate slip from Apple in the mail," my dad said. "It's addressed to me, but I don't remember ever sending in a rebate. You think it might be yours?"

"Yeah, Dad, it's mine," I told him.

"Okay, great. I'll send it to you when I get the chance."

My dad was quiet after that, as if that were all he had to tell me.

"Dad?" I said. "What about Dr. Staddon? What did he say?"

"Oh, yeah," my father said. "What, Mom didn't tell you?"

"Tell me what?"

"Dr. Staddon looked at the MRIs, and he said that he is ninety-nine percent sure the cancer is all gone."

"Are you kidding me?" I said. "*That's* how you tell me?"

I heard my father laugh a hearty laugh on the other end.

So there it was. A ninety-nine percent chance my cancer was gone. Not ten percent. Not seventy percent. Just one percent shy of absolute certainty. I tried to gauge how I felt at that moment. I can't say it was all-out elation. I was happy, yes, absolutely, but more than anything I felt a sense of vindication. Some doctors told me I wasn't doing the right thing—the radiation would weaken my leg; the cancer would spread; I could die. Some doctors scoffed at my questions about playing football again. Some doctors predicted a life of biking and swimming, if that.

They could have still been right, but at that moment I felt as close to being the old Mark as I had in a while. I still had a long way to go, but I felt defiant in the face of all gloomy predictions. There were times I wondered whether I was too stubborn in making my decisions about cancer—as if saying, "I'm going to play football again," enough times would somehow make it come true. There were times I wondered whether there was any logic to my thought process, or if I was just crazy. But maybe, just maybe, I wasn't crazy. Maybe I was right.

For some reason I didn't tell Codi and Molly about the news right away. After the movie, which was awful, we were all walking back to the car near Harvard Square when I suddenly blurted it out.

"Oh, by the way," I said to Codi, "I got an MRI, and the doctor said he's ninety-nine percent sure I'm cancer-free."

Codi stopped in his tracks.

"What?" he said. "You didn't think to tell us that before?"

Codi came in for a hug, and then he did a little dance in the parking lot.

"Cancer-free Day!" he yelled at the top of his lungs, and those words echoed across Harvard Square, into the night.

❦

Then I texted Zack. I don't know why I didn't call him; a text just seemed more appropriate, given our friendship. No need to exchange a lot of words.

"Guess what," I typed. "I'm cancer-free."

Several minutes passed before I heard a little ping on my phone. Zack's response was all of two words.

"That's sick."

I laughed. It was sick that I wasn't sick. The perfect Zack response. I wish he'd been there in person so I could have seen his face, because it was his victory as much as mine. Even so, that was the most satisfying text I ever wrote. And the best text I ever got back, too.

That evening Dr. Staddon called me himself, and we talked over the results. The news was all good. But the very next morning I woke up feeling especially weak and sickly. I had trouble walking and I could barely breathe. I called my mother and told her how I felt. My mother called my chemo nurse, Kathleen.

"He needs to have a CBC test done," Kathleen said. CBC meant complete blood count. The reason I felt so bad might be because my blood-count levels were low. If that were the case, and the cells weren't carrying enough oxygen to my organs, I could go into anemic shock. My mother called and told me to get over to the hospital in Boston and get a CBC.

There was one problem: I was too busy.

I had interviews scheduled with reporters from ESPN, the sports network that had been following my battle. ESPN has an extremely popular show called *College GameDay*, which airs for a couple of hours before important collegiate games. The show travels to different colleges and universities and builds a set right on campus so thousands of rabid college fans can swarm the set and scream like lunatics for their team. Just five days after I learned I was essentially cancer-free, *GameDay* was scheduled to broadcast live from Boston College's main lawn, ahead of our big game against Florida State. The show's hosts wanted to do a segment on me, and they wanted me live on set.

I told my mother I had too much ESPN stuff to take care of to go to the hospital for a long CBC test. She wasn't happy to hear that. The last thing she wanted was for me to feel like I was in the clear because of the MRI results. My mother called the Boston College Medical Center and scheduled the CBC anyway.

"He's supposed to go in and be tested," she explained to a staffer there, "but now he's saying he won't." As if I were a misbehaving kid.

Around the middle of that day, I started feeling guilty. My mother was still making all my appointments, keeping me on track, doing her thing; that wasn't going to change because of one MRI. Deep down, I knew she was right. I raced to the BC Medical Center and had the CBC test. I did it because my mother told me to.

The results came back the next day, and my white-blood-cell count was low. "It's a concern," a BC nurse told my mother. She called Kathleen and read her the numbers, and Kathleen said the cell count was too low for me to have my usual Monday chemo session. Missing a chemo session was not a good idea, especially now. You don't want to give cancer any sort of a toehold; you want to keep doing what's working. Missing my first chemo treatment right after getting the great MRI results was almost like tempting fate. And I didn't want to do that.

But the only way I could have the chemo was if I had a blood transfusion first.

I called Kathleen and asked her how long a transfusion would take.

"Six hours," she said.

"Forget it," I said. "Is there any other way I can get my cell count up?"

Kathleen suggested I eat a lot of iron-rich foods, like red meat. She said I should come in on Monday as scheduled, and she would retest my blood and we'd go from there. But right after that, she called my mother and told her to set up the blood transfusion for Tuesday. The chances I'd be able to have chemo without a transfusion, apparently, were very, very slim. White-blood-cell counts don't just magically go up. My mother let me go ahead and try anyway, and I ate a few rare steaks, hoping for the best.

Right around that time, a couple of days before the *GameDay* broadcast, I got a call on my cell from a Boston area code.

"Hi, this is Tedy Bruschi," the man on the other end said. "Am I speaking with Mark?"

The former Patriots linebacker who'd fought back from a stroke, calling me? At first I thought it had to be a prank. Then I remembered I'd given my number to my friend who was on the Patriots.

"Tedy Bruschi?" I said. "Yeah, it's me, Mark! How are you?"

I could hear my voice cracking as I talked.

"I'm good. I just wanted to call you and let you know that I am very inspired by your story, and that you are in my thoughts," he said.

"It's actually you who inspired me," I said. "And that's why I want you to know that I just got the results of an MRI from my doctor and he said he's ninety-nine percent sure I'm cancer-free."

"Well, congratulations!" Tedy said, clearly surprised and excited. "I'm so happy to hear that."

We talked for a bit about cancer, and about football, and finally we talked about what came next.

"Mark, don't forget—you're a survivor now," Tedy told me. "So be proud of being a survivor. Always be proud of that."

We hung up and I sat on my bed for a long time thinking about what he said.

The notion of feeling pride in relation to my cancer had never occurred to me. Yet here was Tedy telling me I *should* feel proud. He wasn't saying I should be happy that I got cancer. But the accomplishment of fighting it off was something to feel proud about. And with that pride, I realized, came responsibility. As a survivor it fell to me to be an inspiration to others. That was my responsibility now. After talking to Tedy, I realized exactly what I had to do.

I had to go public with my MRI result on *College GameDay*.

❦

My mother was against the idea. She didn't want to do or say anything to jinx my recovery. Like my father, my mother is highly superstitious. When Brad and I were little, my father coached my football team, and he wore the same shorts to every game. He believed that wearing them would bring us good luck. Then my father had back surgery and couldn't coach one of the games. But he still believed the shorts had to be there, to keep bringing us good luck. So my mother had tiny little Brad put on my father's huge shorts and wear them to the game. And wouldn't you know it? We won.

The idea of announcing to the world that I was cancer-free spooked my mom. Plus, my low white-cell count and my trouble breathing were a real concern to her. She didn't want to have thousands of BC students cheering me on because they thought I was home free. *They have no idea how sick this kid still is*, she thought. *We got good news, but the fight isn't over. The cancer might not be gone.*

Saturday, October 3—the day of our game against Florida State—was raw and rainy and cold. The clouds hung gray and low. But the excitement of having *GameDay* at Boston College was palpable. The campus was electric and buzzing. My parents, Brad, and LeRoi drove up and were given seats near the *GameDay* set. Hundreds and hundreds of students in number 94 jerseys and BEAT CANCER T-shirts squeezed onto the lawn. The show's hosts, Chris Fowler, Lee Corso, and Kirk Herbstreit, took their seats to huge wails from the crowd. The unique, surreal emotion overload of a college football game, coupled with news of my appearance on *GameDay*, simply electrified the place.

I spent the morning with the BC team at a local Sheraton hotel, eating a meal and planning the game. Then Barry Gallup drove me to campus. I walked to the *GameDay* set and got my first look at the sea of students on the lawn, waving signs and banners and flags. More students were hanging out their dorm-room windows, shouting my name. I looked left and saw my family. My mother was in a yellow rain slicker with a big button with my photo on it. Brad wore a number 94 football jersey. I was in a yellow BEAT CANCER T-shirt. I was bald and had no eyebrows.

Earlier that day I couldn't walk up a set of stairs without feeling totally winded, but now the energy of the students gave me strength. I walked toward the stage and high-fived every fan I could. I was smiling and nervous and happy. They played a prerecorded video of athletes and celebrities wishing me luck. I sat next to Chris Fowler, and a set director waved at us, letting us know we were live.

I began to tell the story of my phone call with my dad. How he asked me about the Apple rebate instead of telling me my MRI results. The crowd, screaming just moments ago, was silent. They sensed something was coming. I got to the heart of the story, which was me asking my dad what Dr. Staddon said.

"He said he looked at the MRIs," I announced, "and he said he's ninety-nine percent sure that the cancer is completely gone."

Then it happened. The roar. The sweet, beautiful roar.

It's on YouTube, if you want to hear it for yourself. Sometimes I dig up the video just to listen to it again. It went on for nearly thirty seconds, a strong, sustained, exuberant, unifying roar. The sound of relief and happiness. I turned and saw students jumping up and down, out of their minds with excitement. I looked over at the *GameDay* hosts—all gruff football guys—and I saw tears in their eyes. I looked at my parents, who were smiling and cheering and crying. I sat there and tried to soak it all in. I'd said the words now, aloud and in public, and that made everything more real. I was beating this thing. I was really beating this thing.

When the roar subsided I explained that I still had three chemo sessions to go, and after that the titanium-rod surgery, and after that I'd "get the leg strength back, start running again, and get back on the field." The crowd roared again. I didn't ever want to leave the embrace of the students that day, because their love and support and genuine concern were incredibly empowering. Sitting on the *GameDay* set I felt a lot of things, but chief among them was blessed. Blessed to have my parents, blessed to have Brad, blessed to have these fans. I was bald and I was sick and I was still a cancer patient, but most of all, I was blessed.

Boston College was the underdog that day. But we won anyway.

The next day I drove back home to get ready for my chemo. On Monday my mother drove me to Radnor, and on the way she tried to warn me that I probably wouldn't be able to have my session that day. She told me the nurses didn't think it was possible for my blood-cell count to go up without a transfusion. At the medical center Kathleen drew blood for a test while my mom explained that I didn't want to have the transfusion. Like she was talking about a stubborn kid again.

"Mark, you can refuse treatment anytime," Kathleen patiently told me, "but unless the numbers are up, you won't be able to have the chemo."

Kathleen tested the numbers. They were up. I was clear for chemo. Little miracles.

❧

After *GameDay* aired. I got a letter from a man named Doug Day Sr.

Mr. Day was a Virginia Tech fan, and he asked whether he could meet me when Boston College played VT that week. He told me he was battling cancer, and he found my story inspiring. Up to that point, I'd never really sat down and talked with someone with cancer. I'd told plenty of reporters my story, but never another cancer patient. I wondered what I could possibly offer Mr. Day; after all, he was in his sixties and I was twenty-two. Kelly Wheeler, BC's public relations person, told me she'd be happy to set up the meeting, but first she asked whether I'd be comfortable with it.

Honestly, I didn't know. But I told her to set it up anyway.

Right before the game, in Lane Stadium in Blacksburg, Virginia, Kelly pulled me aside.

"Mr. Day and his family are here," she said.

I looked over and saw Mr. Day surrounded by his children and grandchildren. He wore a cap over his wavy white hair, and he had a serious look on his face. He was a proud man and he carried himself proudly. I felt a pang of panic. What could I possibly tell this man to help him in his battle? What did I know about anything?

Mr. Day gave me a firm handshake, and Kelly took us all to a private room in Lane Stadium. Mr. Day and I sat and talked about his life. I was anxious and the meeting felt awkward. I began to think I wasn't cut out for the inspirational part of being a survivor. But I remembered what Tedy Bruschi told me—that was my responsibility now. Still, I couldn't think of anything smart or profound to say. For the first several minutes we didn't mention cancer at all. I didn't know where this meeting was going.

"Mark, I've just been diagnosed with cancer," Mr. Day finally told me. "I'm battling through it right now. But I'm very lucky, because I've had such a good life, and my children are doing great. So whatever happens, I am happy with my life."

When I heard him say that, something clicked. I knew exactly what I wanted to say. Maybe he expected me to sympathize with him and tell him I understood his approach. But I didn't. It was different from mine. *Very* different. And suddenly he wasn't in his sixties and I wasn't in my twenties. We were just two cancer patients, fighting in the same arena. And in that arena, I firmly believe, there is no room for resignation.

"Mr. Day, I understand you've had a great life," I told him. "But you still have a lot of life ahead of you."

Behind him, his adult children perked up.

"I know your treatments are going okay now, but they are going to get harder, and it will be tougher and tougher for you to get through chemo," I said. "And the big thing for me, the only way I was able to get through it, is because I have a goal. That goal is to play football again."

"But, Mark," Mr. Day said, "I'm so happy. I've met all my goals."

"Then make a new one," I said. "Ask yourself, 'What do I still want to do in my future?'" I knew one of Mr. Day's granddaughters was nineteen and in college. "Don't you want to see your granddaughter graduate?" I asked. "Don't you want to be there when she gets her diploma?"

Mr. Day sat quietly for a moment, then looked up at me.

"Yes," he said, "I do want that."

"Okay," I said, "that's good."

"Mark, I am going to make that my goal," Mr. Day proclaimed. "I want to see my granddaughter graduate."

That was the first time I realized I might have a message after all. And it didn't have to do with results and outcomes. It had to do with the *fight*.

I never saw Mr. Day again after that meeting. But two years later I got a package in the mail. The postmark said it was from Virginia. I opened up the box and found a small photo album inside. I leafed through it and at first I didn't know anyone in the photos. Then I recognized Mr. Day. A handwritten note fell out from between the leaves.

"Mark," the note read, "thank you for giving me so much inspiration, and thank you for giving me a goal. I don't have cancer anymore, and I'm feeling great. I'm recovering. I am a survivor. And I wouldn't have made it this far if it hadn't been for you."

I looked at the very last photo in the album. It showed a beautiful young girl in a crisp graduation gown. She was beaming with all the promise of an endless future. And standing next to her, beaming just as brightly, was Mr. Day.

❦

A few days before Halloween, my friends at Boston College started getting their costumes ready. Halloween is a big deal on any campus, and at BC there were tons of parties to choose from. I still wasn't feeling very good—I wasn't yet finished with my chemo—but Codi and the other guys convinced me I should go out. Then one of them had the idea that I should go as Mr. Clean.

"You're already bald," he reasoned. "All you need is white pants and a white shirt and an earring."

I found all those things in the dorm, including the earring, and on Halloween, I was Mr. Clean. At the last minute, I Googled a photo of him, because I had the feeling something was missing. I was right—Mr. Clean has eyebrows. White eyebrows. I found a small bottle of Wite-Out correction fluid and gave myself a pair of white eyebrows.

Everywhere I went that night, people were happy to see me, and that was a really good feeling. The Mr. Clean outfit was a hit. My buddies and I went to a bar near Fenway Park called Who's on First, which was hosting a party organized by BC students. We ran into some friends and stayed for a few drinks.

I looked around the room for cute girls, which is basically what every guy in the bar was doing. At the time I was still pretty beat-up by the chemo, but even so I got approached by a fair number of female students at BC. Like I said, I may have been the single best-known student in the whole college. Being a top athlete at a top sports school gave me lots of opportunities with women. But the fact is, I didn't take advantage of them.

For one thing, as I've mentioned, I wasn't very smooth with the ladies. I just never have been. But I also wasn't interested in quick, meaningless relationships. That never appealed to me. And I wasn't all that removed from my prolonged, painful breakup from Caitlyn. Throw in the cancer and the chemo and the radiation and you can see why I wasn't very active socially. But I wasn't a hermit, either. I was twenty-two, and I wanted to be in a relationship. It just wasn't happening.

At Who's on First, some guys in my group knew some people in another group, and before long the two groups blended into one. I noticed someone I knew: a really nice BC student named Sara. She was dressed up as a cowgirl. She was with a friend, someone I'd never met, who was also a cowgirl. She was in cute overalls and cowboy boots. I looked at Sara's friend, and I noticed right away that she had really pretty eyes. I looked away, but before I knew it, I found myself looking back. After a while I was trying not to stare.

I drifted closer and closer to Sara's friend, but I didn't have the nerve to talk to her. Then someone in the group said he knew about another party, and all of a sudden everyone was leaving. I took a deep breath and made a move.

"Hey, are you coming with us?" I said to Sara's friend, probably too abruptly.

She seemed a little startled. She looked up at me and sized me up. Standing next to her, I noticed the difference in our sizes. I was six-four and she was about five-two. Yet she had a kind of hard shell I picked up on immediately. There was nothing frail or fragile about her. Her manner and posture told me she was tough.

"Who are you?" she finally said.

I could tell she genuinely had no idea who I was.

"I'm Mark," I said. "Your friends said they were coming, and I wanted to see if you were coming, too."

Sara's friend continued to size me up. I got the feeling she had a gut instinct that she really trusted.

"Okay," she said. "Yeah, I guess we're all going."

"Great," I said.

"Yeah," she said.

And with that, we shuffled out of the bar with our big group of friends, a towering Mr. Clean and a tough, sexy cowgirl.

I had no way of knowing that Halloween 2009 would change my life more completely than anything that had ever come before.

CHAPTER FIFTEEN

Danielle, I learned, was the name of Sara's friend. I don't remember whether she told me or if I heard someone call her that. On the way to the other Halloween party, we didn't really talk; everyone in the group was sort of talking to everyone else. We ran into someone who told us the party we were headed to was dead, so our new plan was to head back to campus. But before I knew it, Danielle and her friends were piling into a cab.

I hurried over and grabbed Danielle by the arm.

"Can I have your number?" I asked.

Danielle hesitated. Then she said, "Okay, sure." She gave me her number, and I put it in my cell. I felt a rush of adrenaline. Danielle got in her cab and drove off.

The next morning, before I could even call her, I ran into Danielle and her friends outside Alumni Stadium, where Boston College was playing Central Michigan. My white outfit and white eyebrows were gone; instead, I was wearing an official BC Eagles tracksuit. As I walked toward Danielle, I noticed her looking at me in a funny way. I saw a kind of shock of recognition on her face. She was just figuring out I was *that* Mark. Big man on campus. Cancer Boy. The *GameDay* guy. Mr. Clean was actually Mark Herzlich.

"Hey, Danielle," I said as casually as I could.

"Oh, hey."

We spoke for a couple of minutes about Halloween and what they did later—inconsequential stuff. Then I said good-bye and left. I wanted to play it cool. The next day I sent Danielle a text.

"It's Mark. We met the other night," I wrote. "Do you want to come over and watch a movie?"

It took a while for Danielle to respond. "Sorry. I can't," she finally texted back. "I have a paper to write."

I tried hard to convince myself that was true.

I waited another day, then texted her again. Same offer: a movie in my dorm room. Once again she said no and offered some excuse. If she was giving me a hint, I wasn't ready to take it. A couple of days later, I texted her a third time.

This time, she finally said, "Okay."

❧

Danielle was the eighth person in her extended family to attend Boston College. Her grandfather Domenic had played football for the Eagles and had been a big deal in his day. Her first visit to campus was when she was two years old. Her mother, Robin, an alumna and big Eagles fan, took her back to BC often.

Danielle and her family didn't grow up with a lot of money, but even so, Robin insisted Danielle and her two sisters do a lot of community outreach—same as my mother did with us. Danielle performed something like a hundred hours of community service every year in high school, going to food banks, running book drives, helping the homeless. That was how she grew up, and that commitment to helping others became a part of who she is.

In the eighth grade, Danielle accompanied thirty-five family members to a tailgating party at BC's Shea Field, to celebrate her mother's fortieth birthday. That was the day Danielle set her sights on being an Eagle herself. The first thing she did when she enrolled at Boston College was sign up for the Army ROTC program. No one else in her family had served in the military, so she wasn't keeping with some long tradition. She felt the ROTC scholarship was a good way to pay for college, but more than that, she felt called to serve her country somehow.

"Why'd you go and do that?" some people asked after learning she'd signed up for ROTC. "You have so much going for you."

"*That's* the reason I joined," she said. "I want to do what I can for my country."

Danielle's time at BC neatly overlapped mine, so she knew all about me before we met. She knew I was one of BC's best football players, number 94, the guy who was going to make it to the NFL. She knew I was this larger-than-life figure on campus even before I got sick. Then a friend called her with news of my diagnosis.

"Hey, did you hear Mark Herzlich has cancer?" he asked.

Instantly, Danielle felt sad. She knew me only as a figure, not a person, yet she still felt sad. A lot of people tell me they can remember exactly where they were and what they were wearing when they heard I had cancer. Danielle can remember those things, too. My diagnosis really affected her, though she didn't understand why. It was just one of those sad things that upsets you more than you'd expect.

Not long after that, Danielle broke up with her boyfriend. It was a painful, difficult breakup. Her two best friends were studying abroad, and she suddenly felt very alone. The summer of 2009 was a miserable summer for her, just as it was for me. And when Halloween rolled around, Danielle was in no mood to celebrate either. But her friends convinced her to go, and at the last minute she dug up some overalls and cowboy boots, and she went to Who's on First.

That was when I first laid eyes on her.

About a week after our first meeting, she agreed to watch a movie with me in my dorm room in Ignacio Hall. My roommate, Codi, and his girlfriend were there and were staying for the movie, and I think Danielle was relieved to see that. In her mind, she suspected I had a million girlfriends. She didn't know I wasn't a player.

I set up our big projector screen, and we settled in to watch the remake of *The Taking of Pelham 123*. I sat next to Danielle on the sofa, and I found I couldn't stop talking to her. I don't usually talk through movies, and it annoys me when other people do, but that wasn't the case that night. All four of us joked and laughed and talked easily, and I felt a real sense of comfort around Danielle. She still had a bit of a wall up around her, but I could see her relief that I wasn't a total weirdo. I didn't make a move or anything like that. I just talked a lot and had a great time.

A couple of days later, I texted Danielle again and we went out to dinner, just the two of us. There wasn't a single awkward pause or silence. I was surprised by how loose and confident I felt, how free the conversation was. It felt like I was sitting around chatting with a friend, not a date. A few days later my father came up to Boston for a visit, and I was hanging out with Danielle when he showed up on campus. I introduced him to Danielle, and we all chatted for a while.

"Well, Mark, do you want to go to dinner?" my dad asked.

"You bet," I said.

I saw Danielle begin to slowly ease away from us. She clearly didn't think she was invited.

"Danielle, you want to come?" I asked.

"Yeah, okay, that would be great."

She seemed surprised I'd want her there with my dad and me. But by then, only a handful of days after meeting her, I already felt a real connection to Danielle. I'd never really had a close friend who was a girl. But that's what Danielle felt like—like a good friend. I didn't know how that could be possible after so little time together. Even though Danielle had yet to drop all her defenses, I felt like I somehow *knew* her, in a way I can't explain. It was something I'd never felt with anyone before.

What I didn't know for sure was whether or not Danielle had any romantic feelings for me. A couple of weeks into seeing each other, after three or four official dates, we were in my dorm room one afternoon when I leaned in and kissed her. Danielle kissed me back. That was it for me. After that, I was hooked. I was still bald and sick and weak, still not out of the woods, but all of that suddenly seemed secondary. For the first time in a very long time, neither football nor cancer was front and center in my mind.

Danielle was.

❦

Early on we didn't talk about my cancer very much. I had my final day of chemo only two days after meeting her, and I mentioned that on my Facebook page. Danielle sent me a lovely congratulatory text.

"Woo-hoo! No more chemo! Happy for you, Mark."

Otherwise I can recall us talking about it only two or three times. And when it came up, I always ended the conversation the same way.

"I'm going to beat it," I'd say. "I'm going to play football again." And that was that. There was no more to say.

Danielle would later tell me that during those early days she never looked at me and saw a sick person. She never felt sorry for me, never worried I might die. It wasn't that she was insensitive; in fact, she's very intuitive and empathetic. Maybe it was my positive outlook, or maybe it was because I was especially happy and cheerful because I was around her. Either way, Danielle was able to see past the baldness and the missing eyebrows, past the pale skin and the occasional sickly demeanor, and see something I hadn't felt like in ages—a normal person.

Which, if I think about it, is remarkable. Physically I was just a shadow of myself, so Danielle did not meet Mark Herzlich the strong, powerful athlete. And while I looked a lot more like a sick person than a football player, she did not meet Mark Herzlich the cancer patient, either. These were the only two personas I had, and yet when I met Danielle she didn't notice either of them.

All she saw was Mark Herzlich the *man*.

Not long after our first kiss, Danielle sent me a text.

"My roommates are going out but I don't feel like it. Wanna come by and watch a movie?"

The movie she picked was *Monsters, Inc.* It had been her favorite growing up, and her mother's and sisters' favorite, too. In fact, Danielle owned only Disney movies. Obviously something about them was comforting to her.

We popped in the DVD and sat on the sofa, and we talked and laughed through the whole movie. I noticed Danielle spoke a lot about her mother but never mentioned her father. Without really thinking, I asked, "What about your dad?"

Immediately I wished I hadn't. Danielle tensed up and her smile disappeared. But just as quickly, she gathered herself. She didn't allow herself to betray any emotion. The tough shell was back.

"He doesn't live with us," she said.

Then she was quiet. I knew there was more to the story, but I didn't ask. Danielle opened her mouth to say something else, but nothing came out. She was struggling to find words. She was fighting herself. It was like she wanted to talk but couldn't. Something was stopping her.

Then Danielle did something strange.

She turned her back to me and faced the wall.

I didn't know what was happening. I wondered whether I should get up and go. But before I could move, Danielle started talking in a soft voice.

"I was nine years old the first time I saw my father beat my mother," she said. "Since that moment I witnessed and was the victim of physical and emotional abuse more times than I can count."

I was shocked. I could hear the raw hurt in Danielle's voice. Slowly and softly, she kept talking. She told me the whole story. She told me about how her father's alcohol use and gambling problem had drained her family's savings account; how she had feared for her life every time she walked into her house; how her father had controlled every aspect of her life and her mother's and sisters' lives; how she had had to lie to her friends about the cuts and bruises and even a broken ankle.

She told me about the abusive relationships she had entered into when she got older, because that was all she knew—that was what she thought love was.

It was a terrible litany of pain and abuse, and I almost couldn't fathom such a nightmare existence, because all I knew was the peace and happiness of my own upbringing. My heart broke for Danielle as she unpacked the awful memories and laid them out. She wasn't crying, and her voice wasn't quavering. She was being tough. But it seemed like an unburdening to me. Once she started talking, it all came out.

"When I was fifteen, my mother got me and my sisters out of that situation permanently," she said, explaining how after years of court appearances, restraining orders, and lawyers, her father was finally out of her life for good. "If it wasn't for my mother, and what she did for my sisters and me, I couldn't say for sure we'd be alive today," Danielle said. "My mother is my hero."

It didn't escape me that Danielle's horrific story ended not with anger and bitterness, but with love.

"I just want you to know I don't share this information with a lot of people," Danielle added, still turned away from me. "But for some reason, I feel I can trust you. I feel comfortable with you. You make me feel . . ."

She worked to find the right word.

"You make me feel safe," she said.

Then I saw her hang her head and look down. I knew why she'd turned her back to me—she was too hurt, too vulnerable to tell me her story to my face.

"I hope you don't look at me differently now that you know this about me," she said.

I touched her arm, and she turned and looked at me. She scanned my face, searching for a reaction, and I knew exactly what she was looking for. She was looking for pity. The same thing I looked for in the faces of people I told about my cancer. Danielle worried whether I would start treating her like she was broken now that I knew about her life. But just as I didn't want to be defined by my cancer, I knew she didn't want to be defined by her past. Neither of us wanted to be pitied.

"I do look at you differently," I said. "I look at you as a stronger and more amazing person than I thought you were before."

Danielle smiled, and I could see the relief in her face. At that moment, a lot of things changed for me. Somehow Danielle's trust made me feel strong—stronger than I had in a long time, maybe ever. In my life I'd won a thousand awards, and I'd heard a thousand compliments about my prowess on a football field. I'd been highly valued for my power and tenacity. I'd been called a hero and a leader, and I'd been cheered by multitudes. I knew what it felt like to be larger than life.

But this . . . this was different. This was someone trusting me enough to open her heart to me. Someone who saw the best side of me, even as I was showing the world my worst. This was better than any prize or trophy could ever be. Danielle told me I made her feel safe. And that made me feel like a man.

From that night forward, our relationship only got better. One night we both had cousins visiting from out of state, and we all went to a local bar. Unfortunately my cousin wanted to leave early, so I agreed to take her home while Danielle stayed at the bar. We were disappointed we couldn't be together, but she stayed and showed her cousin a good time, and they closed down the bar at two a.m.

When she came home to her dorm room, she found me fast asleep on her sofa. Next to me was a large cheese pizza from Roggie's, our favorite local place. I'd dropped off my cousin, gotten the pizza, and waited for her to come home. Danielle later told me that when she saw me sleeping on the sofa, a big, cold pizza lying next to me, one thought popped into her head.

I love this guy.

My best move happened when I wasn't even awake.

❦

In early November, I reached another milestone: my last day of chemotherapy. I sat in my usual chemo chair and felt my usual dizziness and nausea, but that was fine, because I knew this was my last session. Sometime around three o'clock that afternoon Kathleen came into room S-6 and disconnected me from my IV tubes. I watched her wheel the IV stand away one last time.

I got dressed and staggered toward the exit, my mother holding my arm. I saw a group of people waiting for me there—it was all the oncology nurses I'd met during my treatments. Some of them had even come in on their day off to say good-bye. I hugged and thanked them all, and I saved the last hug for Kathleen. We didn't say anything particularly profound to each other; it was more of a matter-of-fact thank-you and good-bye. There was a reason for that. Kathleen knew I still had a long way to go in my recovery. There was nothing really final about this moment; it was only one step of many. As Kathleen herself had told me, I would always be a cancer patient. The fight would never really end.

On the way out Kathleen pointed to two little bells near the front desk. She explained that when people finished their chemo, they could ring the bells to commemorate the moment. She asked me whether I wanted to ring the bells.

"Not really," I said. It seemed too much like tempting fate.

"That's okay," Kathleen said. "Almost no one does."

❦

The first thing I did when I got home after my last session was make myself a big, sloppy peanut-butter-and-jelly sandwich. That was my favorite meal, and the one I'd purposely avoided for months. I bit into it and savored the moment. I still couldn't taste food the way I used to, but even so it was the best bite of food I'd ever had.

Now there was nothing standing in the way of my surgery, scheduled for November 23, 2009. After the Boston doctors refused to perform a rod implant, we went back to Dr. Lackman and asked whether he'd still do it. He said that he would, and he sounded confident about it. After that, the decision was up to me. Should I listen to the Boston doctors, or should I trust Dr. Lackman? In the end, neither my parents nor I allowed the Boston doctors to steer us off the path we'd chosen. Long ago I'd decided to have the riskier surgery if it gave me a better chance of playing football, and my folks were on board with that. Even after hearing the Boston doctors discredit my plan, I still felt the risk was worth it. I made the hardest decision in my life a *second* time.

I went with the riskier surgery.

The night before the operation I prayed in my bedroom, and I asked God to give me strength and poise, and to give Dr. Lackman those things, too.

The next morning I was at the Pennsylvania Hospital at nine a.m., to get ready for my eleven a.m. surgery. My parents were there, of course, handling the paperwork and making sure I was okay. One nurse put a hairnet over my bald head, and an anesthesiologist injected me in the arm.

"Mark, I need you to count backward from a hundred out loud, please," he said.

I made it to ninety-seven before slipping into darkness. Then Dr. Lackman got to work.

His sleek, shiny tools were laid out neatly on a tray. He picked up a scalpel and made a long incision on my left hip, starting near the top of my femur. He pulled my flesh apart and kept it separated with a prong. He took something that looked like a screwdriver and drilled small holes at both ends of my femur, then threaded a long wire through the marrow cavern in my leg. Now it was time to bore down through the bone, from hip to knee, to make space for the titanium rod. A nearby monitor provided an X-ray view of the inside of my leg. Dr. Lackman picked up something called a reamer drill—sort of like an expensive screwdriver with a two-foot-long drill bit at one end. Then he started drilling into my potentially still-cancerous leg bone.

It was not easy drilling. Bones are hard, and to get through them you need elbow grease. Nor was there any margin for error. If the drilling went offline they couldn't just spackle over the mistake. This was difficult, precise, painstaking surgery. Dr. Lackman used the drill bit as a kind of guide, placing a thin, sleek titanium rod right behind it in the medullar cavity of the bone. When he was finished with the drilling, he gently hammered the rod into place, then fit screws into holes at each end. The screws went in one end of the bone, through the titanium rod, and out the other end of the bone. They were screwed tight, and my incision was sewn up. The surgery was over. It took two hours.

I woke up a while later in a total haze.

"When are they doing the surgery?" I asked my father.

"They already did it, Bear."

A nurse hooked me up to a morphine drip, and I drifted in and out of consciousness in my hospital room. Then the nurse told us Dr. Lackman was coming to see me. Even in my groggy state this made me nervous. I saw my parents tense up, too. What if there had been a complication with the surgery?

Not much later Dr. Lackman appeared. He was normally a fairly placid guy, like I said, rarely betraying emotion. But now he bounded into the room, like he was all jacked up.

"That was the best surgery I've ever done!" he said, his voice higher than usual. "I left so much good space between the rod and the leg. It went great!"

I closed my eyes and exhaled. I heard my parents profusely thank Dr. Lackman and I heard the relief in their voices. Then I realized why Dr. Lackman was so pumped up. The surgery was his Super Bowl. And he'd won.

"The hardest part of the surgery was getting through the bone," he went on excitedly. "The bone was just so strong! It wasn't easy drilling through it!"

I felt the flush of vindication again. Dr. Lackman was telling me I *hadn't* been crazy. I *hadn't* been too stubborn in making my decisions. I had made the *right* decision. My cancer was gone, and I still had a chance to play football.

The next day, when I was less groggy, Dr. Lackman came to see me again. This time I asked him when I could start my rehab.

"Well," he said, "everything is done on our end, so as soon as the pain subsides, you can start walking. Then you can begin jogging. And then we'll see if you can't play a little football."

This was the first time in seven months a doctor had cleared me to run. It was an incredible moment, and I felt a great relief. I'd been told I might not ever run again, but I would—I *would* run again. Whatever else happened, I would run again.

A few days later, my mother got a call from Dr. Lackman. This time he was even more excited than in the hospital room. He was practically giggling.

"Barb!" he said. "Oh, my God! I just got the pathology report back!"

After the surgery Dr. Lackman had gathered dust from my bone and had it tested for cancerous cells. If you're lucky, all they'll find are some old dead cancer cells.

"You're not going to believe this, Barb," he said. "There are zero cancer cells. Not even dead cells. Zero! *Zero!*"

❖

The last game of the Boston College football season was the Saturday after my surgery. I hadn't missed a single game all season, and I wasn't going to miss this one. I put weight on my left leg for the first time two days after the surgery. It hurt like hell. I had to use crutches to get around, but for some reason—pride, I suppose—I decided not to use my crutches to walk into the stadium in Maryland where BC was playing. I wanted to walk in on my own power.

It wasn't the best idea. It was rainy and slushy that day, and a couple of times I almost slipped and fell. I found myself clambering up muddy hills trying to find tiny dry footholds for my aching leg. Part of me just didn't want to be patient or cautious anymore. I'd had months of that. Still, I probably should have used my crutches.

I watched the game from the press box, because I couldn't really stand on the sidelines. Boston College won that final game against the University of Maryland, but we lost our bowl game to USC in San Francisco. The 2009 season was officially over, and to me that was important. Because the next time the BC Eagles took the field for a game, in nine months, I planned on being there with them.

I had one last postsurgery checkup with Dr. Lackman, my orthopedic oncology surgeon. I took the Amtrak train down from Boston to Phila-delphia and I met my mother at home. When I got there a network cam-era crew was waiting for me.

This was one of the crews that had followed me around on and off throughout my whole ordeal. Now they wanted to be there for the big reveal in Dr. Lackman's office—was I really cancer-free? But my mother wasn't at all happy to see them. I hadn't had an MRI or a CT scan of my chest in three months, and in the world of cancer three months is an eternity. What's more, the first set of scans after the chemo stops are crucial because the active killing of cancer cells is over, and no one knows if new ones will appear. In any case my mother never allowed herself to get ahead of any diagnosis, so in her mind the news could still be bad. And she didn't want either of us to receive bad news on camera.

I'd allowed the camera crews to infiltrate the privacy of not only my cancer battle but my whole family's struggle, and generally my mother had been a great trouper about it. And it wasn't always easy having three burly technicians crammed into your kitchen at the end of a long, tiring day. But this time she put her foot down.

"Mark, I don't want them in there with us," she said. "They can come in and film afterward."

I made the crew wait outside Dr. Lackman's office until we got the diagnosis.

Dr. Lackman didn't waste any time. His smile told me the news before he did. The scan hadn't turned up anything. The tumor was gone. The cancer cells were all gone. I no longer had cancer. We let the camera crew in, and they filmed the moments just *after* the moment that was one of the best of my life.

Not too long after that, I woke up one morning and ran my hand over my head, out of habit. It was kind of interesting to feel how sleek and smooth my head was. Only this morning, instead of smoothness, I felt a tiny layer of fuzz.

My hair was starting to grow back.

❦

My chemotherapy was over. My radiation was over. My cancer was gone. God had answered my first prayer.

But now I needed Him again.

The intramedullary rod procedure was a success, but that still left the rehabilitation of my left leg. To me, that was always going to be the easiest phase. It might be painful, and it might be difficult, but at least it would be within my control. However hard I needed to work to get back to my physical peak, I would work that hard. I knew how to do it. We were in my area of expertise now. Even so, I knew I couldn't do it alone. I needed God to answer my second prayer.

But feeling like you're in control is always a tricky thing when it comes to cancer. Maybe I should have known that by then. Because just when I was starting to get my strength back, just when I was morphing back into the Mark Herzlich I knew, I had a setback. A big setback.

It involved a mysterious yet familiar pain in my leg.

CHAPTER SIXTEEN

"Here's the deal, Mark," Coach told me. "You're going to do a hundred and fifty pull-ups and a hundred and fifty chin-ups. And you can't leave the gym until you do them."

I hadn't been barked at by a Boston College coach in a while, and it felt good. This was about three weeks after the surgery, and I was back on campus for my very first football-related workout since the diagnosis. BC's strength coach, Jason "Loco" Loscalzo, agreed to help kick off my rehab. He looked like what you'd expect a strength coach to look like— wide jaw, buzz cut, thick arms. He was loud and intense and even a little scary. I didn't expect him to go easy on me, and he didn't.

"All right, Mark, you beat cancer," he said by way of a greeting. "So guess what. Back to football."

I was seriously, seriously out of shape. I hadn't run at all in several months, except for the times I'd tried to jog out of the Alumni Stadium tunnel with the football team. I'd jog the first few steps and feel okay, but then I'd have to stop and walk. The pain was just too intense. Even now I wasn't quite ready to start running, so Loco and I focused on my upper body first.

Still, a hundred and fifty chin-ups and pull-ups right off the bat? I wasn't sure I could do it.

I got through the first twenty-five chin-ups okay. Loco loudly counted each one out. I took a quick break and shook my arms loose; they were cramping up. I squeezed out another ten chin-ups and took another break. My lungs were screaming and my hands were shaking uncontrollably. After another three chin-ups I felt like I was dying. But I didn't stop. With all my strength I grabbed the bar and did as many chin-ups as I could do. Which was one more.

After that, I still had a hundred to go.

I kept going. One or two or three at a time. Loco left his post and returned to his office overlooking the weight room.

"Don't think I can't count from up here," he yelled down.

"One fifty," I finally blurted out a good while later. Somehow, I had done it.

"Now the pull-ups," Loco yelled.

The very first pull-up made me feel like I wanted to cry.

It took me another hour and a half to complete a hundred fifty pull-ups, and when I was finished, I fell to the floor and tried not to pass out. My arms felt like lead weights and my eyesight was blurry. But I could still see that Loco was now standing over me. And I could see that he was smiling.

"When I gave you that workout I didn't think you'd be able to do it," he said. "But you did it. Your determination is outrageous. Now I know you're going to be okay, kid. You just wait and see."

❦

Winter gave way to spring, and I started running. Just the sheer act of it was exhilarating. It wasn't easy, and it didn't feel right—my left leg felt sluggish and heavy. I knew I had to keep building up my stamina, but weeks passed without my leg feeling much better. It always seemed like it was lagging behind. Gradually the pain did begin to lessen, and my leg did start to feel stronger. But the progress was much, much slower than I'd expected.

Still, I kept pushing. Stationary bikes, step machines, ellipticals—Coach Loco put me on all of them. Hours and hours and hours in the gym. He handed me a pair of dumbbells and had me do deep knee-bending lunges around the gym and into the corridor. Pouring sweat and out of breath, I'd lunge past giant posters of the great Boston College players—defensive end B. J. Raji, quarterback Doug Flutie, my buddy Matt Ryan. I lunged another six steps and there I was, beneath a huge poster of a fearsome linebacker, his face painted black, his eyes ablaze, his sneer ferocious. It was like the old Mark Herzlich was taunting me.

Look at you, he might as well have said. *Now look what you used to be!*

I turned away from my likeness and kept lunging.

I got so frustrated with my sluggish left leg I decided to see a massage therapist. Someone told me about a remarkable therapist in Canton, Massachusetts, who worked on some Patriots players, and I made an appointment. When I got to the office the first person I saw was a tiny, tan Italian woman who talked really fast. I towered over her by more than a foot. She introduced herself as Ellen, my therapist.

I told her all about my cancer and my surgery, and how I wanted to play football again.

"It's been four months and I can't figure out what's going on with my left leg," I explained. "It just won't loosen up."

"May I?" Ellen asked, before taking her thumb and slipping it into the quadriceps and hamstring of my left leg. It took everything I had not to scream out in pain. Ellen kept digging, and I couldn't believe how penetrating her tiny thumb was. I started to worry I might pass out. Still, I didn't scream. I didn't want her to see how much agony I was in.

"I can't feel any movement in your muscles," she finally said. "What, do you have a wooden leg?"

"Titanium," I said.

"Oh, just like my thumb."

It turned out Ellen had shattered the bones in her thumb after years and years of massage work, and she'd had them replaced with titanium. No wonder the pain was so unbearable. Her thumb was a tiny weapon.

Ellen believed the radiation and surgery might have created scar tissue that was now fused to my femur. The scar tissue could be inhibiting movement and muscle growth. Ellen's solution, I soon learned, was simple but sinister.

"I am going to rip the muscles from your bone," she said.

She went back to work with her titanium thumb and I had to grab the padded massage table so I didn't collapse from the pain. Still, I didn't cry out. Ellen looked at me and asked me whether it hurt. I told her that it did.

"It's okay," she said. "You can show it. I won't think less of you. *Pain is good.*"

Then she dug into my quads and I screamed like I never had before.

After my first hour-long session, I never wanted to see Ellen's face, or thumb, again. But I came back. I came back every Tuesday and Thursday for the next several months. I came back because of something Ellen said at the end of the session.

She said, "I can fix you."

That was all I needed to hear.

❦

The massage therapy was working. All the weights and running and workouts were working. My leg was feeling looser, and I was feeling stronger. Twenty weeks into my rehab, I was starting to feel like a football player again. The Boston College Eagles were set to start training camp in August, two months away. I was on schedule. I had no doubt I would make it all the way back.

On May 12, 2010, I hit the one-year mark since my diagnosis.

Right around then BC's spring game rolled around—the same game I'd played in a year earlier just before I learned I had cancer. I wasn't ready to play in this spring game, but I did attend the team dinner that night. My parents came up, too, as did the parents of a lot of my friends at BC. To me, it felt like a bit of a celebration. My cancer was gone and my rehab was going well, and my family was starting to get back to normal. It had been a while since any of us felt this good.

My father, in particular, was just so happy to see me get physically better. Even at his age his life was all about being active, and he understood how hard it was for me to be stationary for so long.

Sometimes it felt I was making my comeback as much for him as for me.

My dad is a guy who likes to challenge himself, and every few years he picks up a new challenge. One year it was hiking, and every day he'd drag Brad and me up some steep mountain, until we told him we hated hiking, and then he'd go by himself. Another time it was golf, and he'd play obsessively. One day he came home and announced he was going to start running marathons. He began by running one or two miles a day, but quickly jumped to ten and twenty.

Sure enough, he ran his first two marathons at the ages of fifty and fifty-one.

It was during his marathoning kick that my father came home one evening after running twenty miles for the first time. The man could barely walk. Brad and I watched him walk stiff-legged around the kitchen saying, "Oh, man, I hurt so bad."

"You know what you should do?" I said. "You should take an ice bath."

"That really works?"

"Oh, yeah. I take them at BC all the time."

We had a big bathtub just off the master bedroom. Brad and I, teenagers then, filled it with cold water and dumped in buckets and buckets of ice from our fridge. We put our hands in the icy tub water to test it, and it had to be forty degrees or less. It was *frigid*. My dad came in and looked at the tub with frightened eyes.

"You know I don't like cold stuff," he said.

"Don't worry, Dad," I assured him. "This will make you feel great."

My father slowly lowered himself into the ice water, making shrill little breathing sounds as he went in. As he got deeper, the sounds got louder. It took about a minute for him to submerge his whole body, and as soon as he did, he wanted to jump right out.

"I can't do this," he said through chattering teeth. "Too cold."

"Just ten minutes, Dad. You'll be numb and you won't feel a thing."

Brad and I were trying to stifle our laughter but not really succeeding.

"Nope," my dad said. "Can't do it. Got to get out. My feet are *frozen*."

It was then that my father started shrieking. Brad and I couldn't help but laugh. My dad jumped out of the tub, red and trembling. When he saw us laughing, he got kind of mad, so he rushed us to scare us away. But he forgot the bathroom floor was wet from all his splashing around.

My father slipped and flew into the air and landed on his butt. Then he spun around like a turtle on its shell.

I'm pretty sure I've never laughed so hard in my life. My dad got up and chased me and Brad into the bedroom, and when he caught up with me, he tried to tackle me into the bed. Instinctively I wrapped my arms around him, picked him up, and threw him on the bed instead. I was two years into my college-playing career then. That was what I'd been taught to do when someone came at me.

My father was a little stunned at first, but then he started laughing. The three of us lay around the bedroom giggling and trying to catch our breath. It was one of those moments I don't think I'll ever forget—a happy, playful memory. Well, at least for Brad and me.

But the moment meant something else, too. That was the first time I realized I was physically stronger than my father. When I was growing up, he had been impossibly bigger and stronger than me, but inevitably I'd caught up to him, and now surpassed him. Another chunk of his larger-than-life image fell away, and another piece of his humanity came into view. I don't think we can every truly know our fathers until we stop thinking of them as protectors and start seeing them as just men. I think that's part of the necessary ritual of growing up. It's not always easy, but it's something we have to do. My getting cancer just accelerated the process.

So it was a different Sandy Herzlich who showed up in Boston for the team dinner that May. Like all of us, he'd been through something that changed him. He was looser, happier, maybe even more appreciative of the tiny moments that bond families, as we all were. But he was also still my dad. And he still liked a challenge.

Before the dinner my folks came over to hang out with Danielle and me in my dorm. We sat in the backyard and cracked a couple of beers. The guys next door were playing a game my father didn't recognize.

"What are they doing?" he asked.

"They're playing dizzy bat," I said.

"Oh, yeah? How do you play?"

The rules of dizzy bat are simple. You take one of those hollow yellow Wiffle ball bats, cut a hole in the handle, and fill the thing up with beer. Then you chug the beer and stand the bat on the ground with your forehead touching it. Then you spin around the bat for however many seconds it took you to chug the beer. If it took you four seconds, you had to do four spins around the bat. When you were finished, someone tossed an empty beer can at you. You picked up the bat and took a swing. If you hit the can, you won. Simple as that.

"Sounds like fun," my father said, and before I could stop him, he headed over to the neighboring backyard.

I settled in for what I was sure would be an entertaining spectacle. The guys filled up the Wiffle ball bat with beer for my dad and counted off the seconds as he chugged. My mother looked on disapprovingly. After five seconds, my dad was finished. Not too bad. He put the bat on the ground and spun around it five times. When he stood up, he was so dizzy, he couldn't stay in one spot. He was staggering. Someone tossed a beer can at him. My father grabbed the bat and swung.

And wouldn't you know it? He *crushed* that beer can. Hit the thing a mile.

Everyone started cheering, and my father got it in his mind to run a circle around imaginary bases—a home-run trot. But he was still dizzy and wobbly and he never saw the thick, low-hanging elm tree branch to his right.

My father hit the branch dead-on with his forehead and crumpled to the ground. Blood dripped down his forehead. We ran over and helped him to his feet. I should have felt bad that he got clotheslined like that, but instead I found myself laughing. When he got his senses back my father found the humor in it, too.

That evening my father got cleaned up and made it to the early dinner my friends and I were throwing for our families. He had a giant bump on his head but was in great spirits. Just a few minutes into the dinner I heard someone hitting a spoon on a glass. I looked over and it was my dad—he wanted to make a toast. I wasn't even sure his brain was working properly, and my first thought was, *Jeez, this is going to be embarrassing.* I don't think I was the only one who had that thought. My father got to his feet and cleared his throat and addressed the fifteen or so people in our party.

And wouldn't you know it? He crushed the toast, too.

"This has been a rough year for our family," he said. "And you are the people who have been with us and helped us get through it the most. The past four years at Boston College have made us grow so much as a family, and they have helped my son Mark grow as a football player, and as a man. I am so proud of my son. And I am thankful to all of you for what you've done for us. God bless you all."

My father may not have been my protector anymore—after all, no one could protect me from what I was going through—but he was still the most important man in my life.

❧

A month later I was given clearance to work out with the team. It was only light workouts, but for me it was a huge milestone. Finally, finally I was back with my teammates, not just to cheer them on, but to practice alongside them.

One of the first drills I ran was called a sandpit workout. Basically you run quick sprints and turns in big pits of sand, strengthening your legs. I was running alongside my good friend and teammate Alex, and my left leg felt strong. I noticed I was keeping up with Alex.

But then we did a quick turn and I stepped forward and caught my right foot on one of Alex's feet. I landed on my right foot harder than I normally would have, but I turned and sprinted back and kept on with the workout. My right foot felt weird, an insistent, acute pain shooting through it. I didn't think much of it. Soreness, I figured. I finished the workout and tried to walk it off, and that was when my foot started to really hurt. A trainer put some ice on it and gave me a quick massage.

The next day, though, I could barely walk. Something was wrong with my foot. The trainers were extra cautious with me now, considering what had happened a year earlier. They sent me to a foot doctor right away. The doctor took X-rays and looked them over with me in his office in Boston.

"You've got a stress fracture in the second metatarsal," he said.

In other words, I had a broken foot.

I wish I could say I handled the news well, but I didn't. I wish I could say I didn't feel a twinge of self-pity, but I did. *Seriously?* I thought. *After everything I've been through? You have got to be kidding!* The doctor studied the X-rays and frowned and then made matters worse.

"The fracture is on the inside of your foot, so we can't do surgery," he said. "I don't know if this is going to be able to heal."

That was more than I could stand. Not heal? Why would he say that? How could my foot be unfixable? That was the ultimate frustration right there: a tiny fracture nobody could reach.

"What do you mean, it might not heal?" I said, my voice rising.

"We can put you in a boot and get a bone-stimulation machine," he said, without a shred of enthusiasm. "I don't know if that will heal it, but if it does heal, it will take at least four to six weeks."

I took deep breaths to calm myself down. It was June. Training camp started in August. The first game was September 4. I could handle six weeks. I could still play in the opener. All was not lost.

Depending, that was, on the answer to one critical question.

What if the fracture was related to my cancer?

❦

The Boston doctor's pessimism scared me. I began to think all the radiation might have somehow weakened my other leg. Or what if the cancer had spread? My mother got right on the phone and called Dr. Staddon.

"Could cancer or radiation have somehow caused the stress fracture in his right foot?" she asked. "Is this going to keep happening to him?"

Dr. Staddon was emphatic in his reply.

"Absolutely not," he said. "One has nothing to do with the other."

That was a big relief. I started walking around in a fracture boot and wore a bone stimulator designed to speed the healing of my foot with electromagnetic pulses. I had to slather my foot with gel and wrap it in a brown strap attached to a cord and have periodic twenty-minute treatments everywhere I went.

None of that bothered me in the least. What bothered me was that I couldn't work out or practice football. I was right back to being stationary, and it felt like some kind of cruel joke. To alleviate the intense frustration I joined some friends on a trip to Maine.

At one point my buddies went waterskiing and asked whether I wanted to go. I was still in my fracture boot, and my right foot was still tender. My left wasn't yet all the way back. Clearly waterskiing wouldn't be the smart thing.

A day later, one of my friends sent my mother an e-mail back in Wayne. Attached was digital footage of the waterskiing outing. My mother sat down and watched it, looking for me. After a minute or so, she saw me. I was standing on the dock. So far, so good, she thought.

Then she saw a water ski attached to my left foot.

You see, I knew it wasn't the smartest choice. But I was just sick and tired of putting my life on hold. So when I got the chance to live a little, I took it.

My mother held her breath and watched as I clung to a length of rope, and the motorboat ahead of me started to churn. She watched as the slack in the rope disappeared and I got ready to jump in the water so the boat could pull me. She held her breath as I pushed off the dock with my fractured right foot and the boat went full throttle. Then I disappeared. I was in the water, below the surface, hidden by waves. I was bigger and heavier than all my friends, and the boat wasn't going fast enough to pull me. Instead it was just dragging me through the water.

My mother tried to find me in the spray and tumble of the water but she couldn't. She tried not to think of all the bad things that could have happened. Maybe she even said a small prayer; I don't know. But she kept watching, waiting for me to rise up out of the water.

And then, finally, I did.

My mother watched as my body slowly got above the waterline and my water ski came into view. It wasn't very graceful, but it still resembled waterskiing in some way. Then my mother noticed something remarkable. She noticed that as I glided through the water, all of my weight—all two hundred forty pounds—was on one leg.

My left leg.

My mother exhaled and leaned back in her chair and had a thought. *He's going to do it*, she said to herself. *He's going to play football again.*

❦

I survived the waterskiing, but the truth is my foot wasn't healing fast enough. I was otherwise about seventy-five percent back to my precancer condition. I'd lost my fat and found my muscles. And thanks to Ellen, my left leg was coming along. But the fracture in my right foot was keeping me off the practice field. I hadn't been able to really test myself—I hadn't made a tackle or been knocked down or hit on the leg. No one knew whether I was football-ready. With training camp less than two weeks away, I was still a big question mark—to my coaches, and to myself.

The only guy who had the authority to get me back on the practice field was the pessimistic Boston foot doctor. If he didn't clear me, I couldn't play.

After six weeks I went to see him for an exam. He was as glum as ever.

"I'm sorry, Mark. It just hasn't healed," he told me. "You need another two weeks."

I went back to see him two weeks later, and he told me the very same thing.

That was it—I was missing training camp. Watching the other guys suit up and practice while I hobbled around in my boot was painful. It just seemed so colossally unfair. The only thing that kept me sane was seeing Danielle. We weren't supposed to have girls in our dorms during training camp, but I really, really needed to see her. So I sneaked her around the back and into my dorm room whenever I could.

Then I went to see the Boston doctor again, and he told me I needed another two weeks.

Now it was the end of August. I'd missed the entire training camp. The coaches hadn't had a chance to see whether I was back to my former self, or even close to it. Locked into my fracture boot, I didn't know whether I was, either. And all that time a date loomed large on my calendar—September 4. That was the date of BC's season opener at home against Weber State. September 4 was the day that kept me going through long, miserable workouts and endless leg treatments. It was the day I would, at long, long last, be back on the football field.

Number 94, playing on 9/4. It would be so perfect. It had to happen that way.

But it was no longer up to me. It was up to that Boston doctor.

I went to see him again on August 30, five days before the opening game. I desperately needed him to clear me so I could practice for a couple of days and then play. My foot didn't feel like it was fully healed; I still felt pain when I put pressure on it. But I didn't care about that. Some silly foot fracture wasn't about to keep me from playing, not after everything I'd been through.

The doctor looked over my X-rays. It was obvious he didn't like what he saw.

"You're going to need another two weeks of rest," he said.

That meant I'd miss the opening game and probably the next two games, too. I was furious. I got up and left his office as quickly as I could. I guess I'd had my fill of doctors tossing off dire predictions so casually and wiping out two weeks of my life without a second thought. Doctors who couldn't fathom how important it was for me to prove I wasn't damaged goods. I'd just had enough of doctors—enough, enough, enough. I went straight from that visit to the office of the BC medical staff.

"I'm ready to practice," I told the team's trainer.

"The doctor said you're okay?" he asked.

"Not exactly," I said.

"Well, why don't you tell me what he did say?"

"It doesn't matter," I shot back. "I'm not waiting. I'm playing. I don't care if I have a broken foot. I'm going to tape it up and play."

The trainer looked me over. He could see I wasn't fooling around.

"Go see Coach; see what he says."

Forget the doctor. Forget the trainer. The only obstacle left was BC's head football coach, Coach Spaz. If he cleared me to play, I would play. And if he didn't I ran the risk of falling behind the other players and never getting back in the starting lineup again. Our whole season was only twelve games. Missing three was out of the question. I collected myself and walked over to Coach Spaz's office. He was on the phone but motioned me in.

"So what's up?" he said after hanging up. I got right to it.

"Coach, I have a broken foot," I said. "But I'm playing on Saturday anyway."

It was not a question. It was a statement.

"Is that what you want to do?" Coach Spaz asked.

"Yes," I said. "No one and nothing is going to stop me from playing."

Coach Spaz sat quietly for a moment and thought about what I'd said. Or maybe he thought about the day he learned I had cancer, or the day he bestowed his yellow towel on me, or the day he found out I was cancer-free, or all the days he'd seen me grunting and sweating my way back to some kind of shape.

Or maybe he didn't want to be the one to clear me to play and then watch me get injured all over again.

I stared at Coach and tried not to blink. I never took my eyes off his. I needed him to see how dead serious I was. I needed, desperately, to hear him say yes.

"Well, then," he finally said, "I guess that's settled."

Coach Spaz cleared me to practice the next day, September 1.

It was my birthday. I was twenty-three.

CHAPTER SEVENTEEN

September 1—my first official football practice since the diagnosis. Twenty-four weeks of chemotherapy. Fifty rounds of radiation. Eight months of rehabilitation. Hundreds of days of waiting, a fractured foot, and one ignored doctor's warning. Dozens of proddings by an unyielding titanium thumb.

All of it just to get to this day.

I took two thin metal pads and wrapped them tightly around my fractured right foot. I wrapped them so tightly, I was basically cutting off the blood circulation so my foot would go numb and I wouldn't be able to feel it. I put on my football pants and my number 94 jersey and my cleats. Then I pulled on a football helmet for the first time in more than a year. It felt beautifully familiar. I buckled my chin strap and left the locker room. A few minutes later, I was on the football field.

I honestly don't remember too much about that first practice. I was so adrenalized, it all seems like a blur to me now. I do remember I wasn't nearly as quick on the field as I used to be. I felt a step or two slow. But I still knew all the plays, and I held my own. We had a sophomore linebacker, Luke Kuechly, who won Defensive Rookie of the Year honors the season before, and as much as it pained me to say it, he was clearly faster and stronger and maybe even better than me heading into that first practice. But that only gave me more incentive to keep going.

Somewhere in that first practice a lineman came at me and knocked me to the turf. It wasn't one of those pure, blistering hits, but it was a hit. I lay on the ground for a split second, then jumped back on my feet. My left leg had absorbed the hit, and it hadn't shattered. It was still intact. I jogged back to the line of scrimmage and lined up for the next play. "You're not so fragile," I said to myself. "You can do this."

Maybe that was the moment I stopped using the phrase "the bad leg."

After the practice my fractured right foot felt better than I'd expected. I was in one piece, and I was good to go for the next day's practice. The question now was whether I would be starting or not. The coaches didn't have much to go by. If they started me it would be because they reasoned that even at seventy-five percent I was an asset to the team. But I knew they didn't want to do anything to jeopardize my health. To me, however, being named a starter was *hugely* important. I didn't want to begin my big comeback game on the bench. I wanted to be out there like I always was, front and center. But that, too, was no longer up to me.

My parents and Brad came up to Boston a day before the opening game and stayed with friends in town. That day my father went out for a run and found himself outside Alumni Stadium, where the team was practicing. By then our practices were closed to the general public, but that didn't stop my dad. He wanted to get a look at me on the field. My dad knew some of the security personnel at BC, so with a wave and a hello, he basically sneaked into the stadium. He lurked near the tunnel and strained to see the players on the field. After a while he found the number he was looking for—94. He watched for a while, then dashed out of the stadium.

He ran all the way back to where he and my mom were staying and burst in, sweating and out of breath.

"Barb!" he cried out. "Mark is practicing with the starters! I think he's going to start tomorrow!"

Before that practice, Coach Spaz had called me into his office to ask how I was feeling.

"I'm feeling good, Coach," I said. "Great, actually."

"Mark, I'm going to start you on Saturday," he said.

I didn't respond. I just sat there, speechless. I probably broke into a goofy grin. It was happening. It was really happening.

"I don't know how much playing time you'll get," Coach went on. "We want to take it slowly and build up your reps throughout the year. I imagine you'll be playing the whole game soon enough."

I left Spaz's office feeling light as air. My cell phone rang, and I saw it was my mother calling. The timing was perfect—I couldn't wait to tell her the good news. But I didn't get the chance.

"Mark, I'm sorry to have to tell you this," she said, "but your grandfather Roland died."

❦

Roland was my mother's stepfather. He had married my grandmother Gandy after Pop-Pop died of a heart attack in his kitchen when I was four. Roland DiLeone was a cheerful, musical, sentimental Italian-American we called Rubber Ducky, because his initials were RD and because he had a great laugh that sometimes came out as a squeak. Roland was also Gandy's savior. He gave her a second chance at life when she was sure she'd never get one. He had found out he had pancreatic cancer six months earlier, right around the time I was told my cancer was gone. After he got sick, Gandy sat with him and read him the newspapers when he was too tired to read. Or she talked football, because she knew that was what he liked talking about.

When I heard his diagnosis, it struck me as so unfair. Gandy had already lost one husband, and now she risked losing the man who had brought her back to life. I knew instantly that I was going to do whatever I could to help Roland beat the disease and recover.

Roland and Gandy lived in Connecticut, just a two-and-a-half-hour drive from Wayne, and I went to see him whenever I could. We'd been close when I was a kid, and we got even closer after his diagnosis. I felt like we were part of a club none of our other relatives belonged to. Only we understood what we were going through. The thing is, Roland was always the most positive person I knew—always happy, always up. He was the same way after his diagnosis. I never once saw him sulk or complain or go to a dark place, not even right after his chemo sessions. Just like I tried putting my friends at ease, Roland always made me feel like he was going to bounce right back. He had so much life in him, and he had so much living left to do.

"Mark, are you there?" I heard my mother say. "Are you okay?"

"Not really," I said.

"I'm so sorry," she said. "You need to go find someone to talk to right now. Is Danielle around? Or Codi?"

They were both in class. I felt myself wanting to cry.

"Mom, I'm so sorry about Roland," I said. "Don't worry about me. I'll be fine."

I wandered around campus, trying to keep it together. The news was just so stark, so final—Roland was gone. He had lost the fight. I don't think I ever realized how formidable an opponent cancer was until that phone call—not even when I was given as low as a ten percent chance to survive myself. It took losing my grandfather for me to accept that cancer was often a fatal disease. It put my own mortality, my own survival, in a whole new light.

I walked around aimlessly, or maybe not so aimlessly, until I arrived at the BC athletic department. I headed to a particular coach's office and knocked on the door.

"Come in," Govs said.

He saw my face and asked whether everything was okay.

"No," I said, trying but failing to get out more than one word at a time. "My. Grandfather. Died."

Then I started crying. Govs came around and put his hand on my shoulder. He kept it there as I heaved and sobbed. I let it all out, everything—sadness for Roland, sadness for my family, sadness for me. A lot of emotions I'd kept bottled up for months. Govs didn't say anything except, "I know. I know." He just stayed close and let me cry.

After I left, Govs called my mother and told her he was worried.

"I've never seen Mark like that," he said. "With all the camera crews and all the fanfare about his comeback, it might be too much for the kid to handle. It's emotional overload."

My mother knew Govs was right—there *was* too much going on in my life. But the truth is, there had been too much going on for the past sixteen months. My mother worried about me more than anyone else in the world did, because that was part of her makeup—preparing, anticipating, worrying. But she also knew me better than anyone—and she knew nothing was going to stop me from playing the next day.

"You're right," she told Govs, "but he'll be okay. Mark will be okay."

❦

September 4, 2010, was warm and clear. Early that morning, Boston College students began jamming the Alumni Stadium parking lot and kicking off their infamous tailgate parties. Tailgating was such a tradition at BC that for most games the stadium seats were half-empty for much of the first quarter, as students reluctantly stopped partying and went in. But on September 4, every seat in the stadium was filled long before game time at one p.m. More than thirty-five thousand people packed the place.

In the locker room I bore down and got ready to play. I put on my pants and shoulder pads and my maroon-and-gold Boston College jersey. I laced up my cleats and strapped on my helmet. Around my left wrist I wore a yellow cancer-survivor band that said TEAM HERZLICH. Codi's father had made it for me.

I joined my teammates in the dark tunnel leading out to the field. Our tradition was to wait for a signal, then burst on the field together like a pack of wild dogs. In the tunnel my teammates led me to the front of the pack. They had decided they wanted me there. They wanted me to lead them onto the field.

I looked out at the throng of fans in the stadium. Somewhere out there were seventy-five friends and relatives who had come out to see me play. I also saw a sea of number 94 jerseys and BEAT CANCER T-shirts and signs. I felt a chill run up my spine. This was the moment—the *exact* moment—I had dreamed of for sixteen months. The moment so many people said would never come to pass. I looked out at the lip of the tunnel, and I saw a woman in a white shirt and sunglasses and a black nun's habit.

It was Sister Barbara Anne, the cancer survivor.

Sister Barbara Anne had not missed a single Notre Dame home game in *sixty* years. Yet here she was, skipping one so she could watch me play. Our athletic director, Gene DeFilippo, had promised he'd fly her to the game if I ever got back on the field, and he'd made good on that promise. You could not miss the shiny gold Notre Dame watch on Sister Barbara's wrist. Nor could you miss the big Mark Herzlich button over her heart.

I nodded to Sister Barbara Anne, and she smiled back at me.

I saw one of our coaches with his hand in the air, just about to give us the signal to go. I got ready to burst.

Just then I felt someone sidle up next to me. It was my roommate and teammate, Codi. Normally he didn't care whether he was in front of the pack or in the back, but on this day he worked his way past everyone else and made sure he was by my side. He looked up and smiled.

"I want to see this up close," he said.

The noise from the crowd was deafening. My legs felt like two springs. Finally the coach gave the signal. This was it. I ran out of the tunnel as fast as I could. The stadium got even louder. I ran to midfield waving my arms and screaming, and I noticed the rest of the players had let me run out by myself for the first few paces. I took off my helmet and ran to the student section and soaked up the cheers. I kept running and running, not wanting to stop, not wanting the moment to end.

It had been six hundred and twelve days since I last set foot on a field for an official game.

But I was here now. I was on a football field again.

I dedicated that game to my grandfather Roland.

❦

The game itself was a blur. Before the coin toss, a ten-year-old boy walked out on the field with a microphone and sang a beautiful rendition of the national anthem. He had just survived his own bout with cancer. He beat Ewing's sarcoma, just like me.

I took the field for the first time in what seemed like forever. The ground beneath me felt sacred. About midway through the first quarter the Weber State quarterback threw a little slant pass to his senior full-back, Zac Eldridge. The second I saw him release the ball I made my move. I pushed off with my left leg, quickly changed direction twice to keep up with Eldridge, and got within five feet of him as he turned up-field. I jumped in the air, completely leaving the ground, and I stretched out my left arm and grabbed Eldridge by the back of his jersey. I pulled him down and landed hard on the turf, face-first. I bounced back up and went back to the huddle.

I'd just made my first tackle in six hundred and twelve days.

On ESPN an announcer said, "He hasn't lost anything."

I played only part of that first game, but I made five tackles: three solo, two assisted. Most important, Boston College beat Weber State, 38–20. I felt a little slow and I overran a couple of routes, and there were a handful of plays I should have made but didn't. But overall, I felt good. I felt like I was back. "You know, he's had enough of being Mark Herzlich, cancer victim," *Boston Globe* columnist Bob Ryan wrote after the game. "All he wants now is to be Mark Herzlich, linebacker supreme."

Mr. Ryan was only half-right. I would never be just Mark Herzlich, linebacker, again. I would always be Mark Herzlich, linebacker and cancer survivor. Because of what Tedy Bruschi told me, I wanted to be known as both, and I would wear both labels with equal pride.

But when reporters caught up with me after the game, I really didn't want to talk about cancer. What I wanted to talk about was football.

"To get a win, no matter how we played, is huge," I told a reporter from *USA Today.* "Now we have to get in the film room and work."

Afterward I found my mother and father and Brad and pulled them in for a hug. I found Sister Barbara Anne and hugged her, too. There was someone else there, standing with my family—someone who had just watched me play a college football game in person for the first time ever.

My friend Zack.

He'd always been too busy with his own college life to make it to Boston to watch me play. But there was no way he was going to miss me play that day.

"Nice game," Zack said in his quiet, concise way.

"Get over here," I said as I brought him in for a big hug.

❦

My comeback season was a dream come true, but it also had its ups and downs. I wish the ESPN announcer had been right, and I hadn't lost anything. But I clearly had. Dr. Staddon warned me that even long after I was finished with chemotherapy, I could still experience a mental fogginess he called "chemo brain." And he was right. My short-term memory was diminished, and it was harder for me to absorb things. New plays took me much longer than usual to learn.

My body was also in its own kind of fog. There used to be almost no lag between my brain's decision to do something and my body executing that decision, but now there was. Pass drops I'd run a thousand times felt foreign, and blocks I'd shed with ease in the old days I suddenly couldn't get past. In one game I watched the running back take a swing pass and head downfield. I knew exactly what I had to do—push out through the curl, break away to the flat, and make the tackle. That used to be my bread and butter. But that game I was slow off the curl and slow on my break, and when I finally got to the running back he stutter-stepped and ran right by me. My body just didn't do what my brain ordered it to.

From the turf I looked up and saw my teammate Luke Kuechly make the tackle. In that instant I realized I wasn't the same player as before. I wasn't the best linebacker anymore. Luke, for one, was now outplaying me. When he was a freshman I told Luke he would one day feel invincible on the field, and when he did he would know he'd made it as a player. And now Luke was feeling that invincibility. On the field he *was* invincible. And I wasn't.

Dealing with my foggy brain and body was hard enough, but I also had to deal with constant scrutiny of my ability. At every turn reporters reminded me I wasn't as good as I used to be. "Do you think you're going to get back to where you were before you were diagnosed with cancer?" they would ask. Once in a while I'd read a blog about the team and come across a comment like, "Mark used to be good. Now he's just okay." Reading something like that stung; I'm not going to lie. But it also pushed me to work even harder.

During one practice I tried to swat the ball away from wide receiver Ifeanyi Momah, and I hit my left hand on his helmet. An X-ray showed the fifth metacarpal in my left pinkie finger was broken. I had another burst of self-pity, another "haven't I been tested enough?" moment. But I didn't spend a lot of time waiting for an answer. I got a cast put on my left hand and I didn't miss a single practice. I played in the very next game against the University of Virginia. In the fourth quarter, UVA's quarterback was under pressure and tried to throw the ball out-of-bounds. I read his eyes and broke for the sidelines and at the last moment I leaped and got fully airborne. I caught the ball between my cast and my good hand. I made the interception.

That interception was a turning point for me. After that I started to make more and more plays.

I started all twelve of BC's regular season games my comeback season, plus one bowl game. I didn't approach my junior-year statistics, but I did end up with sixty-five tackles, four interceptions, and two forced fumbles. On my very last play as a Boston College Eagle, I caught an interception. But the most important thing about that season wasn't a statistic.

It was that I played. I *played*.

That year I was given the Disney Spirit Award, which goes to college football's most inspiring player, as well as the Rudy Award, named for the famous Notre Dame underdog Daniel "Rudy" Ruettiger and given to players who "demonstrate exemplary character, courage, contribution, and commitment." Later that summer I received the ESPY for Comeback Player of the Year. These were big national awards, and winning them is something I will cherish forever.

But the most remarkable award I won didn't have the stature of the other two. It had something else. The Maxwell Football Club honors high school and college athletes around the nation, and they honored me with that season's Spirit Award. In 2005 they had given the Spirit Award to Tedy Bruschi. That alone made receiving it an uncommon thrill.

But there was another reason it was special. That same year, my brother, Brad, won the Maxwell Club's Jim Henry Award for area high school player of the year. It was the first time two brothers were given Maxwell awards in the same year. My family arranged to attend the awards ceremony in a resort in Atlantic City.

Not too long before the ceremony, we got a copy of the promotional poster with drawings of all the winners. There were about eight players depicted in all, and my likeness was right in the middle. I looked to see where Brad was, but I couldn't find him. I stared at the poster for a long time, trying to see whether it was just a bad drawing, but that wasn't it. The problem was that the artist had left Brad out.

It turned out that when the artist got the list of award winners he saw the name Herzlich twice and assumed I'd won *both* awards. It never occurred to him that there was another Herzlich. So he painted only one.

When Brad got a look at the poster he was clearly disappointed. "Oh, well, that stinks," he said, trying to be casual, but I knew, and my parents knew, that it hurt him to be excluded. He'd been forced to live in my shadow for so many years, and now that he'd finally willed himself out of it, someone had pushed him back in. He had to wonder whether he would forever be the forgotten Herzlich.

We called to ask if the poster could be fixed, but the ceremony was only days away and there just wasn't time. To Brad's credit he really didn't seem to care all that much that he wasn't on the poster. He let it go and moved on.

When we arrived at the resort in Atlantic City, the poster was everywhere. We couldn't help but see it. When Brad stopped to look at one, he noticed something he could hardly believe.

He *was* in the poster.

Brad figured they must have hastily fixed it, even though they'd told us they couldn't. That night we both received our awards, and it felt like a wonderful crowning moment for our whole family. I know that for me, seeing Brad on that stage was one of the best moments of my life.

It was only very recently, when the subject of that awards ceremony came up, that Brad learned the real story of how his likeness made it on that poster.

Two days before the ceremony, I called the event's organizer. I asked him one more time to get Brad on the poster. He began to tell me again how it was too late, and I cut him off.

"If Brad doesn't get on the poster," I said, "I'm not coming."

There was some more discussion, but I held my ground. No Brad on the poster, no Mark at the show.

So they fixed the poster.

❦

My college comeback was complete. My days as a Boston College Eagle were over. The next step was the final step in the long journey of my fight against cancer.

The National Football League.

After my junior year at BC, I was generally predicted to be a first- or second-round pick. Some scouts had me listed in the top ten. But that was history now. That was a lifetime ago. I'd missed an entire year of football, and when I came back I was not the same player I was before. I showed signs that I could be, but that was probably not enough for NFL scouts. I accepted that I wouldn't be drafted in the first round, and maybe not even in the second round. I told myself where I was drafted didn't matter. All that mattered was that I get picked to play in the NFL. Once I got there, I would prove everyone wrong.

The NFL commissioner, Roger Goodell, invited my family and me to come to the first day of the 2011 NFL draft, which was being held in Radio City Music Hall in New York City. The entire first day was devoted to the first round of picks, with the six other rounds spread out over the next two days. The first day was for the big dogs, the future stars. No one expected me to be picked that early, but the NFL invited me as an acknowledgment of everything I'd overcome. I had mixed feelings about going, but I went anyway. A camera crew from the NFL Network tagged along.

I watched from a seat near the stage as the Carolina Panthers picked Auburn quarterback Cam Newton with the first pick. Then the Denver Broncos, with the second pick, selected Von Miller—a linebacker, like me. I'd dreamed of being in Von's shoes—the best college linebacker in the nation. It wasn't the happiest feeling for me to see him picked number two. In all, thirty-two players were chosen in the first round. To no one's surprise, I wasn't one of them.

That night LeRoi, Danielle, Zack, Codi, and I went out to dinner in New York City with my agent, Howard Skall. We laughed and joked about what I would buy with my first NFL paycheck. We stayed up late and had a great time, and we all couldn't wait to hear my name called sometime in the next forty-eight hours.

We didn't stay in New York City for the rest of the rounds. Instead we went to Providence, Rhode Island, where Brad—then a freshman at Brown University—was playing in a spring football game. Danielle came with me, and so did the NFL Network camera crew. They wanted to film my reaction no matter what round I got picked. I made a decision not to stay in a room and watch the televised draft results. I wanted us all to walk around and relax and have fun, and when we found out what team picked me, then we could celebrate.

The first day in Providence, we walked around the campus and went to grab a bite. Throughout the day we'd get updates from someone listening to the draft on the radio. Sometime in the middle of the day, we heard the second round was over. No NFL team had picked me yet.

The rest of that day we did what we could not to think about the draft, even as we kept getting updates. "San Diego takes Vincent Brown," I'd hear. "The Rams just picked Austin Pettis." That evening, we learned the third round had come and gone without my name being called. I could tell Danielle was upset. No, not upset—she was angry. She did her best to contain it, but I knew what she was thinking.

Really? Don't you people know how good Mark is? Don't you know what he's made of?

Inside, I was asking the same questions.

But there was still another day, and four more rounds to go.

That day, a Saturday, I woke up anxious and uneasy. We went out for breakfast and then we went to watch Brad play in the spring game. In the stands we got more updates on the final four rounds of the draft. "The Colts picked Delone Carter." "The Bills take Chris Hairston." None of us talked about the draft at all. We just watched Brad play and laughed and joked about other things. But as the day wore on, the tension built. The camera crew shadowing us didn't help.

The fourth round ended, and then the fifth. I was starting to feel a real pit in my stomach. I kept thinking I felt my cell phone ringing, but it never did. They were phantom rings. I tried to will myself to forget about the draft altogether. *Just put it out of your mind,* I thought, *and when someone calls with news, then you can think about it.* There were still two full rounds to go.

I can't remember who it was who whispered the words, "That's it."

In all, two hundred fifty-four players were selected by NFL teams. Thirty-two of them were linebackers.

But the name Mark Herzlich was never called.

CHAPTER EIGHTEEN

The thing about a journey is, you never really know where it will take you. You might think you know, and you might even end up where you planned. But the journey will hit bumps and stops and detours you never imagined, and the destination will be different from what you expected. A journey is a passage, and in all passages things happen that change who you are. So by the time you get to where you're going, you're not the same person as when you began.

Not being selected in the draft was a hard thing to accept. It had briefly crossed my mind that I might not get picked, but I'd brushed that thought away just like I'd brushed away all those predictions I'd never run again. The draft was a painful moment, just as much for my family as for me. We had to say good-bye to the camera crew guys, who genuinely felt bad for us, and watching them pack up without getting the one shot they wanted was strange and awkward. Danielle was probably madder than any of us. She'd become very protective of me, and she was angry at all the football executives who passed me up. She desperately wanted a happy ending for me so that I could feel I'd made it all the way back. But that wasn't how things worked out.

I quickly realized I wouldn't be able to put on my usual brave face, so I told everyone I was going for a walk alone. I shuffled around from street to street and thought about what had just happened. After my junior year, I would have walked straight into the NFL and made millions of dollars. But cancer wiped all that out. Cancer might have just cost me my chance to play in the NFL. And in a way that felt like the end of the world.

But I had walked only a few blocks before I realized the error of my logic. No one is guaranteed a spot in the NFL. A million things can happen to derail you, and not just cancer. The ones who get there are the ones who get there. The ones who find a way—any way—to make it happen. The door to the NFL wasn't closed for me. It was just going to be a whole lot harder to get through. Not getting picked wasn't the end of the road. It was just the beginning of another part of my journey.

By the time I rejoined my family and Danielle I felt better. "It wasn't meant to be," I told Danielle. "But I'm fine. Let's move forward." We had dinner that night and talked about everything but football. We did what we could to put the day behind us. Still, I could see the reality of the draft weighing on my parents, and particularly on my father. You see, football isn't just a game to my dad. When he was in his forties he and some friends got together to play touch football, and my dad came home with a bloody, banged-up face. He needed seven stitches to close a nasty gash he got in a game of *touch* football! But that's just who my dad is—he's as passionate about football as I am. He wanted to see me play in the NFL just as badly as I wanted to play there.

Two days later I was contacted by an executive from the United Football League, a small offshoot league based in cities without NFL teams. He asked if I would join their team if they picked me with the first overall pick in the UFL draft. It was a flattering offer, but I politely said I wouldn't. The UFL just wasn't the NFL. Another two days passed, and I got a second call from the executive. He told me I'd been selected fifty-first out of fifty-two players by the Omaha Nighthawks. "Mark Herzlich is a special person and we feel a special football player," Omaha head coach Joe

Moglia tweeted. "We would like to offer Mark the opportunity to show-case his talents."

I called and thanked Coach Moglia for his kind words, but once again I declined.

Besides getting picked in the NFL draft, there was one other way to get in—you could be an undrafted free agent. NFL teams always invite a handful of unsigned free agents and players who didn't get drafted to their training camps, hoping to find a diamond in the rough. It's not easy for someone like this to make a team; you get only a few practices and four preseason games to prove you belong. But undrafted players do make the NFL. It does happen.

Before the draft I started working out at the IMG Academy NFL Combine training program in Bradenton, Florida. After I didn't get picked I went right back to working out again. I started a strenuous pro-gram with a strength-and-conditioning coach name Jeff Dillman. Like my BC coach Loco, Jeff was a character. He walked around like he was hooked up to an IV caffeine drip. Jeff would bang on my door at six a.m., screaming, "Wakey Wakey Eggs and Bakey!" He'd run me relentlessly until he figured I'd pass out; then he'd run me some more.

"If I had a farm, this boy right here would be my prized ox!" Jeff once yelled loud enough for everyone in the gym to hear. "He can't be broke!"

That was just what I needed. I needed someone to keep me intensely focused. Someone to push me beyond my limits. Someone to help me believe I could still do it. All I needed was one interested NFL team to call me and give me a chance. And so, once again, I spent a lot of time waiting for my cell to ring.

There was one big complication—the NFL players had been locked out in a labor fight. Players weren't allowed to train at team facilities, and teams weren't allowed to even speak with free agents. That meant I wouldn't be hearing from teams until the players and the NFL struck a new collective bargaining agreement. The lockout stretched through the summer of 2011: from the draft in April, through all of May and all of June, and then through July. After months and months and months of waiting, I had to wait some more.

The truth is, I had no idea whether any NFL team would call me. I didn't know whether anyone believed I could play.

Finally, on July 25, just six weeks before the scheduled start of the 2011 season, a new agreement was signed. The lockout was over and the waiting game began. My cell phone became the sole focus of my life.

Would anyone call?

The day the lockout ended, my cell rang. It was a call from someone with the Baltimore Ravens. The Ravens of the National Football League.

More calls came. One from the Philadelphia Eagles, and another from the New York Giants. At the Herzlich household, it was like someone had pulled back a big black curtain and let the sunlight in. Teams were interested in seeing me play. The NFL hadn't forgotten me. I would get my chance to make it after all.

That was when a camera crew from *60 Minutes* started following me around.

When it became apparent that more than one team wanted to bring me into training camp, I had to make a choice. In a way the Eagles were my hometown team, and the thought of playing there was tempting. The Eagles were also Zack's favorite team, and that alone was almost reason enough to go there. But one of the other teams held a special interest for me.

The New York Giants.

The Giants were my *father's* favorite team. He had grown up in an area that was near both Boston and New York, and he could have rooted for either city, and in fact he loved the Celtics and the Bruins and the Red

Sox, all from Boston. But when it came to football, it was always about the Giants. His own dad had been a Giants fan, and he was, too. When I was a kid he'd nearly knocked me off his lap when the Giants won the Super Bowl in 1991. And now, if somehow I wound up on the Giants, my father would be the happiest guy in the world.

In my talks with Giants executives they made it clear they wanted me in their training camp, which was starting in just one day. The time for me to make a decision was all but over. I spent an entire evening on the phone with executives from all three teams, trying to figure out what to do. That night, I made up my mind.

The next morning, at my family's home in Wayne, I got a call from a New Jersey area code. My mother and father huddled around me as I answered it.

It was Tom Coughlin—head coach of the New York Giants.

"Hey, Mark, how are you?" Coach said.

"I'm good," I said. "It's nice to see you."

See you? I was really nervous.

"So, Mark," Coach went on, "I know your story and it is very inspirational to me. But I don't want you on the team because of your story. I want you on the team because I think you can help us win a Super Bowl. So what do you say? Are you ready to be a New York Giant?"

I took a deep breath to calm myself.

"Yes, sir," I said, "I am."

My father was ecstatic. He popped Brad and me in the car and drove us straight to the mall so he could buy us all New York Giants caps. He couldn't put his on fast enough. I'm pretty sure my dad was more excited than I was. That day I tweeted the news.

> Decision is made. I will be a #GIANT. Can't wait
> to get to #NYC. Thank you for everything.

Then I had to tell my best friend, Zack. He wasn't just an Eagles fan; he also hated their archrivals, the Giants. *Hated* them. When I told him I was going to the Giants training camp his reaction didn't surprise me.

"Aw, no," he said. "Not the Giants. The Redskins, the Cowboys, *anybody* but the Giants."

But those were just the words he said. That was not how he really felt. I knew how he felt without even having to ask him.

He was happy for me because I was getting my shot.

❦

I spoke with Coach Coughlin on July 24 and I reported to camp the next day. When I got there, team officials put all the rookies and free agents on a bus and drove us to the Hospital for Special Surgery in Manhattan for our physicals. We broke up into two groups and got poked and prodded and MRI'ed and X-rayed. Some of the rookies were high draft picks and walked around fairly cocky. Some other guys seemed overwhelmed. I was not one of the cocky guys. I wasn't thrilled to be back in a hospital getting examined, either, and my old fear of MRI results came back. I was happy when we finished and got out of there.

The rest of training camp was a blur. Because of the lockout the training schedule was compressed, and I would have even less time to prove myself to coaches. Every game, every practice, every play counted. On our first day they handed us a huge document, thicker than a phone book, and told us to start learning it. It was the Giants playbook. We had two weeks to learn every play. I studied harder than I ever had in college. I was the first one in the gym in the morning and the last one, I hoped, devouring his playbook at night.

Pretty quickly I bonded with three other players looking for their break. One of them was the guy I was assigned to bunk with, Henry Hynoski Jr. Henry was a thick, rugged guy from Pennsylvania coal country. His dad had played in the NFL, and now that was Henry's dream, too. I also got to know an undrafted linebacker named Spencer Paysinger. He was a warm, soft-spoken guy from California. Rounding out our gang was Tyler Sash, a buzz-cut defensive back from the University of Iowa. The Giants picked Tyler in the sixth round of the draft, but he still had to fight for his spot on the team, same as me. The four of us became inseparable, eating together, training together, helping one another with the playbook. The only downside to our friendship was that we all knew the odds were against all of us making the team.

We had four preseason games to play, leading up to September 5—the day the Giants made their final cut. That was the day I'd learn whether I was in the NFL or not. For our first preseason game I was the team's fourth-string linebacker and also on the special team squad, chasing runners on punts and kickoffs. I was sent in for only five plays the whole game, compared to the dozens of plays I'd get every game at Boston College. Still, I had two tackles and a forced fumble. I didn't see much more action than that in the second and third games, before being sent in for all of ten plays in our fourth and final preseason game.

When that fourth game ended I thought for sure I was going to get cut.

Physically I felt good on the field, but the truth is, professional football is played at a much, much faster speed than in college. And I just wasn't sure I'd convinced anybody I could play at that speed. All I wanted was more of a chance to prove myself, but I didn't know whether I was going to get it.

For me, training camp with the Giants was even more stressful than having cancer. I know that sounds crazy, but it's true. I had such confidence that I would beat cancer, and I knew I'd do whatever it took to beat it. But now there was always *more* I could do to impress the coaches. I could study more, play harder, play longer, make fewer mistakes, watch more film, and on and on. I was constantly harping on my errors and worrying I'd run out of time. For four weeks I was *always* stressed.

Every once in a while I would also feel bitter that I was in this position. Again, if I hadn't gotten cancer, and if I'd been drafted after my junior year at BC, there would have been no stress at all. First- or second-round draft picks almost always make the team. Yet here I was, scratching and clawing to get noticed. It was easy to get angry at my cancer. But it was also pointless.

On September 5—final-cut day—I truly had no idea whether I'd made the team or not. The way the Giants operate is, if they're going to cut you they give you a call. So if you don't get a call by six p.m. that day, it means you made the team. No news is great news. I told my parents I was just going to hang around by myself that day, and if I got cut I'd call them. I also warned them not to call me, because every time my phone rang I'd think it was the Giants cutting me and my heart would sink.

That morning Henry, Spencer, Tyler, and I went to IHOP. I usually put away a big breakfast, but I was too anxious to eat much. We all were. We knew full well that one or two or maybe three of us were likely to get cut. On our way out Tyler's cell rang. It wasn't a Giants coach—it was his agent.

Tyler had made the team.

After that, Henry lost patience and called his agent.

He found out he'd made the team, too.

That left Spencer and me. Neither one of us wanted to call our agents; we just wanted six p.m. to come and go. Spencer went back to his room, and I went to a local Chili's to watch Boston College play a game. I ordered a quesadilla and poked at it. I later found out that as soon as Spencer got to his dorm his phone rang. It was a Giants coach. Spencer nearly passed out.

"Spencer," the coach said, "is your roommate there?"

It was his roommate who got cut. Spencer was safe—for now.

I went back to my dorm. It was around three p.m. At that time my mother was visiting her mom in Connecticut, trying to keep her anxiety under control. But it was no use. She was as restless as I was. She got in her car and drove to East Rutherford, New Jersey, where I was staying and waiting. *I have to be with Mark*, she thought. *I know he told me not to, but I have to go. I don't want him to be alone for this.*

On the way she called my father. He was supposed to be back in Wayne, working.

"Sandy, I couldn't wait," she said. "I'm driving down to see Mark now."

"That's okay; I couldn't wait either," my father said. "I'm in my car driving up to see him, too."

My mother showed up first, then my dad. Honestly, I was very happy to see them. A few minutes later Danielle showed up, too. She'd been at the Boston College game in Chestnut Hill, but she hadn't been able to wait, either. I hugged her tightly and told her I was glad she had come.

It was now five thirty p.m. Thirty minutes to go. The four of us talked nervously about whatever it was we talked about, trying desperately not to look at our watches. My cell phone sat like an explosive device on a table. But then a funny thing happened. I was so happy to see my parents and Danielle that for a moment I forgot about the phone call altogether. I didn't think that was possible, but that was what happened. I just got lost in the sweet feeling of being around the people I love. Time stopped mattering. Only they did.

"Hey, guys," Danielle said all of a sudden, "it's six-oh-three."

We looked at our watches. I looked at my still and silent phone.

"Is that it?" I said. "Does that mean I'm on the team?"

I looked at my mother, and saw that she was crying.

"I guess so," she said. "Looks like you're a New York Giant."

❦

The four of us got up and hugged and laughed and cried. It was such an incredible feeling of relief. It had been nearly nine hundred days since I learned I had cancer, and in that time there were so many dark and frightening moments. But there were also many beautiful moments, and this might have been the most beautiful of all. Against the odds, against the predictions, maybe even against all logic, I had made it to the NFL. God had answered my second prayer.

After a while I called my buddy Spencer and found out he made the team, too.

The moment called for a celebration, but we were too emotionally spent for any sort of night out. Instead we all went to Pizzeria Uno and devoured my favorite pie, the Numero Uno—with no mushrooms, of course. Then we got a hotel room in town. My folks slept in one bed, and Danielle and I slept in the other. When I was little my father had always sat and told Brad and me a bedtime story. He gave us a choice of three stories—Mark and Brad the superheroes, Mark and Brad the policemen, or Mark and Brad the animal trainers. We tended to favor Mark and Brad the superheroes.

Having my folks in the hotel room with me reminded me of those nights.

"Hey, Dad," I said, "how about a bedtime story?"

"Sure, Bear," my father said. Then he came up with a new one. "How about Mark the football player?"

And that was the story my father told to me that night, with Danielle fast asleep by my side. So my big celebration was pizza and a bedtime story. Sometimes when I do silly stuff with my family, Danielle rolls her eyes and jokes, "Mark, you are the lamest." I can see she has a point.

❧

My first official game as a professional football player was against the Washington Redskins. It was the tenth anniversary of the 9/11 terrorist attacks, and before the game, volunteers unfurled a giant American flag that stretched across the whole field. Standing in the stadium tunnel in my new Giants jersey and helmet, seeing that beautiful flag and waiting to play in my first NFL game, is a moment I will always treasure.

The game itself was even faster and fiercer than preseason had prepared me for. NFL games are played at a breakneck speed you can never really replicate in practice. I didn't start, but I got in on special teams. On kickoffs I hurled my body downfield at lightning speed, recklessly and with abandon, because that is the only way to play pro football. Your body exists to be sacrificed to the play. That first game was exhausting and exhilarating and unlike anything I'd experienced. I was in on some tackles and I played reasonably well, but the Giants lost 28–14. Almost immediately afterward I had to start cramming and studying for our next game.

That first season I watched a ton of game film and analyzed countless plays. I fell into the trap of thinking too much, both before and during games. My old BC coach, Coach Spaz, used to say, "If you think, you stink." By that, he meant that if your mind is too busy during a game you won't be able to play fast enough to be good. You have to know exactly what you're supposed to do on every play, and then forget about it once you're on the field and let instinct take over. I kept trying to find the balance between thinking too much and being underprepared.

Halfway through the season, Danielle got called for active duty. By then she was a second lieutenant in the U.S. Army, and she was assigned to Fort Jackson in South Carolina for three months. That meant I wouldn't see much of her for the rest of the season. Having Danielle with me was such a blessing; she helped calm my anxiety, and she always made me feel like I would succeed. I can't imagine how things would have played out if I hadn't met Danielle. But I respected her so much for her military service, and I knew this was what she had to do. Still, it wasn't easy saying good-bye.

A couple weeks later I got word Coach Coughlin wanted to see me in his office.

"Sit down, Mark," Coach said when I walked in. "How're you feeling?"

"Really good, Coach," I said.

"Mark, we're going to give you a chance to start this week. So you'll be the starting middle linebacker."

How about that? The game was against the Philadelphia Eagles, the team I rooted for as a kid. It would be nationally televised on Sunday night. And I was a starting linebacker for the New York Giants.

The Giants lost that game, and I made some mistakes I shouldn't have, but overall I played my best game yet. It was the first game where I felt like my old self—quick, instinctive, powerful. On one play I burst through the scrimmage line and brought down the Eagles All-Pro running back LeSean McCoy. It was like the old days, when I lived for that half second of pure, perfect contact. That was a turning point for me. That was the game that made me feel I belonged in the NFL.

After that, it seemed my fortunes were changing. Coach Coughlin picked me to start the next game, too, against the New Orleans Saints on Monday night. Before the game I tossed a ball around with all the other linebackers and I felt loose and relaxed, maybe for the first time as a Giant. The feeling I had was that I was right on the cusp of finally showing everyone the kind of player I was.

But like I said, journeys don't always take you where you want to go. Sometimes they take you where you least want to be.

Against the Saints I made two or three really good tackles early on and I sensed more were coming. I felt light and strong. In the third quarter I blitzed up the middle, trying to sack Saints quarterback Drew Brees. I jumped in the air, anticipating a pass, but instead Brees tucked the ball away and started running upfield. I fell to the turf and tried to scramble after him, but before I could get up someone pushed a Saints offensive lineman and knocked him over. The lineman—all three hundred pounds of him—landed on my right ankle. I felt a sharp, instant, shooting pain. I ran off the field and had my ankle taped up, but before long I couldn't even stand.

The next day an MRI showed a fracture in the bone.

I had broken my ankle.

❦

The doctor told me recovery would take six to eight weeks. There were only four games left to play, so that meant my season was over. I was crushed—*crushed*. Being debilitated, getting relegated to the sidelines, losing touch with the other players—it all brought back terrible memories of when I had cancer. I was back in that awful, familiar position—I was a patient again. The waiting, the inactivity, the unbearable frustration, even the bouts of self-pity—all of it was back. The Giants signed a guy named Chase Blackburn to fill in for me at linebacker, and to be truthful it was hard for me to watch him play. Every good play he made was a play I felt *I* should have been making. I tried to stay as close to the team as I could, but much of the time, hobbling around on the sidelines on crutches, I was just in the way. A week after feeling like I finally belonged, I now felt like an outsider.

The Giants had a rough season my first year, and with one game to go, against the Dallas Cowboys, we had eight wins and seven losses. The only way for us to get into the playoffs was to beat the Cowboys and finish at nine and seven. The Giants won that game and, contrary to most preseason predictions, made the playoffs. Still, no one gave the Giants much of a chance going forward.

At Fort Jackson in South Carolina, Danielle told her supervisor that if her boyfriend's team made it to the Super Bowl, she was going to put in for a leave so she could go to the game.

"What team does your boyfriend play for?" he asked.

"The Giants."

"Oh, they're not going to make it," the supervisor said. "Don't worry about taking a leave. Dismissed."

I watched the first playoff game, against the Atlanta Falcons, from the sidelines. The Giants won easily, 24–2. The Giants' defense—*my guys*— were starting to play really well. But we still had to beat two great teams, the Green Bay Packers and the San Francisco 49ers, to make it to the Super Bowl. Again, no one gave us a chance. Because I was injured I didn't even travel with the team to Green Bay. I guess I could have made a point of it and gotten the team to let me go, but I was so angry about not playing, I stayed home and watched the game on TV with my teammate Spencer, who was also hurt for that game.

That day the Giants beat the Packers 37–20.

After the game, a wild thought came to me. My ankle wasn't close to being fully healed, and most of the time it still hurt. But if the situation arose, if the football gods could make it happen, I was more than willing to play against the heavily favored 49ers. I told the coaches I was ready to go if they needed me. They told me it was unlikely, but they didn't rule it out. I was back to waiting for a call to tell me whether I'd been reactivated. My season might not be over yet.

Back at Fort Jackson, Danielle approached her supervisor again.

"If the Giants beat the 49ers, then we'll have this conversation," he told her. "But they're not going to win, so we won't need to talk."

I traveled with the Giants to San Francisco for the game. It was a close, tense, hard-fought game, but on the sidelines all I felt was anger. I didn't want to feel that way; I just couldn't help it. I could barely stand to see other guys playing in such an incredible, meaningful game while I was banished to the land of the injured yet again. In the third quarter the Giants were losing, and I left the field to check on my teammate Tyler, who had suffered a concussion in the game and was in the locker room.

Then, on a TV in the locker room, I saw Giants linebacker Jacquian Williams make a beautiful hit on a punt return and cause a fumble. It was the kind of play I would have loved to make. Something clicked for me with that play. We still had a chance to win the game, and if we did, we'd be going to the Super Bowl. I thought about what it would mean to my father to see his son win a Super Bowl ring with his favorite childhood team.

Then I thought about what it would mean to me.

Football is a team game; no one player can decide the outcome. You win only if a whole *lot* of players do well. And you get to the Super Bowl only if the whole *team* plays well. And not just in one game, but throughout the whole season.

Well, I was part of the Giants. I had contributed. My journey to the Super Bowl wouldn't be anything like I planned, but the journey could take me there nonetheless. *The journey was not mine to orchestrate.* It hadn't been when I got cancer, and it wasn't now. But it was still my journey. And it wasn't over yet.

I hustled back to the field on my crutches and watched the Giants score a fourth-quarter touchdown. We were ahead by three. The 49ers tied it with a late field goal, and the game went into overtime. Seventy thousand people at Candlestick Park were screaming, the Super Bowl in their grasp. On the sidelines, I was limping and jumping and yelling and trying to fire up our players. All of a sudden the Giants' defense forced another fumble. Our kicker Lawrence Tynes lined up for a field goal that would win the game. I watched the ball jump off his right foot and sail toward the goalposts. If he made the field goal, we were going to the Super Bowl.

The ball went straight through the uprights.

CHAPTER NINETEEN

On January 30, 2012, the Giants' team plane left Newark Liberty International Airport in New Jersey and flew to Indianapolis, site of Super Bowl XLVI. I was on that plane. My plan was to practice with the team and hope to get activated. But deep down, I knew that was unlikely to happen. The Giants squad that had just beaten three great teams was in place, and it didn't make much sense to change it now. Still, I held out hope. Anything could happen.

When we landed I grabbed my phone and sent out a tweet.

> 2 years ago I was told I might never walk again.
> Just WALKED off plane in Indy for the #Superbowl.
> #TakeThatCancer

The Giants chartered a plane for the players' families, and my parents and Brad took that plane to Indianapolis. But by Thursday of Super Bowl week, with two days to go before the big game, I still didn't know whether Danielle would make it. After the 49ers game her supervisor put in for a leave of absence for her, and sent it up through the chain of command. But days passed without Danielle getting an answer. She had no plane ticket, and no idea whether she should buy one. She just had to wait to hear whether her leave had been approved.

The week leading up to the Super Bowl passed quickly. With each passing day the excitement and electricity around our team got more intense. We were playing the New England Patriots, winners of three previous Super Bowls and one of the great NFL teams of the last twenty-five years. Their record was thirteen and three, compared to our nine and seven. They were favored to win the Super Bowl, too, but only by three points. Just four years earlier the Giants had faced the Patriots in Super Bowl XLII, and going into that game the Giants were *huge* underdogs. Most people expected the Patriots would win by two touchdowns or more. But the gutsy Giants, and our remarkable quarterback Eli Manning, pulled off the upset of the decade and beat the Patriots. We knew it could be done. The question was, could we make lightning strike twice?

I never fully appreciated the significance of the Super Bowl until I got to one. I found its true meaning in the faces of my teammates. There were players on the Giants who had been in the NFL for years and never been to a Super Bowl, and I could tell how emotional it was for them to finally make it. You see, every player in the NFL had to overcome great odds to get to where they were. They all had people in their lives who told them they couldn't do it. And yet they fought and fought and never gave up, and now each of their journeys was reaching a magical conclusion. The Super Bowl is not just a football game—it is the culmination of all the hopes and fears and wishes and struggles of hard, proud, determined men. Going to the Super Bowl is the dream of millions of kids. And for us it had come true.

If you are on a team that wins the Super Bowl, whether you play in the game or not, you will be a champion for life.

The morning of the game, February 5, 2012, I still didn't know whether I'd be activated. Early in the day, many of the players went out on the Lucas Oil field just to soak up the Super Bowl excitement. As soon as I walked on the field I was transformed into a ten-year-old boy. We all were. Many of us started tossing footballs around, pretending to make one-handed catches in the end zone—just like we all used to do when we were kids! And we were professional football players! That is the magic of the Super Bowl. It made a team of grown men feel like little boys.

Back in the locker room, I looked for my shoulder pads. If the trainer drapes your jersey over your pads, that's how you know you're playing. If the jersey isn't there, you're not.

My jersey was there.

Before I let myself get excited, I looked around. Right away I noticed that *everyone's* jersey was there. Coach Coughlin wanted everyone on the team to suit up for pregame warm-ups. That included players on the injured list, rookies who hadn't played very much, even guys who were on the practice squad and not actually on the roster. Coach knew what it meant for a player to buckle up his chin strap on the day of the Super Bowl. He wanted all of us to have that memory.

I walked over to the whiteboard. That was where trainers wrote the list of inactive players. Deep down, I already knew my name would be there. And it was.

I was disappointed—extremely disappointed. But I wasn't crushed. After all I'd been through, it just didn't make sense to feel sad anymore.

That afternoon I put on my pads and cleats and helmet and joined the entire team for warm-ups on the artificial turf at Lucas Oil Stadium. My ankle still hurt a lot, but the adrenaline soon wiped out the pain. Just after the warm-up, I got a text. It was from my father. My dad texted me before every game I'd ever played in high school and college and the NFL. He always sent a pick-me-up message: "Hey, buddy, good luck today"; "Have fun and play hard today"; stuff like that. Super Bowl day was no different.

"Keep your head up and stay in the game," my father texted. "Enjoy this moment."

My father knew that if I didn't play I'd have a lot of different emotions swirling inside me. He wanted to make sure I didn't let those emotions ruin my day.

After warm-ups I showered and got dressed in my street clothes. That was one of the strangest feelings I've ever had. Every fiber in my body, every instinct I possessed, told me I should be putting on my pads and cleats and joining my guys on the field. Doing the opposite of that was painful. This was not the way any fairy tale was supposed to end—with a player in sweatpants on the sidelines. It was not the way I'd pictured my journey would go.

I ran out of the tunnel with the team. That was more thrilling than I expected it to be. I searched the crowd for my family, but there were some sixty-nine thousand people in the stands, and I had no hope of finding them. I stayed on the field for as long as I could, until it was time to go to the sidelines. Kelly Clarkson sang the national anthem; the Patriots won the coin toss. The Super Bowl began.

The game was epic.

The Giants went up by nine; the Patriots stormed back. My friend Henry Hynoski jumped on a fumble. Chase Blackburn, the linebacker who replaced me, intercepted a Tom Brady pass. With three minutes and forty-six seconds left to go in the game, the Giants got the ball. We were losing by two points, 17–15, and we were all the way back on the Patriots' twelve-yard line. We had a long way to go to get in scoring range, and not much time to do it. If we didn't score on this drive, we would likely lose the game.

That was when our quarterback Eli Manning went to work. That whole season we always believed that in close games all we had to do was get the ball in Eli's hands and he would find a way to win. He had done just that in the Super Bowl four years earlier, throwing a late touchdown and earning the game's MVP award. Under extraordinary pressure, Eli is able to work magic. Now he faced the most pressurized situation imaginable—one last drive to win the Super Bowl. With less than four minutes to go.

Eli got to it. He completed one of the greatest Super Bowl passes ever, a thirty-eight-yard throw to Mario Manningham along the left sidelines. If he'd thrown the ball an inch shorter or farther or left or right, it wouldn't have been caught. The Giants worked their way down the field, and with one minute to go our running back Ahmad Bradshaw scored a touchdown. The Giants went ahead, 21–17.

On the sidelines I was a wreck. The emotion and intensity were overwhelming. The Patriots still had one minute to score and win the game, and they had one of the great quarterbacks of all time, Tom Brady. It was up to our defense—my guys—to stop them.

With just a few seconds to go, the Patriots had advanced the ball only to midfield. Their only hope was to throw a Hail Mary pass into our end zone and pray one of their players caught it. Tom Brady heaved the ball into the air, and I watched it as it floated across the sky. It seemed like it hung in the air forever. Then it came down, and a cluster of Giants and Patriots were there to try to catch it in the end zone. The ball got batted around and stayed afloat for another second or two. At the last moment Patriots tight end Rob Gronkowski lunged desperately for the ball. From where I was standing it looked like he had a chance to catch it. If he caught it, the Patriots would win the Super Bowl. If he didn't, we would win.

I lost sight of the ball. I couldn't tell whether Gronkowski caught it or not. For a brief moment my heart sank. And then I saw the ball.

It wasn't in Gronkowski's hands. It was rolling around on the turf, uncaught. The game was over. The Super Bowl was over.

The New York Giants were champions.

What happened next was bedlam. I ran onto the field beneath a rain of confetti and screamed out of complete euphoria. I jumped in the air and flailed my arms and looked for someone to grab. I saw my buddy Henry and I ran up behind him and put him in a bear hug. Then I saw Spencer and Tyler, and I grabbed them and hugged them and danced with them on the field. The confetti kept falling, so much of it I could barely see. The sense of elation, the pure, powerful joy of the moment, was unlike anything I'd felt before.

Back in Pennsylvania, in the library of her warm, comfortable home, Kathleen, my chemo nurse, watched the game with her husband and a pitcher of Bloody Marys. She cheered so hard for the Giants, she was almost hoarse. Her husband, a rabid Eagles fan, let it slide. A few days later, Kathleen joined all the other nurses at the medical center in Radnor and watched the Super Bowl ticker-tape parade on TV. She and the nurses wiped away tears when they saw me riding on a float, wearing a smile they'd never seen before.

And over in South Bend, on Super Bowl Sunday, a Franciscan sister left room 109 of Our Lady of Holy Angels convent and sat squarely in front of a large-screen TV in the common area. A week earlier Sister Barbara Anne sent me the latest of her more than one hundred letters, wishing me luck in the game.

"Know that we have more Giants fans here than ever before!" she wrote. "Welcome to Indiana! We will be watching you and rooting for you, my Football Man. Love and prayers, Sister Barbara Anne."

And when the Giants won, Sister Barbara Anne let out a holler that woke the Holy Angels.

And up in the seats in Lucas Oil Stadium, a set of proud parents completely lost their cool. Sandy and Barbara Herzlich didn't even wait for the game to end; they left their seats early and headed down to the field with Brad. They were in the tunnel when Brady's last pass hit the ground. My father ran ahead of my mother, desperate to get onto the field, but a ring of security guards stopped him. In the chaos my father broke through their arm chain and dashed onto the field. He scampered through the deluge of confetti, looking for me. I was running around looking for him.

I saw him first. I ran his way and he turned around and saw me and then he ran toward me. We met on the forty-yard line.

"Bear, we did it!" my father yelled.

"We did it!" I yelled back.

Then I gave my father a long, long hug.

Then I saw my mother, and I hugged her so hard, I picked her up.

"We did it, Mom," I said. "I love you."

"I love you too, Mark," she said. "I love you too."

Then I saw Brad, and we both screamed, and the confetti washed over us as we hugged. This was my family. This was my team. These were the people who saved my life. Two years earlier, in the kitchen of our home in Wayne, I'd heard my father say, "Let's do this."

Now, two years later, at the Super Bowl, I heard him say, "We did it."

❦

And then I saw Danielle. Her leave of absence had been approved, and she had made it to the Super Bowl. She'd spent a fortune on airfare, but she got there in time. She ran on the field, looking for me, a few steps behind my parents, and our eyes met through the confetti. She walked toward me and I walked toward her. She looked like she wanted to say something, but there was nothing to say. I couldn't find any words, either.

So we just held each other and we kissed near the fifty-yard line.

That might be my favorite moment ever on a football field.

Everything that came before—all the setbacks and all the bad news, all the chemo bags and the MRIs, the fears and frustration and night sweats and bad dreams, the moments when hope seemed lost—all of it, *all* of it, no longer mattered. The only thing that mattered were three little words.

We did it.

CHAPTER TWENTY

Two years after the Super Bowl, I sat at a desk in a conference room in the Giants' training facility in New Jersey. It was our regular Saturday meeting, when the defense goes over all the plays for the game the following day. My best pal on the team, Spencer Paysinger, sat in a desk to my right. We both had our notebooks open and were scribbling down plays.

Halfway through the meeting I reached over and wrote something in Spencer's notebook. It was something that had been on my mind for a while, and I wanted to get his advice about it. I wrote:

I'm thinking of asking Danielle to marry me.

Spencer read my message, turned to a fresh new page in his notebook, and wrote a heading on it.

Proposal ideas.

Then he gave me a multiple-choice question.

Where? Home. Vacation. In public. Circle one.

I circled *home.*

Family there? Friends there? Just you two?

I circled *family.*

Fancy or casual?

Casual.

Next Spencer wrote down an idea.

New Year's Eve. When the clock strikes midnight.

I want her to remember it, I answered. *She'll probably be hammered by then.*

Spencer came up with more ideas, and I came up with a couple, too. Then, out of the blue, it hit me. I reached over and wrote two words in Spencer's notebook.

Scavenger hunt.

He wrote down a one-word response.

Cool.

I had my plan. I was going to propose to Danielle in a scavenger hunt. Now I just had to hope the coaches hadn't put in a new defensive scheme in that meeting.

❦

Maybe it strikes you as funny that two big professional football players were passing notes about a girl like a couple of grade-school kids. But then, if you knew NFL players like I do, it might not seem that out of character.

One of the most eye-opening discoveries I've made since joining the NFL is how the toughest guys on the field can be the biggest softies off it. Being tough does not mean being heartless or unfeeling; like my friend Sister Barbara Anne said, you can be both tough *and* have a gentle spirit. One of my teammates on the Giants, David Diehl, looks like a ferocious, snarling monster when he puts on his pads and uniform. But then, just before game time, he grabs his cell phone and Skypes with his young daughter.

"Hey, sweetie," the three-hundred-pound beast says in a soft voice, "how's my little girl?"

There are tons of guys like that. After practices you see kids running around everywhere, getting scooped up in the massive arms of their dads, just like my dad scooped me up at that lacrosse game. I had no idea how important family is to NFL players until I got there. Everyone at the NFL level is hugely devoted to their craft—to learning more and playing harder and getting better—and at times it can seem like football is the one and only thing NFL players live for. But that's just not true. On the list of consuming interests, family is ahead of football.

Another important value, I learned, is friendship. The camaraderie among players, the sense of being brothers, is one of the most special things about being a professional athlete. When I got hurt a few weeks before the Super Bowl, and the Giants brought in Chase Blackburn to replace me, I had a hard time feeling anything but bitterness toward him. I didn't root for him to fail or miss tackles, but I wanted my job back, and it was hard to get excited when he made great plays. That's just human nature, I guess. In those early weeks it was apparent that Chase and I weren't going to get along. He could tell how I felt about him, and I assumed he felt the same way. We were two guys fighting for the same job. How could we be friends?

Then something amazing happened. I noticed that as the weeks went by, Chase made an effort to involve me in the games. He'd come off the field and find me on the sidelines and say, "Did you see that block? See how that happened?" Or he'd grab me after games and ask me about certain plays and situations. He took me under his wing, and it made me feel better. Only much later would I learn that, earlier in the season, watching me play had been as hard for Chase as watching him play was for me. I'd been picked for the team over him, so he sat at home and watched me make plays he felt *he* should be making—just like I did later. We were more alike than we realized. We were both driven, fierce, competitive—and human.

At a golf outing after the season, Chase and I played together and laughed and joked around like friends. Without knowing it, we'd *become* friends.

"You know," Chase said after we'd had a few beers, "I used to hate your guts."

"I know," I said. "I used to hate yours."

"I never expected we'd become friends," he said.

"Me neither."

"But I'm glad we did."

Chase and I are good buddies now, and Danielle is good friends with his wife, Megan. They come over to our place, and we hang out at theirs. Chase really surprised me. He took my job and he fought hard to keep it, and that's exactly what he should have done—that's football. On the field you have to be cutthroat. But off the field you treat one another with respect, and you recognize that you're all in the same trench together. And when you start to realize this, that's when you start to become a leader. Chase figured all that out before I did, and he taught it to me.

He made me a better football player and a better person.

❦

One thing cancer does is teach you how little you really know about life. Since I got my diagnosis I learned so much about so many things. For one thing, I got to really know my parents, because I got to see the burdens they have to carry. I got to see their pain and hurt and hopes and fears, even though they did their best to hide those things from me. Very early on in the ordeal, when I went to see a doctor about my biopsy results, my mother sat next to me in the waiting room, phoning relatives to tell them about my diagnosis. As she made the calls, she couldn't help but cry.

Well, I was in a terrible mood. I didn't yet know if my cancer had spread. So I said something rude.

"Mom, I don't mind if you cry," I told her, "but can you do it over there so I can't hear you?"

My mom got up and went somewhere I couldn't hear her. And after that, I don't think I ever heard her cry again—until, finally, I heard her cry with happiness.

What we all went through opened my eyes to the kind of people my parents are, as opposed to the image I had of them growing up. I came to appreciate the incredible demands made on them by my illness. How my mother would drop me off at a gym after a chemo session, only to have me call her five minutes later and say, "Mom, I'm too sick; come back and get me," or how, early on, my parents ended a family vacation after just one day because I didn't feel well, and quietly said to themselves, "Oh, so this is how it's going to be," yet bent their lives around mine dozens and dozens of times after that without a single word of complaint.

Or how I'd hear my folks say, "I'm going to the shed for a minute" before I even knew the shed was where they went to wallow in sadness, only to realize later that they suffered as much as if not more than me, because they took my pain and frustration and purposely made it their own. They didn't shy away from what was happening to me. They dug in.

And because I got the chance to appreciate the great sacrifices my parents made for me—not just as parents but as flesh-and-blood *people*—I also got the chance to rediscover, with grown-up eyes, how much they love me, and how much I love them. I'll never forget the day when, after it was clear I'd beaten my cancer, I heard my mother say, "Well, no more trips to the shed!" That was such a happy, happy moment. But the truth is, the shed—that dark, dank place of pain and sorrow—changed us all, profoundly and forever. And as it changed us, it brought us closer together. And that is a very special kind of gift to receive.

❦

I'd like to say my cancer brought me closer to my buddy Zack, but I don't know how that's even possible. Since the day we started trading little Crazy Bones plastic action figures in elementary school—and I came

home and randomly announced to my mom, "Zack is my best friend"—
we've been like brothers. Before my cancer, we shared a million adventures—
playing little games on our TI-83 calculators instead of solving calculus
problems in class; building ramps on nearby hills and launching our
bikes all of five inches in the air while thinking it was more like five feet;
betting on every conceivable contest known to man, yet never collecting
on a single bet; going to the mall to chat up girls when we were sixteen
but never having enough nerve, and settling instead for eating pizza and
telling corny jokes. If there was an adventure out in the world that called
to us, we would take it together.

So when I got cancer, Zack and I went on that ride together, too. We
didn't talk about it. We didn't plan it out. We just did it. Together.

At some point I realized I hadn't really thanked Zack for all he was
doing for me, at least not properly. As you know, we don't waste a lot
of words when we're together. Then I wound up leading a Boston College First Year Experience retreat called "48 Hours." For the freshmen
on the retreat one of the exercises was writing a letter to someone
important in their lives. I sat quietly in a candlelit room as the freshmen pulled out pens and paper and thoughtfully wrote their letters. I
felt inspired to grab a pen and write my own letter to my important
person—Zack.

Half the letter was about how grateful I was that Zack had been with
me during chemo. The other half was about our lifetime of friendship
outside my illness. It was the first time I let him know just what he meant
to me. I thanked him for everything I could think to thank him for, and
finally I just thanked him for being my best friend.

I'm sure Zack was surprised when he got that letter from me. We've
never been touchy-feely kind of friends. But I'm guessing he knows how
sincere I was when I wrote it. True to form, we didn't talk a lot about
it, if we talked about it at all. But I hope Zack knows every word came

from my heart. To make sure, I've looked for small ways I can try to pay him back. I bring him along to every cool NFL party I get invited to, and at one event he got to meet Larry Bird and Magic Johnson. For a basketball junkie like Zack, that was huge.

And today the competition between Zack and me goes on. I remember us playing a video game—Madden again, probably—after I broke my hand at BC my last year there. I was in a hard cast, so I could hold the game controller with only one hand. After a while I started working the right joystick with my teeth. And I *still* beat Zack that day. If you ask him about it his memory might fail him and he'll say he can't remember, but he does. I didn't collect on our wager on that game, because, as I explained, with Zack and me it's not about the cash. It's not really even about winning. With Zack and me, it's about taking the adventure together.

❧

One of the most important lessons cancer taught me is humility.

To succeed at football you have to be uncommonly confident. You have to truly believe you are indestructible. Sure enough, for much of my life my identity was inseparable from my physicality. I *was* my strength, my power, my size. I was so athletic, one of my early gym teachers made me throw the dodgeball left-handed, just to make it fair for the other kids. I suffered my share of injuries—broke both wrists on one ski trip, fractured an ankle jumping into shallow water, busted finger after finger playing football, and on and on. But I bounced back quickly from those injuries, and I played through plenty of them—including the concurrently fractured foot *and* hand I played with at Boston College. You see, a tough guy plays with pain. I was critical of teammates who weren't as tough as I was or didn't work as hard as I did, and sometimes my cockiness veered straight into arrogance. I lacked empathy—I'd think overweight people just needed to exercise, or homeless people just needed to get a job. It was easy for me to think of myself as an indomitable force: faster, stronger, better than others. And because I was, nothing out there could stop me.

Then I got cancer.

The entire foundation of my identity came crashing down. Every outward vestige of my toughness got stripped away. I was exposed, and my weaknesses revealed. As doctors X-rayed every inch of my body, they literally got to see right through me. The real Mark Herzlich was laid bare.

And that, I would learn over time, was a good thing.

Because what I learned is that, much as we think we might be, we are ultimately not in control of our lives. Like I said, the journey takes us where it takes us. Learning that, and truly understanding it, is a very humbling experience. It means you are ceding control to some other force. For some it's fate, for others the universe. For me, it was God.

I was always someone who didn't like to ask for help. I controlled my own destiny; I worked hard and made things happen. I didn't need a handout from anyone. But when I got cancer I quickly learned I needed help after all: from my parents, from my brother, from doctors and nurses, from Danielle. And also from God. In my very first prayer to Him, I begged for His help. And, looking back on it, I believe that was when the tide began to turn.

In football it's all about being "the man." You hear it all the time—"Be a man!" "Man up!" But ultimately your manhood has nothing to do with how hard you tackle people. You can be the most brutal hitter in the NFL, but that just makes you great at hitting people. It doesn't make you a great man. Cancer made me realize that no matter how strong I get or how hard I hit, I will never be "the man." I can't control everything in my life. Only God can.

Danielle, who was a theology major in college, helped me understand my cancer ordeal better. She knows the Bible a lot better than I do, and sometimes a Scripture will strike her as appropriate to my story. "I know the plans I have in mind for you, declares the Lord," it says in Jeremiah 29:11. "They are plans for peace, not disaster, to give you a future filled with hope." In other words, it is not always for us to know the plan for our life. We have to have faith that God's plan is good. We may never understand why good people suffer so much. Or why beautiful, innocent kids get cancer. Sometimes it's hard to accept that that can possibly be God's plan. But the truth is, we can't even comprehend what God is capable of, or how he's going about it. "God can do anything," it says in Ephesians 3:20, "far more than you can ever imagine or guess in your wildest dreams. He does it not by pushing us around, but by working within us, his spirit deeply and gently within us."

Stay faithful in the face of a challenge, and trust that God's spirit is in you—that is the message. But when times get really, really hard, that's not so easy to do. And the truth is, I'm still working on it. My cancer brought me closer to God, but I can get closer still. I pray a lot more now: before every game, at night, or just randomly during the day. I concede that God is more powerful than me, and I ask him for his help. It's nothing too heavy—it's just me talking to God. It's me understanding how we all face challenges—the poor, the weak, the obese, the homeless—and how we aren't always in control of what happens next. It's me feeling empathy for others in their time of pain. It's me being humbled by God's plan for me, even if I don't always understand it.

It took my being stripped of all my strength and power and dignity to come to that place of humility. And while the journey was often dark and painful, I can honestly say I'm glad I got to take it.

❦

For the longest time, however, there was one question I had a hard time finding an answer to.

Why did I survive cancer, while so many others don't?

During my last season at Boston College we traveled to San Francisco to play in a bowl game. I'd been contacted by a young boy, Matt, who was in a hospital in San Francisco and, like me, had Ewing's sarcoma. Two days before the game I drove a half hour to see him at his hospital. When I walked into his room I saw a boy who was really sick. He was bald and pale and weak. His entire family was in the room with him, because, I learned, his condition was so critical, he could pass at any time. Apparently the doctors hadn't given him much of a chance.

When he saw me, though, his face lit up. His smile was beautiful. I sat on his bed and we talked about cancer and football.

"I'm a big Boston College fan," Matt explained, "because I see what you went through and it gives me hope."

I stayed with Matt and his family for a couple of hours, and Matt told me how happy he was that he got to meet me.

"My goal," he said, "is to see you play in the bowl game."

"See you there, then," I said.

When I left his father pulled me aside outside the room.

"We haven't seen him that alive and happy in months," he said. "Thank you so much."

The bowl game was two days away. I planned to see Matt and his parents there. But the next day I got a call.

Matt had passed away.

The day before the bowl game, I attended a player panel. It's an event where players get to eat and hang out and get up and talk about the game. I got up and told them Matt's story. Suddenly the room got very quiet.

"He was such a big BC fan," I said. "He wanted to hold on to watch us play tomorrow. But he didn't make it. Not because he didn't fight, but because cancer sometimes doesn't care how hard you fight or how strong you are. Cancer is cruel and people like Matt remind us to always, always fight, even when fear tries to stand in our way."

I got to meet or correspond with many truly remarkable people like Matt. After my *GameDay* announcement, a girl from California contacted me on Facebook and told me her friend had cancer. She asked whether I could write a letter to her friend to give her inspiration. I sent her friend a letter and we wound up exchanging messages a few times. I remember seeing a photo of her wearing a MARK HERZLICH BEAT CANCER T-shirt that Boston College had made in my honor.

But then I didn't hear from her for two months. Finally, I got another Facebook message from her friend.

"I'm sorry to have to tell you that she died yesterday," the friend wrote. "She fought hard and you gave her a lot of inspiration. But she didn't make it."

Then the friend told me something I could hardly believe.

"Before she died, she requested that she be buried in your MARK BEATS CANCER T-shirt."

I stared at my computer screen for a long time after reading that. I didn't feel honored, or happy I'd helped her, or anything like that. I just felt sad and confused.

Around then I began to grapple with survivor's guilt. I couldn't understand why I made it while so many others didn't. Matt's family loved him as much as my family loved me, and he fought every bit as hard as I fought, yet he lost his battle. Why did that happen? How could anyone explain the outrageous unfairness of that? And if you could fight hard and still die, was I giving people false hope by telling them to keep fighting? Was it all just a random spin of the wheel?

I have learned there is no satisfactory answer to the question of why I made it and others didn't, except that cancer affects people in different ways. Mine was caught just before it spread; others aren't so lucky. And even people who fight like crazy sometimes pass quickly. There is a kind of randomness to the disease.

But that doesn't mean you shouldn't fight. Because the fight has *meaning*.

I got the chance to talk to Kathleen, my chemo nurse, about this subject. Kathleen herself once nearly died of a staph infection, and at one point her doctors said she was touch-and-go. Fortunately she fought her way back to health. She has seen death up close, both as a nurse and as a patient. I wondered whether maybe she could help me with an answer.

"If someone fights as hard as you did, Mark, then they will be okay—regardless of the outcome," Kathleen said. "Because you should always fight. And when there is no more fighting to do, then you can stop, because that is the reality. Dying is part of living. It's not always about the result."

That made sense. We can't always control the outcome—the journey takes us where it takes us. But we can control how hard we fight. And the reason we fight hard is because it gives us hope. And hope is too precious a thing to ever surrender.

While we are alive, we fight for life. And the fight gives our lives meaning.

And whether or not you make it, you are still considered a warrior. Matt is a warrior. The beautiful young girl who was buried in my T-shirt is a warrior. We are all warriors.

Not too long ago, a teenage boy walked into the offices of POHA in Radnor for his first day of chemo. He was way too young to have cancer, everyone around him said, but he had it nonetheless. Kathleen gave him a tour of the place, same as she did with me. The boy was scared and anxious, and he didn't talk very much. He just shuffled around, looking at what would be his home for the next several months.

Halfway through the tour, he stopped. Then he pointed at room S-6. "Is that Mark Herzlich's room?" he asked.

"Yes, it is," Kathleen said, surprised he knew.

"Can I have it?" he asked. "Can I have my chemo in there?"

"Sure you can," Kathleen said, and she knew just why he wanted that room.

The kid was ready to fight. He was ready to be a warrior.

❦

What helps us find the energy to fight is inspiration. Inspiration powers hope. For me, inspiration came from so many places. One of the most remarkable sources of all was children and teenagers.

I received hundreds and hundreds of letters and cards from young people around the country wishing me well. I still have them all, and the thoughts and sentiments on those cards continue to inspire me. Like the letter from a little girl named Carly, who drew a small scoreboard at the bottom of her note.

"Cancer: 0," the scoreboard read. "Mark: 1."

Or the note from a boy named Max, who chose to write a school essay "about finding a cancer cure for you." Max also told me he wore a fake Mohawk and put on eye black so he could go trick-or-treating as Mark Herzlich. Or the girl named Kennedy who wrote: "Like my mother always says, 'Energy flows where intention goes,' and you are the best example of this. Your belief that you would get better and play football again made all the difference. You inspire me."

There's also a little blond boy named Sean who was diagnosed with an inoperable brain tumor. I met Sean at an event at the Giants' training facility, and we hit it off right away. "Hi, Mark Herzlich!" he says when he sees me now, because for some reason he uses my whole name. "What's up, Sean?" I say, and we get to talking school and family and football.

After we spent time at one charity event, Sean disappeared for a minute and came back with a note for me.

"You're my hero," he wrote on the napkin. "I love you, Mark Herzlich."

Warrior Sean was there when the Giants played our final game last season. It was a cold, rainy, miserable day, but Sean was all smiles. He always is. We hung out a bit and I asked Sean whether he wanted to try on my helmet. His eyes got really wide. I helped Sean slip the big helmet on his head, and his parents snapped photos. When they were finished we hugged good-bye and promised we'd see each other soon.

Just a few minutes later I got a text from Sean's mother.

"He is beaming," she wrote. "He said, 'Now I can never give up because Mark Herzlich let me wear his helmet.'"

I know his mother thinks I inspire Sean, but really it's the other way around.

I have met so many remarkable children like Warrior Sean, and that has been one of the great blessings of my ordeal. These kids truly taught me what it means to be tough. They are the real superstars. Now, when I get the chance, I ask them for one thing—their autograph.

"I gave you mine," I say. "Now I need yours."

❦

I was lucky, too, to have an endless source of inspiration right under my nose—my family.

My mom and dad and Brad are all doing great now. Brad went on to become a pretty good football player at Brown University, but in his junior year, after he tore a joint in his shoulder, he decided to give up the sport. He has other passions that are more consuming. He spent a year abroad in Copenhagen, drawing, painting, and sculpting. He also co-founded the nation's first all-athlete collegiate a cappella group, called, naturally, Jockappella. He's incredibly smart and creative and driven, and he has the chance to accomplish some truly great things. He's completed internships with top hedge funds and agencies, and I'm excited to see what will come next for him.

My father is his typical self—the backbone of our family. He is still my hero, but that's not all he is. A long time ago he told me he was my father, not my friend, but that is no longer true. He is both now. We have found new ways to communicate besides sports, and we are closer than ever. I'm a lot more like him than I ever knew, right down to his fondness for corny jokes. "What time is it?" is one I like to tell these days. "*Tooth hurty.* Time to see the dentist."

As for my mom, well, she's my mom. She is our family's beating heart. I can't even begin to summarize everything she did for me, and does for me still. When I was a teenager I tended to wear my blue jeans extra saggy and low on my waist. So did Zack, and both our moms hated that. One day they decided to give us a taste of our medicine, and they walked into the kitchen with their own pants nearly falling down. Zack and I were horrified and traumatized. I'm sure we hitched up our pants for a while in response, but just the other day, when I drove down to visit my parents in Wayne, I felt someone come up behind me in the kitchen and pull up my jeans by a belt loop. It was my mom.

"Mark, you know I don't like your jeans this way," she said.

I may be a big and tough NFL player, but my mom still likes to pull up my pants. She will never *not* look out for me, and that is, as it has always been, incredibly comforting to me.

My mother and father and Brad—they were my inspiration. Without them, I don't know where I would be.

❦

And then there's Danielle.

Just two weeks after the Super Bowl I flew down to South Carolina for

Danielle's graduation from Army training. I already knew she was one of the top officers in her class, but I didn't know just how remarkable she is. At the ceremony she won not one but three big awards: two physical fitness awards, and an honor-grad certificate for finishing with one of the highest GPAs in her class of forty-five graduates. She hadn't told me about the awards, so I sat there stunned as she kept getting called to the stage. After the ceremony her colleagues all came up to me, one after another, to tell me what a great officer Danielle is.

This is her Super Bowl, I thought. *And she is a champion.*

Afterward I could hardly articulate how proud I was of her, but I gave it my best shot. Then I just hugged and kissed her. With her awards and honors in tow, we got into her Ford Escape and drove fourteen hours up to New Jersey, to the house where we live with our happy bulldogs, Champ and Scout.

To me it's something of a miracle that I met Danielle when I did. I was still in chemotherapy, and I was physically at the lowest point of my life. I was bald and weak and a shadow of myself. Yet somehow Danielle saw past all that. Somehow she fell in love with me anyway. And when she opened her heart to me she filled me with strength—just when I desperately needed to be strong. Danielle taught me what it means—what it *really* means—to be a man. It does not mean being tough and strong just for you. Being a man means being tough and strong for *someone else.* Danielle gave me the chance to be strong for her, and in that moment I discovered the best part of myself. Her love was a gift I never saw coming and can't imagine living without.

This past Christmas Day my family drove up to be with Danielle and me in our home in New Jersey. We opened our presents until there was nothing left under the tree. But there was still one more gift *in* the tree. I steered Danielle to a homemade card tucked between two branches.

"What's this?" she asked.

"Just open it; you'll see."

Danielle opened the note and read my handwriting.

"As a part of this family you will begin to realize that we sometimes find it fun to make the simplest tasks, such as giving a gift, extraordinary. . . . I ask you to partake in a Christmas scavenger hunt."

Danielle had no idea what the hunt was all about. Earlier that year we had talked about getting married, and we'd even gone to look at rings. But right before Christmas I told her I'd made another appointment at the jeweler's in January so we could see more rings. The scavenger hunt, as far as she knew, was just a silly stunt.

The first card gave her a clue that led her to the second card. The cards and clues kept coming, nine of them in all. They led Danielle from the tree to the ottoman to our Wii console to the backyard to her makeup drawer to my Jeep to the refrigerator and to the front door. The card taped to the door gave her the final clue.

"I represent family, hope, and life. I start from something small and grow into something magnificent. Every nick and cut I endure heals and makes me stronger. The deeper my roots, the more unshakable I become. At my center is a heart with many rings."

Danielle figured it out. I was leading her back to the Christmas tree.

There she found the last card, which had only a few words on it.

"I love you with all my heart," it read, "but unlike a tree my heart has only one ring."

When Danielle finished reading the card she looked up and saw me bending to one knee. I was so nervous, I wasn't sure which knee to bend, and I almost toppled over. Somehow I didn't. I pulled out a small black box and opened it. Inside was a ring with a marquise diamond surrounded by trillion-cut stones.

"Danielle, will you marry me?" I said.

Danielle put her hands to her mouth and said what every guy hopes to hear.

"You're kidding me," she said. Only she said it with an expletive between the *you're* and *kidding.*

Everyone laughed, and Danielle stood there in shock for a while, and then, in a soft voice, she finally said, "Yes."

The journey takes you where it takes you. Sometime the place it takes you is home.

❧

For a long time I stopped thinking about my future, beyond my goal of playing football again. Cancer doesn't allow you to think too far ahead. But now I've begun to give it some thought. I'd like to keep playing football for as long as I can. Most football careers last only three or four seasons, and playing much beyond that is a long shot. Then again, I have a little experience with long shots. I've played in the NFL for three seasons now. We'll see how far I can take it.

I'm planning ahead in other ways, too. At Boston College I got a degree in marketing and a master's in administrative studies. It's hard for me to picture myself as a suit-and-tie guy, but I can see myself transferring my competitiveness from the football field to the business world. The NFL and the Giants have programs that help players prepare for a life outside football, and I've been taking advantage of them. My dream would be to open a gym and rehab center that is available to the public but also caters to cancer patients and wounded warriors. Danielle, a personal trainer on top of everything else she does, could whip our clients into shape.

Whatever else I end up doing, one thing I will always be is a cancer survivor. That's what my business card says—cancer survivor. I'm coming up on five years of being cancer-free, and that will be a huge milestone, but it's like Kathleen told me—there's no such thing as a cure. There is only remission. When I look at my left leg I'm reminded of what was once inside me. I have three nasty scars, and the skin along my femur is hairless. Cancer is a part of me now, a part of who I am. And as I've learned, that's not a bad thing.

I recently attended a fund-raiser for the Jay Fund, a charity founded by New York Giants head coach Tom Coughlin. It's named for Jay McGillis, a Boston College safety who died of cancer. I'm on the advisory board, and all the money we help raise goes directly to families of cancer patients to help pay medical costs, travel bills, and other expenses. At the fund-raiser one of the other board members came up and asked to talk to me.

"You know, Mark," he said, "you're a great football player, but you have to know God didn't put you on this earth to play football."

He had my attention now.

"He put you on this earth for another reason—to help people. Football is your platform. But your purpose is helping people with cancer. Because of who you are, you can work miracles for them. And that is your real purpose."

Those words hit me square in the heart, and I only hope that I can live up to them. Today I travel around the country, meeting people with cancer and other illnesses and giving motivational speeches. I realize my story is an inspiration to others, and I've made it my job to do whatever I can to help them in their battles. Everywhere I go, I deliver the same message—the very message of this book.

Have hope. Fight hard. Be a warrior. Believe in yourself.

Believe that you have what it takes.

ACKNOWLEDGMENTS

With enormous gratitude, I would like to thank:

God for showing Himself to me in the form of a blue M&M and never leaving my side.

My mother, Barb, my father, Sandy and my brother, Brad, for your endless, unwavering love. LeRoi for being an inspiration to me while you achieve amazing things in your own life.

Dr. Bradley Smith, Dr. Arthur Staddon, Dr. Richard Lackman, Dr. Stephen Hahn and all of their nurses for your skill and courage to give me a fighting chance at life. Kevin Mahoney for leading me in their direction, and Dr. Mark Scarborough for his guidance in the process.

My grandparents, cousins, aunts and uncles and my Wohelo family for their support.

My childhood friends from New Eagle, Valley Forge and Conestoga, including but not limited to Reggie Pierce, Zach Jacobs, Brandon Winters, Will Sutton, Duwann Clarke, Mike Jones, Brian Creghan, Scott Deakins and Brian Ikeda for growing with me and never treating me differently during the best days or during the worst.

Jen Schuster and her team at New American Library and Cait Hoyt at CAA for taking a dream of mine and creating a book that I am greatly proud of.

ACKNOWLEDGMENTS

Tom Condon for believing in me as a player and finding me a home in the NFL.

Codi Boek for always being able to put a smile on my face, and Nathan Boek for being a beacon of hope for me.

Sister Barbara Anne for her prayers, Ellen Spicuzza for her titanium thumb and Steve Bushee and his staff of medical trainers at BC for constantly trying to get me in front of the right doctors who could alleviate my pain.

Father Joe Marchese, Peter Folan and Tedy Bruschi for helping me realize that my story could help guide and inspire others.

The entire BC community, Gene DeFilippo, Barry Gallup, Warren Zola, Father Leahy as well as the other ACC schools for their support.

Mike Creghan, John Vogan, Brian Sampson, Tom O'Brien, Jason Swepson, Jim Herman, Frank Spaziani, Jason Loscalzo, Jeff Dillman and all of my other coaches for keeping my fire burning and my push for excellence constant.

Tom Coughlin, thank you for giving me the chance to prove to myself that cancer cannot stop me. Bill McGovern, thank you for defying stereotypes and taking me in to your family as a son.

The military men and women who, like Danielle, have made it their purpose to let us live safely in the land of the free.

Alex Albright, Damik Scafe, Mike Morrissey, John Lowel, Roderick Rollins, Jordan McMichael, James McCluskey, Ryan Lindsey, Rich Lapham, Justin Jarvis, Jack Geiser, Jeff Smith, Chris Fox, Billy Flutie, Wes Davis, Thomas Claiborne, Darius Bagan and Anthony Castonzo; my class of teammates at Boston College for being nothing short of brothers during my bout with cancer.

Stephen Fiorella for offering to be a gargoyle outside of my house, and the entire Tredyffrin/Easttown community for the meals and support they brought to our family.

Zack, there are more than eighty thousand words in this book and that still isn't enough to portray the love and gratitude that I have for you. I read a bible verse the other day, and I thought of you. John 15:13 says, "There is no greater love than to lay down one's life for one's friend." You have showed me that love and have made me a better man because of it. Thank you.

Danielle, I cannot wait to dream with you, grow with you, suffer with you and thrive with you. My father made a commitment to me with the word "let's" and he created a bond that could never be broken. I cannot wait to make my commitment to you with the words "I do." I love you. Thank you for seeing *me* when all I felt was fear.

Lastly I would like to thank the Warriors, who, like me, have battled or are battling seemingly impossible obstacles in their lives. I want to leave you with a quote that stuck with me during my treatments and hung in our locker room at Boston College. Each one of you is excellent and each one of you has inspired me to push to achieve that excellence that you have portrayed.

"Excellence is the Result of Caring more than others think is Wise,
Risking more than others think is Safe,
Dreaming more than others think is Practical,
and Expecting more than others think is Possible."

—RONNIE OLDHAM